Caught
IN THE
Middle

Caught
IN THE
Middle

Border Communities
in an Era of Globalization

Demetrios G. Papademetriou
Deborah Waller Meyers
EDITORS

Carnegie Endowment for International Peace
WASHINGTON, D.C.

MIGRATION POLICY INSTITUTE

✗ 47893580

Carnegie Endowment for International Peace   Tel. 202-483-7600
1779 Massachusetts Avenue, N.W.   Fax. 202-483-1840
Washington, D.C. 20036 USA   www.ceip.org

To order, contact Carnegie's distributor:
The Brookings Institution Press   Tel. 800-275-1447 or 202-797-6258
Department 029   Fax. 202-797-2960
Washington, D.C. 20042-0029 USA   www.brookings.edu

Printed in the United States of America.

Interior design by Jenna Dixon. Text set in FB Wessex.

Library of Congress Cataloging-in-Publication Data

Caught in the middle : border communities in an era of globalization / Demetrios
G. Papademetriou, Deborah Waller Meyers, editors.
    p.   cm.
Includes bibliographical references and index.
    ISBN 0-87003-185-6 (pbk. : alk paper)
    1. Regionalism. 2. Boundaries. I. Papademetriou, Demetrios G. II. Meyers,
Deborah Waller.
    JZ5330 .C38 2001
    320.8–dc21

2001005347

07   06   05   04   03   02   01   5   4   3   2   1   1st Printing 2001

Contents

Illustrations

TABLES

Foreword

ALTHOUGH INTERNATIONAL BORDERS have long existed, the study of borderlands is a relatively recent field, its growth sparked over the last decade by the post-Cold War opening of borders and tremendous worldwide growth in cross-border traffic of goods, people, and information. Many of the rapid changes are seemingly contradictory: borders have grown less relevant for many functions but have increased in importance as a symbol of national identity and sovereignty and as the locus for an intensifying regime of inspections directed both at people and goods. In some places, for example the German-Polish border, the border is on its way toward elimination; in contrast, the U.S.-Mexican border is being fortified, and the size of the U.S. Border Patrol has more than doubled in the last eight years. Communities on opposite sides of an interstate border whose economies are intertwined must work around laws and regulations that often ignore realities on the ground. Are border community residents living at the periphery? Or are they really at the center—at the intersection of international commerce and acting as an integrated social and economic unit?

This volume takes a fascinating tour of the inner workings of border communities along five international borders—United States–Canada, United States–Mexico, Germany–Poland, Russia–China, and Russia–Kazakhstan. It grew out of research engaged in by the International Migration Policy Program for a project titled "Self-Governance at the Border," whose initial aim was to study the United States-Canada border in order to better inform policy discussions regarding the United States-Mexico border. It soon expanded, however, in order to learn from the experiences and perspectives of border communities along other international boundaries as well.

The project initially catalogued "best practices" in each of the chosen communities with regard to managing migration-related issues and then pulled together local and federal officials with academics and business and community leaders to discuss these findings in two regional seminars. There, information-sharing networks were created among stakeholders of different nationalities, and ideas were exchanged among constituencies from various points along the borders. The project's directors then drew tentative conclusions that were presented to North American and other foreign government officials, the media, border communities, researchers, and business and community leaders at a June 2000 conference titled "Managing Common Borders."

The chapters in this volume began as field reports and evolved into essays on various migration-related, community-level cross-border practices and the factors that enhance or obstruct them. Background and context are provided for each of the border communities studied and for the myriad interactions of stakeholders involved in these issues. Some essays also consider the extent and likelihood of future cross-border cooperation while others make recommendations regarding emulation and expansion of the best practices. It is striking that the researchers on different borders and parts of borders in a variety of widely dissimilar countries independently found border communities to be dealing with many of the same challenges, and often wanting to devise their own solutions consistent with their unique, local circumstances, rather than having the wrong solution imposed from their capitals.

Overall, this volume describes the day-to-day challenges and opportunities faced by communities that straddle a border, and how these are being dealt with. It offers a comparative general perspective on border management and a better understanding of the interactions and tensions between federal and local governments, community leaders and government officials, and various border communities, and how these tensions may be overcome. We believe these insights will be useful to policy makers in many settings and to a variety of academic disciplines in this era of devolution.

JESSICA T. MATHEWS
President, Carnegie Endowment for International Peace

Acknowledgments

THE SELF-GOVERNANCE AT THE BORDER PROJECT, and this volume, would not have been possible without the support and contributions of a variety of people and institutions. First, we thank our funders, particularly Taryn Higashi at the Ford Foundation and Marguerite Rivera Houze and Nan Kennelly at the Bureau of Population, Refugees, and Migration at the United States Department of State, who provided the initial funding to begin the fieldwork and turn our concept into reality, as well as the support to publish our findings. To our binational partners in the Canadian and Mexican governments, particularly Daniel Jean, Terri Colli, and Dan Abele at the Embassy of Canada and Maria Elena Alcaraz and Omar de la Torre at the Embassy of Mexico, we thank you for making available to us your network of contacts and for your financial assistance in support of the regional seminars.

Of course, this volume also would not have been possible without the tremendous effort of all our authors. We greatly appreciate the time they spent in the field, writing and editing their findings, and attending the various seminars. We also appreciate the substantive and logistical advice and support of our colleagues in the International Migration Policy Program and the dedicated efforts of the Carnegie Publications staff in turning the manuscript into a book.

Finally, and most importantly, we thank all the people who agreed to be interviewed for this project and who were kind enough to share their experiences and perspectives regarding life along the border. It is these people, who live at the crossroads of two nations, or who work on these issues on a daily basis, who best understand the dynamics and who, facing the daily benefits and challenges, often have the most commonsense approach to border management and its related issues. We dedicate this book to them.

INTRODUCTION

Overview, Context, and a Vision for the Future

Demetrios G. Papademetriou and Deborah Waller Meyers

IN TODAY'S GLOBAL ECONOMY, the increasing flow of goods and people across international borders is a topic of intense interest and incessant discussion. These intertwined phenomena are forcing a conversation about the changing nature of nation-states—a rather recent political construct, at least by historical standards—and, in essence, they may amount to the frontal assault on sovereignty many imagine. This conversation has been difficult to have in the abstract despite the array of forces pointing to its necessity, ranging from advances in technology and the steady devolution of political power to lower levels of government, to the long-rising power of multinational corporations and, more recently, that of civil society—which seems to be becoming increasingly important as a transnational force. Some observers point to an additional set of institutions and activities as further evidence of the systematic erosion of the power of the nation-state, particularly the various supranational institutions—such as the World Trade Organization or the European Union's (EU) bureaucracy in Brussels (the European Commission, EC)—as well as the increasing web of sovereignty-delimiting treaties, international agreements, and joint international actions of many forms. For the purposes of their arguments the fact that this loss of sovereignty occurs with the participating states' consent (whether given freely or obtained through pressure) does not change the basic logic.

These and similar analytical trends—the result of the vast increases in economic and political interdependence (one may even say "integration") that underlie a state's robust engagement of the international system—seem to have sprouted philosophical roots consistent with the possibility that a Kuhnian "paradigmatic shift" in the conceptualization of the state may be in the offing. That is, we may be at the early stages of a process whereby the persistent questioning of a dominant construct (the nation-state) leads to the articulation of an alternative construct around which analytical agreement begins to coalesce (Kuhn 1962). If indeed we are witnessing such a shift, two of the interrelated philosophical constructs that have undergirded the modern nation-state—exclusive sovereign license over physical territory, and social and political "membership" (these constructs are frequently associated with such giants of modern Western thought as Max Weber and Hannah Arendt but in fact predate them by centuries)—may be among the twenty-first century's many likely targets for reconsideration.

Other analysts, however, seem skeptical about both the validity and value of the preceding analysis. In some ways, they too sense the onset of a hinge point in how a state is likely to behave in the future toward the twin exclusivities of physical and socio-political "territory"; the change they perceive, however, is toward greater exclusivity and control, rather than their opposites. In defense of their perspective, these analysts point to compelling evidence that, in the post–Cold War era, most advanced industrial states have sought to strengthen their control capabilities by devoting ever-larger shares of their physical and political capital to a multifaceted regulation and control model. Although not all of these states employ all of this model's facets with equal zeal, two of its components are widely used—those of "saturation policing" (Andreas 2001) and the massive investments of domestic and foreign policy capital made on issues of control. Others of the model's components, however, are used with varying degrees of diligence and enthusiasm. For instance, the United States has been erecting physical barriers at its southwest border with relative abandon and has created substantial obstacles for both legal and unauthorized immigrants to gain access to its social safety net—while showing extreme ambivalence about other forms of interior control. Most other advanced industrial societies have so far avoided relying on physical barriers and have shown considerable discipline in resisting the urge to adopt U.S.-like cutoffs in social benefits—but show no reluctance to apply most forms of interior control.

To be sure, for most people, maintaining (some will say "reasserting") control over both entry and membership may be less a philosophical litmus test about one's stand on sovereignty and more a test of the state's willingness and ability to respond to a pronounced challenge. That is, the effort may have less to do with a philosophical or ideological need to "recapture" control of the state (presumably, from the grasp of transnationalism and its apostles) and more with an attempt to find an antidote to the increasing power of organized private interests seeking to exploit the weakening of national authority for illegitimate purposes. Without demeaning in any way the importance of political symbolism on these issues (Andreas 2001), it is the striving for effective governance and the responsible stewardship of public goods and resources that is likely to be behind current behavior in these respects.

At this writing (spring of 2001), there is little doubt which side is winning both the analytical and the political contest over whether or not the state is in retreat with regard to border (and membership) controls: advanced industrial states are indeed making ever-greater capital and political investments in ever-greater controls. To employ a sometimes useful academic expression, the state seems to have "come back in" with a vengeance. (Relatively little academic effort is devoted to examining whether the state was ever really "gone" or where it might be "going.") As the state does so, however, there is a troubling lack of interest in applying an "effectiveness" test to the recent rush to controls through the independent evaluation of whether the effort is succeeding by any but the most counterfactual of measurements (see Andreas and Snyder 2000). More disturbingly, there is even less effort to think systematically about whether alternative responses to the challenge might have a greater or lesser chance of success. (A recent report on the U.S.-Mexico relationship is a notable exception to this trend—see U.S.-Mexico Migration Panel 2001.)

This seemingly mindless adherence to doing "more of the same" has had several perverse effects. Two of them seem particularly relevant for this analysis. First, it has largely papered over the human effects of the new enforcement status quo. One reputable academic team estimates that nearly 500 persons died at the U.S. southwest border in 2000 (Eschbach, Hagan, and Rodriguez 2001), a number that goes well beyond the ability of some to dismiss border deaths as regrettable but unavoidable "collateral" damage—"desperate people doing desperate things." Second, the current control regime has had a similar disregard for the policy's effects on the communities in which people live and through which these goods and people pass—communities that have become the terrain where the manifestations of numerous conflicting perspectives play themselves out.

It is indeed the residents, businesses, and public and private institutions of border communities who most directly absorb the costs and benefits from both freer movement and greater controls. How do these communities navigate these issues, conflicting aims and all? What is life like for those who live and work at the interface of two countries? What is the local perspective on the movement of people and goods that pass through a community; does anyone else care about it? Does the perspective vary from one community, or one border, to another, and what accounts for any variance? What input, if any, do local communities have into national policies that ultimately affect them? What creative solutions have they found to address the challenge of such policies? This volume attempts to shed some light on all of these questions.

Two points of departure have been most dominant in informing the conceptualization of the research project whose results are reported on and analyzed in this volume. The first was a clear sense that, left on their own, national governments and bureaucracies would do what comes most naturally to them: national governments will reassert control in response to popular fears associated with the by-products of diminishing state authority and controls, and the relevant agencies will seek to convert such fears into additional resources—allowing them to grow in size and gain in influence. (Such influence, in turn, allows bureaucracies to inoculate themselves against attempts to reduce either their budget or their authority.) The U.S. Border Patrol and Germany's border guards are excellent examples of this process at work.

Of course, responses will not be identical across all types of borders. For instance, when national borders are still the subject of some dispute (such as the Russia-China border or some of the Central American borders), are recent creations (such as the Russia-Kazakhstan border), or are separating two states that view each other with suspicion (such as Russia and China), the control impulse will easily trump most institutional forms of cross-border cooperation. More interesting may be, however, that notwithstanding that tendency, local cross-border initiatives continue to occur, even flourish, under all of these scenarios. The work of Solis (2000) and Kosach, Kuzmin, and Mukomel, this volume, point to many such examples.

The project's second point of departure was an attempt to examine an initially notional idea that after several years of upping the enforcement ante along the U.S. southwest border and elsewhere, many border communities had become concerned with the fact that decisions that affect them directly on issues of borders and their management were being made without their participation. In an era of pronounced devolution, much of it admittedly more rhetorical than real, that decision locus—exclusively in the national capitals, with little pretense of consultation with local communities—struck us as worthy of further investigation. We suspected that the continuing function of borders as the physical location where real and symbolic expressions of state sovereignty meet probably explained why domestic decisions about them are seemingly made "unilaterally" by central governments.

A related observation raised an additional red flag for us. Clearly, the urgency of securing a particular segment of the border and the availability of resources were the best predictors of where the border authorities would focus their efforts and how extensive and intensive the effort would be. Remarkably, however, there was seemingly little difference in how, from an enforcement methodology perspective, a government approached communities distressed by a loose border or those having no particular border-related problems—other than by focusing first on the former. In both instances, the management model seemed to be the same; if the manner in which it was applied seemed to be different in some places, such differences were principally a function of resources and of the personalities of and interactions among the relevant national agencies' local managers.

In fact, as we had hypothesized, a state's configuration as a unitary or a federal form of government and the degree to which it emphasized power devolution seemed to have had only a marginal effect on the inclusiveness (within a single state) of substantive decision making about the management of borders. For instance, Canada's at times seemingly pre-determined march toward confederation, its large and clearly defined areas of provincial power sharing and, indeed, primacy, and its abundant mechanisms and processes of federal/provincial co-decision making seem to lead to decisions about borders which do not seem to be appreciably more or less unilateral than those of the United States or, for that matter, Mexico or Russia.

Two interrelated differences, however, remain most relevant among all borders studied in this volume. The degree of threat a state feels from a particular border determines how many resources it will commit to the border control effort. The effectiveness of the effort, however, seems to have only an uncertain association with the re-sources committed to border controls unless the nation is on a war footing. (The Israeli borders are a classic example of this last model.) In fact, and perhaps somewhat paradoxically, saturation policing and other forms of vigorous control seem to produce numerous perverse by-products. Most significant from the perspective of this volume may be the boom in official corruption and the growth in powerful black markets in virtually all aspects relating to the defeat of the control effort—from false documents to sophisticated smuggling networks. (Increases in human rights violations and, in the case of the U.S. Southwest, in the deaths of would-be illegal immigrants, as well as the increased potential for over-reactions to provocations of all types by either side, point to another set of perverse effects.)

The lesson? Unless the politics makes it absolutely impossible, gov-ernments are better off working cooperatively and with the market to expand the legal means for the entry of their nationals in other states' territories. The premise behind this course of action is that, as a rule, acknowledging the economic and social facts on the ground and regu-lating a practice thoughtfully stand a much better chance of achieving important public-policy goals than denying the legitimacy of some of the reasons for the practice's existence and trying to stamp it out through force.

A final aspect of the research further sets this volume apart. Rather than simply providing a case study of a particular border, the volume offers a broadly comparative perspective, reporting on research under-taken as part of the same effort on three different continents. It covers five international borders, over a dozen border regions, and dozens of crossing points. The research thus presents a unique opportunity to discern commonalities and differences among these regions, allows a better understanding of the opportunities and challenges differently organized border communities face, and identifies a broader range of local initiatives from which it is possible to cull "best practices" for testing in other communities. In addition, the two-year project of which this edited volume is the culmination has strengthened existing networks of parties interested in this issue, has seeded new networks, and has promoted the widest possible sharing of information and experiences. Though the greater focus of the project has been on the management of migration-related issues, doing so was impossible without considering the broader context, including other kinds of cross-border interactions and cooperation between communities.

Research Aims

A state performs an array of inspection functions at the border, some of them obvious to any traveler. These include immigration and customs controls, as well as controls against the entry of certain agricultural products. Most of the functions, however, are much less visible. Among the latter are public health and public security functions, currency and financial control functions—still only a few of the nearly two dozen agency interests represented at a border inspection facility.

Many of these functions are clearly essential to good government; all serve some public interest. This fact, however, does not obviate the need to ask whether the functions are all essential, whether they can be done only at the border, whether the manner in which they are done is the most appropriate one, and how the lives of border communities are affected by how functions are delivered. Most importantly, perhaps, and like most governmental functions that are both very costly and intrusive, the delivery of the functions itself demands that the relevant agencies meet stringent effectiveness and accountability standards.

The region of most immediate interest for this research was North America, more specifically the North American Free Trade Agreement (NAFTA) region. The research sought to gain insights in three broad policy areas: first, how the NAFTA partners perceive and conduct their border "inspection" responsibilities; second, whether such inspections are done in the most effective and efficient manner—as well as in a manner that is consistent with interests in other important public policy priorities; and third, the effect of these actions on the life of communities that straddle NAFTA's international borders. It was both intellectual curiosity and interest in comparative inquiry that broadened the scope of the research beyond its North American focus.

The expanded research maintained its focus on border community life as a consistent priority across all research sites. Hence the specific focus on the following three subjects: (a) cataloguing and understanding existing local initiatives toward greater cooperation between border communities located on different sides of an international border; (b) better understanding the similarities and differences in that regard among such communities; and (c) extracting and contextualizing "best practices" in local self-management with regard to cross-border matters. Field research results were then used to assess and develop a perspective on the state of integration within North America, and particularly within the North American Free Trade Agreement space, and to articulate a vision for such integration in fifteen or twenty years.

Review of Findings

The project's principal research hypothesis was that at the local level, communities on both sides of a common border were thinking (and when allowed, acting) creatively and often collaboratively in response to common problems and in pursuit of common interests. Although the degree of cooperation varies significantly across borders and border regions, in almost all instances examples of cooperation were found to exist—thus validating the hypothesis. In fact, the hypothesis held firm even in instances of fractured relationships between national governments—although cooperation under such circumstances typically takes place below the political radar screen of formal, government-to-government relations.

The motivation for cooperative contacts between cross-border communities varies widely. In some instances, the strongest factor tends to be a shared sense of abandonment by each state's national government and, in the new environment of power devolution, a sense that the central government may have turned some power over to them, but not the resources to implement properly the governmental functions they are required to perform. In that regard, necessity or the sense of shared disenfranchisement is at the root of cross-border community cooperation. An attempt to organize the myriad of additional motivations yields the following: the need to address pressing community or intercommunity issues (such as environmental or law and order problems); scarcities in natural resources (especially water) and understanding the advantages of joint stewardship over such resources; practical matters such as maintaining and improving a shared physical infrastructure or using more efficiently whatever social infrastructure may be available to each side (such as medical and educational facilities and fire-fighting and emergency services); and, of course, the sense of a shared economic destiny.

The following are among the most robust general findings of the research. Although not all observations apply to all borders (many individuals and identifiable interests in border communities celebrate their distinctness), most border communities share a surprising number of the sentiments and practices identified below.

1. *The interests of border regions typically receive inadequate and at times unwelcome attention from national governments.* This is generally due to the fact that central governments think of their responsibilities toward borders within the framework of "reasons of state." Such thinking, especially when "security" concerns enter the mix, reinforces the tendency of bureaucracies to make decisions unilaterally and leads to the devaluation of local dynamics and preferences.

Examples of this tendency abound. For instance, along the U.S.-Mexico border, anxiety about drugs and unauthorized immigration has led to fortifications and an active policing framework that gives short shrift to the border's other principal function: facilitation of legal traffic and trade. The dominance of security concerns leads to roughly similar actions (minus the fortifications) at most of the European Union's external borders, as well as at several of Central America's borders (see Witt, this volume, Blatter and Clement 2000, and Solis 2000). In general terms, actions along much of the Russian-Chinese border and at some of the Russia-Kazakhstan border crossings, also discussed in this volume, follow similar patterns. As one might expect, unresolved issues about the demarcation of borders and strained political and military relations between contiguous neighbors further intensifies security concerns, which in turn enhances the "value" of borders as defense perimeters and further downgrades local border community interests and community-initiated cross-border cooperation.

Conversely, when borders are not in dispute and when there is no particular sense of a security threat, light regulation tends to be the norm and facilitation becomes more important than controls. In such instances, local community interests tend to find greater space in which to grow and, under the right circumstances, to be heard. Among all borders studied in this project, only the Canada-U.S. border can be said to approach this latter model—although, until very recently, the two national governments' interest in or capacity to listen to community concerns had been remarkably limited.

2. *National government policies toward border control tend to be inconsistent, even erratic, with patterns often ranging from inattention to the "wrong kind" of attention.* Both extremes kindle discontent and, except in emergencies, both can generate calls for more autonomy on transborder issues of greatest concern to a locality or region. Communities along much of the U.S.-Canada border, as well as in some parts of the Germany-Poland and Germany-Czech Republic borders, desire greater autonomy—as do many communities along the U.S. southwest border. In many instances, however, communities make fundamentally contradictory demands. For instance, along the U.S. southwest border, many U.S. communities, while calling for greater order and security, simultaneously call for easier commercial access to consumers and to workers from across the border. This has been the norm also with some communities along the EU's eastern borders.

Alternatively, rapid population growth (through natural increase, but especially through cross-border migration) and "unplanned" economic growth along a border contribute to pressures on the physical and social infrastructures and the environment that typically go unaddressed. This is a pattern seemingly typified along parts of the U.S.-Mexico border. Neighbors of similar (high) levels of development, however, seem to be better able to manage these issues—in large part because the "burdens" are more likely to be shared (through two-way traffic and use of public goods) and the resources for their amelioration are more readily available, but especially because local governance structures are more mature (see also below, point 10). Hence, disputes along the U.S.-Canada border, as well as at intra-EU "borders," seem to be much more capable of being handled cooperatively than those in either the Near or Far East of the former USSR, or for that matter, Central America.

3. *Most central governments use symbols and language that reinforce the imagery of borders as "zones of exclusion."* One is often struck by the lengths to which some governments go to establish and demarcate their state's distinctness and identity—from the display of massive flags to the creation of a no-man's-land and the building of actual fortifications. Such views, however, often contrast sharply with those of the locals, who are much more likely to consider the border a place of commercial, social, and cultural interface, part of an often single community some of which just happens to be in a foreign political jurisdiction. Many communities along both U.S. borders feel (and act) this way, as do some of the German eastern border communities studied for this research project. Such perspectives and actions, however, appear to be rarer in the border communities of Central America and much of the former Soviet space. Lack of resources to build or maintain the physical infrastructure of border inspection facilities there, however, in some ways translates into less of a sense of a state of siege than is experienced in some parts of the U.S. southwest border!

4. *The adoption of a model of tight controls and the empowerment of border officials to exclude people with little accountability have become breeding grounds for arbitrary behavior by national government personnel; they also create more opportunities for corruption and encourage the growth of market forces designed to defeat border controls.* Nowhere is this phenomenon more evident than along the U.S. southwest border, although behavior at other borders follows the same general rule. As an example of arbitrariness, U.S. immigration officials at different crossings seem to interpret their authority to exclude inadmissible entrants quite differently, resulting in dramatically different outcomes. With regard to official corruption, international smuggling networks are now widely thought to be able to corrupt government officials virtually anywhere. Sometimes, corrupt behavior is broadly institutionalized and involves receiving community public officials at all levels (see Larin and Rubtsova, this volume).

5. *Border communities typically approach both the challenges and the opportunities of deeper cross-border relations in a remarkably pragmatic fashion.* Communities along the U.S.-Canada border typify this behavior;

although below the radar screen of newspaper headlines and the rhetoric of politicians, this is now a nearly universal phenomenon along uncontested borders (see Rodriguez and Hagan, this volume). In fact, as cross-border contacts increase, local officials from both sides, in partnership with business interests, religious organizations, and community-based and other nongovernmental actors, seek to play increasingly significant roles in the ongoing discussions about and the making and implementation of policies that affect their lives.

Clearly, not all communities are equally active in this regard and few are successful in influencing their fate in measurable ways. However, the existence of institutional frameworks that encourage and formalize input, such as those in the EU, can make a significant difference in outcomes. Two other factors also facilitate better cross-border understanding: the growth in cross-border civil society contacts, and official efforts to consider local perspectives along borders. Civil society contacts are growing seemingly by leaps and bounds, even if they are not always able to overcome vast asymmetries of experience and resources (see also del Castillo, this volume). Official efforts to better understand local perspectives are rare but, when agreed upon, can become an important impetus for change—if at least one of the parties commits its political capital and some of its treasure to that goal. The current U.S.-Mexico dialogue holds precisely such a promise, as does, to a less clear degree, the Canada-U.S. Partnership (CUSP) initiative agreed to in 1999.

6. *Business and commercial interests are the drivers of better cross-border relations across all research sites.* In fact, some observers argue that many border communities share a single business culture in what often amounts to symbiotic, even single, markets. This holds true regardless of the degree to which business contacts are formal or informal. Not everyone shares the enthusiasm of commercial interests for more cross-border openness, however, and, as a result, the vision of cross-border relations promoted by business interests can complicate matters when it is in conflict either with that of other local interests or with national priorities and regulations. Such conflicts typically involve issues of whether facilitating the entry of commercial products should take precedence over strict inspection goals, easing access by potential customers from across the border, and the ability to hire workers from a binational labor pool. These conflicts are further exacerbated when national regulations, or the way in which they are im-

plemented by representatives of national bureaucracies at the border, are internally contradictory or are thought to be at significant variance with the broader local economic life.

At times, local communities seek to take initiatives to redress the perceived imbalance. When this happens in the absence of clear national government mandates on an issue it can lead to "cowboy" behavior by local interests. The two studies appearing in this volume on Russian borders provide the most direct examples of such behavior—with the de facto devolution of the visa function in the Russian Far East to regional and local authorities, something that has occurred mostly by default, being the most direct example. Less pointed examples were found throughout the research sites, however, and were most often associated with the national governments' "reach." An example from internal NAFTA borders is the unusual zeal with which U.S. immigration authorities seem to apply the NAFTA rules on the entry of professionals from its NAFTA partners. The implementation of these rules leads to substantially different outcomes along the U.S. borders—which in turn leads to charges of arbitrariness by Canadian professionals.

7. *There is a remarkable degree of community-devised cross-border cooperation on issues such as public health, access to education, environmental protection, joint regional planning, and law enforcement.* In most instances, such cooperation seems to be unaffected by the ups and downs of the national conversation on borders and, more precisely, the conversation within a state's capital. Local concerns about the tone and flavor of these conversations have been heightened by a growing appreciation that discussions about borders inside national capitals often are driven by caricatures and national political slogans and seem always either to over- or under-react to the real issues. Examples of these tendencies were found in all research sites—from Moscow's conversations about a "silent invasion" by the Chinese and the EU's gross overestimates of the likely migration effects of its eastward expansion, to America's on-again, off-again preoccupation with Mexican migration.

Community views, on the other hand, are typically closer to the facts on the ground than is political rhetoric, and are better attuned to local needs and nuances. These range from a finer sense of increasingly common destinies and, perhaps to a lesser degree, human and ethnic solidarity. (As many of the authors of this volume make clear, however, this should not be interpreted as suggesting that cross-border communities somehow share common worldviews or are either unaware of or unconcerned with the economic, social, identity, and governance issues that closer contacts imply.) The most pronounced examples of these forms of cooperation may be found along both U.S. borders, where legalized forms of deep cross-border cooperation abound; however, several communities along Germany's eastern borders and certain aspects of the Russia-Kazakhstan border relationship also show similar tendencies.

8. *Investments in the economic and social development of border regions and cities are at best an intermittent affair and tend to be inadequate even in the best of circumstances.* Models of how to invest in a border region include first, the distribution of significant funds through supranational institutions (the EU "Euro-regions" model—see Irek, Witt, and Schmidt and Salt, all in this volume), and second, the potentially very significant U.S. investments in transportation corridors (see Meyers and Papademetriou in this volume) which allow investments in Canada and Mexico—and to a more limited degree, vice versa. A third model, worth mentioning more for its potential than its concrete progress to date, refers to the embryonic U.S. development efforts at its southwest border, recommended in 2000 by the U.S. Government's Interagency Task Force for the Economic Development of the Southwest Border (President's Interagency Task Force 2000). Despite the change in administrations, many expect some of the Task Force's ideas to be converted into binational initiatives through the expansion of the capital base and the mandate of the binational North American Bank (NADBank), created by the NAFTA and charged primarily with addressing border environmental tasks. A final model comes from the Pacific Northwest, where remarkably well-organized cross-border public/private efforts have been able to make considerable progress in securing funding from state, local, and U.S. federal sources to pursue the objective of adapting national policies to the region's unique requirements and opportunities.

9. *There is an increasing array of experiments with a variety of "extraterritorial" arrangements designed to facilitate commercial and sociocultural interests.* Most of the examples we found are in Europe and in North America, although certain Russia-Kazakhstan transborder activities fit this mold, as do many aspects of the German-Polish coopera-

tive activities outlined by Irek in this volume. For instance, the United States has experimented with permitting Mexican border inspection functions to be performed deep within U.S. territory during the Christmas season (in order to reduce delays at the border as large numbers of Mexicans return home for the holidays). The United States and Mexico have reciprocally expanded the zone for the less restricted movement of Mexicans in Arizona to 65 miles (and for Americans into Sonora for 100 kilometers), mostly as a means of encouraging access by Mexican nationals to U.S. commercial establishments. Furthermore, in most major Canadian airports the United States has a deeply institutionalized pre-clearance system for customs, immigration, and associated agencies for travelers to the United States, and together with Canada it is taking the first tentative steps toward sharing inspection facilities and related items.

10. *Next to being given short shrift by national authorities and the lack of resources, lack of "capacity" may be the border communities' greatest problem.* It may be difficult to overemphasize this point. The capacity gap spans the gamut of activities along borders. It is clearly more pronounced in poorer countries, in remote border communities, and in the communities most recently delegated political power, although it also exists in communities lacking sufficient physical capacity to handle the ever-expanding traffic.

In some ways, the most relevant gap may be in governance—the ability of a community to organize itself to deliver in a relatively competent manner even the most elementary functions a government is expected to deliver. Making progress in this regard is very important: it can earn the confidence of the people and inspire private institutions to invest in the life of the community. Naturally, the lack of resources greatly intensifies the problem. The governance gap also manifests itself in the ability of a community to manage its relations with its national government with some effectiveness. Many parts of the U.S.-Mexico border (often on both sides of the border), Central American border communities, and most of the Russian borders studied for this project fit this pattern all too well.

However, the need for capacity building goes beyond governance and beyond the public sector. Institutions of all types are needed to undertake and complete any number of essential activities—from creating a functioning credit and financial market and maintaining and enhancing the physical infrastructure, to beginning to plan and make the investments needed for setting up the most elementary components of a system of social infrastructure. And no social infrastructure gap is felt more strongly than those in the fields of education and health services. Frequently, a bad situation is made worse when domestic politics dictates that public goods controlled by the national government be distributed on the basis of party affiliation—"freezing out" states and localities that may have sided electorally with the losing side.

Gaps also are pronounced in the development of a culture of civil society that can hold the government accountable for its decisions and can play a part in the development of a broader base of social activism. In the absence of such "checks and balances," corruption, much of it petty but no less entrenched, goes unchecked—and widens the public sector's capacity gap. Examples of such gaps are revealed in the sharpest possible relief in this volume's U.S.-Mexico border research (see especially del Castillo).

Recommendations for the NAFTA Partners

The rich and intricate tapestry of complex interdependence stitched together by the case studies in this volume makes clear that generalizations and, ultimately, policy recommendations need to exercise extreme care not to oversimplify. The case studies also make clear, however, that at borders where local communities engage in transborder relations, there is a great deal more going on than many analysts have suspected and, more to the point, than either national leaders or the national press have bothered to recognize.

In some instances there are a myriad of examples of building transborder "community"—an essential first step to the process of building the "North-American Community" that scholar-activist John W. Wirth envisioned in his 1996 essay. In other instances, residents themselves seemingly desire greater and more organic cross-border "integration," as well as greater autonomy from the national government—or at least closer consultation with them by it—in affairs that affect them. This tends to be the case even though many communities simultaneously articulate desires for two seemingly contradictory policy responses.

The first aspires to the orderliness of tighter management and controls—a promise that governments seldom seem to be able to deliver effectively on, in an intensely interdependent world where economic competitiveness and economic well-being are closely tied to trade and commerce and to the speed and efficiency of those transactions. The second demands greater contact and openness, even going so far as to argue for opening the border to the far greater movement of people. This interest was documented most directly in a 2001 survey of the residents of communities on both sides of the U.S.-Mexico border by the Tomás Rivera Policy Institute. The survey found that border communities along both sides of the border seem to be well ahead of or at significant variance with (a) how politicians see further "integration" (substantial majorities from both sides favored greater freedom of movement) and (b) how much and how quickly they think that U.S. border policies should be adjusted. (As one might expect, the majorities in favor were greater on the Mexican side of the border.)

What, then, might one recommend that is consistent with and moves toward the more open and cooperative future the research results discussed in this volume imply?

1. *Border controls should be conceptualized as a means to an end, rather than as the ultimate policy goal portrayed in political rhetoric and reflected in bureaucratic initiatives.* Put differently, the explicit end-goal of regulatory and enforcement efforts at the border should be to manage the border effectively enough to prepare the ground for the serious conversation about how best jointly to accomplish each neighbor's principal public policy priorities while allowing more organic forms of integration to proceed at a reasonable pace. One implication of this recommendation is that the current set of discussions and initiatives regarding the NAFTA partners' internal borders should continue to proceed roughly along the paths they have been following in the last year or so; *this must be accompanied, however, by an explicit reconceptualization and articulation of the desirable end point.* Focusing squarely on the greater use of technology and on management innovations that improve both facilitation and regulation and control must be part and parcel of this process—but, again, they must not be the end points of the NAFTA relationships.

The recently adopted (2000) Canadian Customs Action Plan, for instance, makes great strides toward these twin objectives. Yet, by the

Canadian authorities' own reckoning, these risk-management-based changes will overwhelm the initiative's capacity as early as 2004 (Policy Research Initiative 2001). This suggests the need for deeper changes. Stephen Flynn (2000, 58) also suggests an approach that centers on risk management, starting from a similar point of wishing to facilitate commerce while improving "security" in most ways. He sees the need for a three-part "paradigm shift" that focuses squarely on upstream, preventive approaches that stress mostly off-the-shelf technology, such as "smart" documents, and cooperative international mechanisms. Flynn's three prongs are as follows: (a) tightening security "within the international transportation and logistics system"; (b) insisting on transparent systems for "tracking regional and global commercial flows" that allow regulators to "conduct 'virtual' audits of inbound traffic"; and (c) developing "faster and stronger capabilities to gather intelligence and manage data."

For the U.S.-Canada border, continuing along the previous path but with a reconceptualization of the end point means ever-closer and more organic cooperation, a more explicit focus on understanding and addressing differences, and particularly, far more experimentation. For the U.S.-Mexico border, this means that Mexico's deeper engagement of the United States over the past decade must not just continue in earnest but in fact must accelerate further, and it must shift gears. This bilateral relationship is too important for either country to become distracted by the differences between them. Both President Fox and President Bush seem to understand this basic principle well enough, and have started on a negotiating course that shows extraordinary promise. Although that course's centerpiece is the migration relationship, the border cannot be left too far behind—if for no other reason than that it is deeply intertwined with the migration issue.

In fact, these discussions of the border must eventually be engaged in by all three NAFTA partners. The discussions should be initially bilateral and should explore interest in and set the parameters for negotiations about changing the current border-management paradigm. The fact that both the United States and Mexico have new executive leadership which, in the case of Mexico, is willing to ask for the reevaluation of the current border "management" paradigm[1] and in the U.S. case appears somewhat receptive to that request, should be embraced as an opportunity to start the relationship anew—while acknowledging and building upon many of the mostly procedural breakthroughs the previous governments had made.

Similarly, newly re-elected Canadian Prime Minister Chrétien must decide whether his often "improvisational" (Cooper 2000) relations with the United States are likely to work as well with Mr. Bush's administration as they apparently did with Mr. Clinton's. Mr. Chrétien's policy of "calculated ambivalence" (Cooper 2000) has been clearly rooted in the Liberal Party's traditional ambivalence about the relationship with the United States and in the need to distinguish the Liberals' policies from those of the predecessor Mulroney government. The question Mr. Chrétien and his advisors must now answer is if this posture moves Canada toward making real progress toward a worthwhile vision of the U.S.-Canada (and, eventually, NAFTA) relationship fifteen or so years from now.

2. *All three national governments must show uncharacteristic adeptness in adapting their border management and enforcement practices to local conditions.* While in the U.S. context this recommendation may raise important field-management concerns about the U.S. Immigration and Naturalization Service (which has proven unable to rein in its field managers and deliver many of its functions with consistency), the principle nonetheless remains a powerful one. Whenever possible, field managers should be encouraged to work in tandem with local communities to deliver the various components of the immigration function in a manner that is sensitive to and builds upon the particular circumstances of an area.

Currently, hardly any border communities have either a strategy or a mechanism for building their capacity to aggregate and articulate their interests. Developing such strategies and investing in mechanisms — such as a regular annual or biennial meeting of public and private-sector interests along and across a single border — could address this weakness. (Some U.S.-Canada border interests are served by a number of useful fora, but more needs to be done, particularly in terms of inclusiveness — see Meyers and Papademetriou, this volume.) Such a regular forum would institutionalize the exchange of views, facilitate the process of learning about each other's interests, priorities, successes, and failures, and offer an opportunity to build relationships and impanel issue-focused groups, as appropriate, to promote common interests. Central governments also should initiate regular, systematic opportunities for local interests to be brought into the decision-making process about issues that affect them. Such an initiative would address a second systemic weakness of the status quo—the lack of a formal mechanism for communities to convey their interests to the appropriate central government policy-making bodies in a manner that is timely and thus enhances the prospects of a fair hearing.[2]

Such courses of action will not solve all of the problems identified in this volume. They do hold substantial promise, however, to improve upon two central attributes of the status quo: the failure of border communities to organize themselves in ways that allow them to learn from each other's experiences, and their lack of success in narrowing the pronounced democratic deficits that national border policies have created and perpetuate.

3. *There should not be a one-size-fits-all approach to the issues at hand —not even along a single border.* History, topography, economy, and the level of local engagement with the issue (both that of the public sector and that of the for-profit and not-for-profit private sectors), lead to enormous variability in the delivery of border inspection functions, as do differences in outlooks and management and personal skills of the local managers of national bureaucracies. For instance, the history of Germany's eastern border is quite different from that of the U.S. southwest border, even though both resulted from wars. The German eastern border is only about half a century old, and has been contested, shaped, and drawn and redrawn many times over the centuries; the U.S. southwest border, on the other hand, has been stable for about a century and a half, and the U.S.-Canada border was created through negotiations about two centuries ago.

It is the condition of the bilateral relationship and each state's strategic objectives that are most dominant in how a government will see its border. Germany's appreciation of the long-term value of the markets of its eastern neighbors inclines its policies toward working with them on all issues, as the day fast approaches when these countries will become its full partners within the EU. In addition, Germany's experience with its own divided past makes it almost inconceivable that it would erect fortifications. The United States, on the other hand, is only now beginning to think in terms of a partnership model regarding Mexico—although its view of Canada probably approximates Germany's view of its eastern contiguous neighbors.

But even along a single border, differences demand border management approaches that use more of a surgeon's scalpel than a butcher's meat-cleaver. Until relatively recently, California's view of the border, or for that matter of Mexico, was dramatically different from that of Texas, whose enormous two-way trade relationship and large Mexican-American community dictated a more measured rhetoric and policies. And the U.S.-Canada border is anything but a single entity—in cross-border relationships, in community engagement, in the opportunities and limitations created or imposed by topography (see Meyers and Papademetriou, this volume), and so forth. These differences demand, and sometimes in fact result in, sensitive and thoughtful approaches that respect and take advantage of differences. These approaches, however, still need to be informed by a single policy frame of reference and reflect the levels of shared goals and objectives between the two countries—that is, building upon, rather than undermining, the increasingly seamless cooperation between the two countries in a vast array of policy areas.

The importance of policy clarity and, more importantly, of policies that have a real purpose—an end-goal or a vision—cannot be overemphasized, nor can its absence, from virtually every border this project has studied, be more pronounced. (Germany has been the principal exception.) It is, in our view, the most fundamental explanation for the relative state of confusion about the management of borders, and for the inconsistency with which it is proceeding. As a result of this failure of imagination, states do not seem able to learn from and successfully incorporate innovations in managing borders, using different management models and alternative methodologies.

To summarize, both U.S. and most other borders studied in this project are undergoing enormous—and extremely fast-paced—social and economic transformations. In light of those transformations, the public sector in the capital city may be the least well-prepared entity effectively to shape and manage such changes. Among the reasons for this are the national capitals' frequent locations far away from the borders, and the national governments' tendency to think about issues, and set priorities, in ways that often militate against giving localities the space and flexibility they need to set and pursue their own priorities within the overall framework of national objectives.

The Concept and Vision of North American Integration

We understand integration in the Churchillian sense of a "living organism"—always in need of nourishment and tending, of active support, and of management of its growth and progress. (Conversely, inattention, or the "wrong kind" of attention, can stunt its growth and even lead to its demise.) It is in this conceptual framework that we call on the three NAFTA partners to commence initially domestic processes that will test the idea that a North American Integration "Project" is worth pursuing, and to develop a strategic plan for changing the terms of the debate about the border relationship with their immediate neighbors. If the decision is to proceed, bilateral negotiations should be pursued with an aim of agreeing on the kind of border relationship each pair of countries wishes to see by an arbitrarily set target date (say, 2015 or 2020).

Whatever is agreed to must proceed from the assumption that if these negotiations are to succeed, they must recommend activities that are gradual and evolutionary, and in each instance take into account the interests of the affected communities. This implies much deeper levels of national government, state (provincial), and local government cooperation. It also implies far greater and more systematic consultations with local stakeholders than any of the three national governments is either familiar with or perhaps comfortable in undertaking.

What we envision here is a set of processes that asks the question, does sufficient support either exist or can it be generated for a bold vision of a North American "Project"? Such a vision imagines the NAFTA's internal borders gradually (and in temporal and substantive terms, unevenly) becoming irrelevant to the point at which their abolition could proceed without any measurable losses in any of the important security, revenue collection, and even "identity" priorities of each partner, at least relative to the results of the present course of action. The vision also imagines small actual additional losses in "sovereignty" for any of the partners that would be offset by substantial democratic surpluses for all three NAFTA countries.

Such a vision could be best approached from two distinct, yet ultimately converging, tracks. The first focuses on continuing the multiplicity of contacts, the deepening of bilateral engagement, and, in some instances, the focus on pragmatic problem-solving that has been the operational model for the past few years. While this track has at times produced an almost mindless continuity (simply doing more of the same but somehow expecting much better results), at other times it has led to occasional progress toward the often competing goals of each pair of partners.

The second track should focus on the kind of North America the citizens of the three countries have a legitimate right to expect in the not-too-distant future—and on how best to achieve it. Some of this track's required elements will of necessity be "defensive" in nature; that is, they must "protect" citizens from unwanted activities, practices, and products. Other elements will be forward-looking and will be advancing broader citizen interests in terms of prosperity, adherence to rules, protection of rights, and fundamental conformity with the principles of humanitarianism. In its totality, the proposed vision should hold the promise for doing better by most people in each of the NAFTA partners along most of these goals.

Such a vision should include the following among its main elements: (a) greater security from illegal activities and unwanted products from *outside* the NAFTA space—including terrorism, illegal immigration, drugs, and more; (b) protection from illegal activities and undesirable products that may be found *inside* the NAFTA region that will be no less reliable than what each NAFTA partner enjoys now; (c) the nearly seamless movement of legitimate goods and people seeking to cross internal NAFTA borders; and (d) protection from the political ups and downs (the political "mood swings," as it were) of one NAFTA partner or another and, perhaps more importantly, from bureaucratic "ad-hocism," affecting the vital interests of the other partners. Of course, such protection would be best guaranteed by some institutional mechanisms, especially "dispute resolution" measures similar to those developed for the NAFTA.

There is nothing in our vision that interferes with building greater prosperity within the border region. In fact, we anticipate greater intraregional economic growth, both as a result of gains in the international competitive position of the NAFTA region's products and services, and from greater freedom and democracy for the people of the region. We, of course, are convinced that these latter gains will be much more robust if border communities are encouraged to reach their own levels of integration—both along and across intra-NAFTA borders.

Is our vision realistic? We think so. Will critics think that it is realistic? Probably not. In many ways, there are few things easier than shooting down a vision. The three NAFTA capitals are full of people who know how to say "no" a million ways. (Bureaucracies of all types are particularly adept at saying "no" to changes in their mission or culture. Ultimately, since it is bureaucracies that will implement any vision, working with them will bear more fruit than working against them.) Getting to "yes," however, requires great political courage and uncommon qualities of leadership. Nor can a vision of a different future immediately provide fully satisfactory answers to all the questions—legitimate or not—that people may pose. Fears, hopes, self-interest, competing institutional mandates and priorities, different senses of self, diverging Weltanschauungen (worldviews), and a whole host of nuances and different perspectives guarantee that the road to realizing the vision proposed here will be rocky and that the outcome frequently will seem uncertain. Furthermore, as with the early stages of any ambitious new initiative, there will be winners and losers—and each NAFTA partner will have to give priority to developing policies that address the concerns of those who will likely lose at the beginning.

Preliminary Steps to Pursuing the North American Integration "Project"

Further integration of North America will not occur overnight. Integration, Wirth's building of "community" (1996), is a gradual process involving a myriad of incremental steps and the building of trust. To begin, we suggest that each border inspection agency be required to analyze each one of the functions it performs at the border along three lines: First, must each of its functions be done only at the border? Second, what are the costs and benefits of doing that function at the border versus doing it elsewhere? Third, can any of its functions be performed by an inspector from a sister agency? (An advisory citizens' panel could review each agency's report for responsiveness to the mandate.)

The following might be among some of the issues to be examined:

- What if the Customs Service re-deployed its resources to perform many of its inspections and collect all applicable duties at the point where the cargo is loaded in North America, and employed available technology to seal the container(s) and transfer all the relevant information about the cargo electronically to any other inspection point?

- What if Customs were then to employ a "risk-management" methodology for performing its inspection functions and in return re-deployed some of its newly "released" personnel to joint investigative task forces with agencies from either side of the border in order to uncover violations of various types?

- What if all inspections and the collection of tariffs, for all of the NAFTA partners, were done either by one partner on behalf of the others or jointly—but always once—at the initial point in which a cargo from a non-NAFTA country enters NAFTA space? And in this context, why not explore the concept of "unified port management" for its potential to use resources most efficiently while improving both services and the quality of inspections?

- What if the remaining border customs inspections also were done once—by either national customs service—so as to accommodate variances in staffing, physical infrastructure, and topographical idiosyncrasies? (Isolated instances of "sharing" are already in place, but they have proven to be politically very difficult.)

- What if the United States were to copy the Canadian model of having only one agency staff the primary inspection lanes, rather than having both Customs and the Immigration and Naturalization Service, as presently occurs? All necessary inspection agencies would retain a presence at the border to perform secondary inspections, but after appropriate training and negotiation this might simplify some of the existing staffing and personnel issues.

- What if the existing systems of customs brokers and private bondsmen were utilized to an even greater extent and were given both greater power and greater responsibility—and, by extension, were made more accountable (and penalized more severely) for failures of either omission or commission? And what if it were thus the private sector that grew to accommodate the growth in commerce, rather than the public sector agencies whose growth depends so very much on the budgetary and policy priorities of the national government at any given point in time?

- What if the private sector were to be relied upon even more consequentially in areas ranging from technology to the building of better infrastructure wherever it might be needed, through liberalized public-private partnerships and pay-as-you-go projects?

- What if the Immigration Service were to move in the same direction as Customs, that is, if it did all third-country (non-NAFTA) immigration controls at an individual's first point of entry into NAFTA space? Pre-clearance technology and intelligence cooperation are in many instances already significant enough to expect that this method can be accelerated without any loss of control relative to the status quo. In fact, airport inspections are more accurate and can be more efficient than virtually any system of inspections at land borders, where visa and identity checks are rather perfunctory.

- What if Canada and the United States initially were to agree to a common visa regime for the widest band of countries each country could accommodate, and exercised much greater care in the issuance of visas for the citizens of countries for which visa-free entry could not be agreed to by the other country?

- What if Canada and the United States initially, the U.S. and Mexico at a later point, and, eventually, all three NAFTA partners and contiguous neighbors, agreed to gradually liberalize the movement of each other's nationals? Considering the special treatment that each has offered to the other's professionals, businesspersons, and investors, for example under the NAFTA, and in view of the extraordinary—and increasing—degree to which the two pairs of economies and their associated labor markets are integrated, formalizing the greater movement of people may be a relatively small step to take. In fact, as the U.S.-Mexico Migration Panel report (2001) referred to earlier points out, the U.S. labor market can probably absorb effectively greater numbers of legal workers from both of its NAFTA partners. (Much better controls on unauthorized entries and employment would be an extra incentive for greater openness in legal visas.) It might be instructive to note in this regard that despite having reached absolute freedom of movement, intra-EU migration by EU citizens is minuscule, at between seven and eight million persons, or about two percent of the EU's population. Concerns about the potential exploitation by the nationals of one country of another country's more generous social support systems can be addressed in a variety of ways, including the EU's method of a foreigner continuing to be protected by the social protection mechanisms of the country of origin for the first three months after "relocation." A migrant can also be required to leave the country to which he or she has moved unless (s)he has found a job within a specified period of time or has his or her own means of support.

These recommendations are not made in a vacuum. Some tentative steps toward the directions recommended here are already being taken, the technology is readily available, and the large business sector that accounts for most of the transborder initiatives and energy is thought to be fully primed for cooperating in return for more timely and predictable results. A vision, and political will, seem to be the major missing ingredients.

Comparisons of Our North American Vision
with the European Integration "Project"

The repeated references to the EU beg the question of how closely our vision for a North American "Project" relates to Europe's own integration project. The answer is that, in the matters most important for North Americans, the differences between the two concepts may be greater than their similarities. Three differences may be most consequential.

First, because of the degree of integration that is likely to have been reached prior to achieving the vision promulgated here, and the United States' strong distaste for supranational bureaucracies, we see no place for a "Brussels" in North America. Although we do not claim that the sovereignty of each partner will not be somewhat diluted, our model does not envision the direct transfers of sovereignty so central to the EU concept.

Second, our conception has a strong bias toward an integration process that is organic and is thus built from the bottom up—and from the periphery to the center, that is, from border regions to capital cities. Although the final push must still come from the top down—if for no other reason than that this is how national bureaucracies become energized—our model differs dramatically from the top-down approach the EU practices even today. It is these fundamental differences in the source and location of the energy for integration that are responsible for the EU's enormous democratic deficits—unlike what we believe to be the significant democratic surpluses of our approach.

Finally, unlike with the EU, there is nothing in our concept that envisions the creation of a new political entity. Nor is there any expectation of untoward rates of change in areas each of the three NAFTA partners considers nearly "sacred"—such as issues of national identity or specific components of a model of public governance, or Canada's attachment to (an eroding) system of social protections. After all, even in the absence of an EU-like Social Charter or an outright emulation of the relative largesse of Canadian social benefits, the defense of individual freedom, the promotion of social rights, the commitment to democratic pluralism, and the importance of civil society are dominant values in both the United States and Canada—and Mexico is clearly moving toward them.

Outline of the Volume

The essays on the individual regions that were studied in this project begin with a section on North American borders, involving three areas along the U.S.-Canada border and four along the U.S.-Mexico border. In the former, Meyers and Papademetriou discuss the three regions they studied (Buffalo/Niagara, Detroit/Windsor, and Seattle/Vancouver), describe the myriad of cross-border ties and cooperative initiatives they discovered in their research visits, and highlight some of the "best practices" they culled from both the public and private sectors. They found that the border relationship is greatly shaped by the degree of shared cross-border interests, the levels of informal and interpersonal relationships between the principal actors, the presence and degree of engagement of stakeholders and networks—especially those of business—and the national political skills of local and federal officials.

Meyers and Papademetriou also catalogue and discuss the many opportunities and challenges faced by communities along the U.S.-Canada border. For example, many border community residents take advantage of dining, entertainment, and shopping in the other country, while businesses use their locational advantages to appeal to and serve a binational clientele. Among the many challenges are delays in crossing the border and their effect on peoples' schedules, business productivity, pollution (which is heavily linked to crossing delays), and mostly petty illegal activity. Overall, the authors' respondents had a positive image of the border, although the role of the federal government (in terms of staffing, infrastructure, and policy issues) was identified as a repeated frustration. The most common refrain of their interviews seemed to be the need for a much better balance of facilitation of legitimate crossings with prevention of illegal ones.

Meyers and Papademetriou conclude that the communities' differences in levels of social and economic integration, geography, types of crossing points, and population compositions are substantial enough that "one size doesn't fit all" when it comes to crafting a policy for this border. Instead, a framework that incorporates a national policy—yet allows local flexibility—and thus takes each area's commonalities and differences into account, would be a more appropriate approach. They argue for greater vertical and horizontal consciousness raising to help mitigate the challenges border communities face, and suggest a two-track approach to problem solving. The first would focus on technical improvements and building further on existing discussions; the second would be more conceptual, challenging the conventional wisdom by stepping back to think more broadly about the goals of border policies and the best ways to achieve them. They recommend greater and more systematic input by local communities and businesses into both tracks.

Moving south, Rodriguez and Hagan focus on the variety of formal and informal local practices that transborder communities have created along the Texas-Mexico border, often despite national regulations. After profiling Laredo/Nuevo Laredo and El Paso/Ciudad Juárez and providing a better understanding of their histories and present-day interactions, they catalogue by sector the "best practices" they discovered. These include cooperation in local government, law enforcement, business, public health, education, and community grassroots. Rodriguez and Hagan note that strong social, cultural, and economic ties have evolved in these four cities which straddle the border, and that local cooperation between individuals is the key to successful initiatives. They conclude that cooperation between these communities may be predisposed to occur, however, because of their integrated economies, historical ties (social, cultural, and familial), common concerns over health and the environment, and the sense that they share a common destiny despite obvious economic asymmetries.

Del Castillo's study of the region further west along the U.S.-Mexico border draws a relatively pessimistic portrait of the border landscape. He finds few stable cross-border institutional, corporate, or community ties along either the California-Mexico or the Arizona-Mexico borders. He attributes this, in part, to the extraordinary pace of economic growth in, and asymmetries between, these particular regions. According to del Castillo, the "understandings" that are reached in these regions often are short-lived. Combined with an increasing and constantly changing number of private actors (often acting as public sector substitutes), cross-border mistrust, and poor-quality governance in the region, cross-border interactions and initiatives are understandably both episodic and limited.

For del Castillo, the two countries' different political and judicial systems exacerbate the problems, as does the fact that as problems remain unaddressed they increase in complexity until their resolution becomes both more difficult and more costly. He urges the development of a unified vision for the region and the formation of "rapid response structures" to address short- and medium-term problems. Such structures could mediate among the multitude of actors and institutions, perhaps even serving as a clearinghouse for binational planning on such issues as population growth, access to natural resources, environmental degradation, and industrial growth.

The reader will notice certain striking differences in the findings between Rodriguez/Hagan and del Castillo along the same national border, not only in the extent and nature of cross-border interactions, but also in attitudes. This is exemplified by the quote of a Mexican official referring to the two Laredos as a single city compared to a San Diego decision maker's comment of "no existe" when asked about transborder understandings. Perhaps the common origins and apparently common economic destinies of the two Laredos and the El Paso/Ciudad Juárez region may be responsible to a large degree for the Rodriguez/Hagan findings—in addition to continuing linguistic ties and deep familial and cultural ties, which translate into most "Americans" having family on the "Mexican" side.

The El Paso/Ciudad Juárez topography and the understanding that their survival and their prosperity are inextricably linked may also have contributed to efforts to develop successful coping strategies. Further, it contributes to the sense that each city has more in common with the other than with others in their respective states or countries, as well as to a feeling that dealing with the federal government is a burden —perhaps even an impediment to carrying on their daily lives. The links are additionally strengthened through numerous joint efforts—ranging from the role of both cities' business communities in the establishment of a Dedicated Commuter Lane at the border crossing to the creation by the sister cities' local governments of a joint urban growth plan and their sharing of medical information and equipment.

By comparison, San Diego is a much larger city, located 12 miles away from the border (San Ysidro is actually Tijuana's neighboring city.) Rapid population growth in both cities has stressed the local infrastructure tremendously, while sharp differences in the ethnic composition of the populations of these two cities reinforce their separation. Though family and business ties clearly exist, they are not nearly as many and not nearly as deep as those in Texas. Nor are the economies of Tijuana and San Diego as closely interdependent as they are in Texas. The absence of joint planning and information sharing in Tijuana-San Diego typically means that initiatives often become overrun by events, while the contrast between "hardened" border enforcement and the continuous expansion of trade and economic ties seem to have had a larger and more negative impact on the populations and relationships in California (and somewhat less so, Arizona) than in Texas.

Witt provides the transition to the volume's second section, on European borders. She offers a thoughtful comparison of issues along the United States-Mexico border with those of the European Union (EU), noting that the EU has a distinctly top-down approach to integration that includes an endless array of institutions and substantial amounts of financing to support them and their initiatives. Witt believes that North America could learn from certain aspects of the European experience and suggests incorporating border regions into the policy process for decisions that affect them and creating funding and institutional structures to support cooperation on security and non-security issues.

Witt speculates that while the NAFTA has raised expectations in the Arizona-Sonora border region which remain unmet, informal cooperation is thriving, in contrast to the German-Polish border, where communities and authorities seem to be lagging in terms of informal cooperation. Witt reports that many border communities in the Arizona-Sonora region view federal policies as a barrier to cooperation or as the cause of particular problems, and want increased representation in the decision-making process in ways that will enhance the federal authorities' understanding of the border, its culture, and the local perspective. For instance, an overly intense focus on border controls and enforcement may be harming the border economy and the building of trust between communities. Witt believes, nonetheless, that border functions remain important for sovereignty and security, and points out that the EU has transformed them into instruments of integration and solidarity rather than barriers.

The European section continues with Irek's detailed study of the border between Germany and Poland, a border rich in informal contacts despite its history of conflict. She details many of the local initiatives that have grown along the German-Polish border, including the self-declaration by two neighboring towns as one *Europastadt*, Internet links between town halls, joint bus lines to facilitate cross-border shopping, a border university, and binational business ventures. Irek suggests that the success of these efforts may be attributable to such factors as the urgency of problems, the degree of economic necessity, the common sense of local authorities, the good will of inhabitants, and the international political climate. In addition, she notes that two of the towns studied used to be one until the penultimate redivision of the borders. In addition, their multiethnic populations and the signing of an international treaty of friendship by the respective national governments have paved the way and provided some funding for local initiatives.

Irek acknowledges that many people are profiting from the current open nature of the border. She observes that common sense and flexibility are required when national governments deal with border communities and that the former are too far from the border to really either understand the situation or improve it—although they certainly can hinder cooperation. She recommends that local communities in border areas be granted additional autonomy in addressing some of the local, border-related challenges.

The third section of this volume focuses on a part of the world noted for its newly opened and newly created borders, the Russia-China and Russia-Kazakhstan borders, respectively. Larin and Rubtsova report on regions along the Russia-China border, which has little history of cross-border interactions due to the Soviet era's closed borders. They note the large asymmetries in population and the primarily one-way flow of people from China to Russia. The traffic is composed largely of shuttle traders, and many residents of that region feel that the Russian government does not appreciate the importance of this trade to the Russian Far East population, as evidenced by restrictive legislation.

Clearly, an atmosphere where only one country sees the border as an economic opportunity is not an atmosphere conducive to two-way cross-border initiatives. Language and political differences pose further obstacles to cross-border initiatives, although Larin and Rubtsova do detail some successful initiatives achieved by local authorities exhibiting some flexibility (such as the 24-hour Chinese market) and describe the generally appreciative attitude of local Russians toward the Chinese who bring many needed goods. They conclude, however, that at present the border is being managed ineffectively, it is challenged by poor infrastructure, extensive corruption, and crime, and it lacks a means to collect and disseminate accurate information about the actual numbers of Chinese migrant entries—data that, in the authors' view, might counter prejudices and security concerns.

Kosach, Kuzmin, and Mukomel conclude this section with their discussion of various crossing points along the Russia-Kazakhstan border. Shedding light on a little-known area, they describe a border that is only ten years old and noteworthy for its limited contact between cross-border communities. In some ways, the border communities the authors studied could not be more different from the communities along the North American and European borders. The authors attribute this to the lack of shared interests, poor transportation and other physical infrastructure, and a paucity of cultural or economic connections. Exceptions include substantial economic cooperation in raw materials in the Orenburg region and cooperation in hydrocarbon production in the Astrakahn region. Moreover, Kazakh citizens regularly use medical and educational cross-border facilities in Russia and some business ties also exist, although they tend to be unstable. By and large, however, the authors describe a region rife with interethnic tensions and territorial disputes, trafficking of drugs and weapons, and substantial crime and corruption.

The contrasts between the two Russian borders studied in this section of the volume are very significant. One is forced to speculate that the far greater cross-border connection between Russia and China is largely the result of business and tourist contacts along the Russia-China border, the greater economic dependence of Russians in the Far East on the Chinese petty traders, and on the business acumen of the Chinese.

Although the section on Russian borders concludes the volume, the appendix provides an opportunity to learn from yet another experience, that of the evolution of the European Union. Schmidt and Salt provide a brief retrospective on European integration, summarizing the EU's steps toward the free movement of people since its inception and discussing the obstacles in continental integration the European project has had to overcome—obstacles that at the time had seemed insurmountable. In particular, the appendix traces the fifty-year incremental process that made free movement a reality, and the evolution of Europe's regional policies. The appendix also serves as a reminder that the free movement of people in the European Union grew as much from a political as from an economic rationale—a reminder that is useful as the United States and Mexico embark on their conversations on the bilateral migration and border relationship. The appendix thus encourages states to manage their borders jointly and reminds the reader that progress on even the most intractable issues may come down to creativity, leadership, local input, an overarching vision, common sense, and a willingness to experiment and learn from others.

Concluding Thoughts

Few issues in the international system are as complex as those surrounding borders. As this volume demonstrates, the roots of that complexity include but go beyond the reality that borders are the most direct physical manifestation of "statehood" and sovereignty—of the continuously evolving Weberian notion of the ability to exercise (near-) monopoly control over entry (and by extension, membership). They also are inextricably linked with competing policy priorities that simultaneously expect border inspection systems to allow the swift and efficient passage of legitimate people and products while unerringly stopping illegitimate traffic and undesirable products. The research conducted for this project has spotlighted another, and typically forgotten or ignored, facet of borders: as concepts which in their practical manifestation divide communities, exacerbate differences in approach between localities and national governments, and interfere with the ability of public and private sector "on-the-ground" actors to pursue their own paths toward ever greater integration.

At their very root, however, borders and their "management" or "protection," however much these last functions may have changed in recent years, are first and foremost *political* concepts, and can only be addressed politically. Hence this project's search for a vision that might maximize the benefits while containing the undesirable elements of the extraordinary—and increasing—economic, social, and cultural exchanges among the peoples of the NAFTA region.

Returning to the "North American" partnership—this project's region of direct interest—what have the years since the NAFTA came into force (1994) meant for the relationships that have been the focus of this volume? At the national level, Mexico has seen gains in what it has chosen to emphasize as its own top priorities: protecting the human rights and dignity of its nationals and inoculating the rest of the bilateral relationship against the infectious potential of disagreements about immigration and drugs. Canada has been largely insulated from America's often wild and unpredictable tilting at the windmills of illegal immigration, drug trafficking, and more recently, foreign terrorism—although not without a great deal of effort and skilled diplomacy. Canada's ultimately successful effort in 2000 to reverse the entry/exit control provisions of a 1996 U.S. law that was universally thought of as a clear threat to the economic relationship of the United States with both Canada and Mexico will become a classic case-study of successfully navigating between the American equivalents of the proverbial Scylla of U.S. domestic politics and the Charybdis of improper interference in U.S. affairs. In engineering and quarterbacking (even if through various surrogates) the reversal of Section 110 of that act,[3] Canada protected its economic interests with extreme efficiency. The United States managed regularly to impose its will on an at times passive Zedillo administration on an array of law-and-order issues relating to the border (such as illegal immigration, drug trafficking, the return of criminal aliens, and so forth). Simultaneously, the United States worked closely and, in all but a handful of instances, effectively, with Canada to address issues of common concern in what is by now in many ways a seamless process of bilateral cooperation across a remarkable number of potentially contentious issues.

Considering these facts, and in view of the unfolding of a more organic and equitable U.S.-Mexico relationship between the Fox and Bush administrations, what relationships might one anticipate within the NAFTA-space in the years ahead?

Canada's understandable preoccupation with its U.S. relationship will continue to motivate that country to ensure by any means necessary that the economic relationship continues to grow in ways that guarantee the prosperity of its people. This does not preclude the periodic flare-up of any of the by now typical disagreements over fishing, softwoods, or other issues, but it does "pre-determine" their outcomes. It is in fact our contention that, substantively at least, the U.S.-Canada border is likely to disappear before any politician finds the political courage to negotiate its removal. Symbolic issues, of course, will need to be addressed, as will the significant strengthening of police functions both along the outside perimeter of North America and—an important policy development—in the interior of each country, an intensification that is already occurring.

Mexico, buoyed by and ready to draw on the democratic dividend created by Mr. Fox's defeat of the candidate of the Institutional Revolutionary Party (PRI) in the 2000 presidential elections, has found the confidence to enter into bilateral negotiations with the United States about a tough binational "bargain" on migration and border issues. That bargain, if finalized, would offer Mexicans much greater access to the part of the U.S. economy and labor markets in which it is already a major player—in combinations of Americans of Mexican descent and Mexican legal and unauthorized immigrants—in return for far greater and much more active cooperation in addressing the primarily "law-and-order" issues of concern to the United States. (These focus mainly on organized criminal networks of every type.) Mexico's ability to deliver on the responsibilities it would undertake under such a bargain would in turn determine the pace at which it may begin to catch up with the U.S. treatment of the U.S.-Canada border.

Finally, and from a decidedly U.S.-centric perspective, where might the United States come out in all of this? U.S. interest in the North American "project" envisioned here ("acceptance" may be a more appropriate term than "interest") is likely to be tepid until it is convinced that it can accomplish its own policy priorities less expensively, more efficiently, and much more effectively than under the status quo. The negotiations with the "new" Mexico, if concluded successfully and implemented with determination, will have taken the United States further along in that "project" than it is initially likely to appreciate. And in getting there from here, the greatest obstacles are still likely to be drug and immigration issues, rather than those of customs or even "terrorism." In that regard, it is the limits of thicker and infinitely more expensive controls—and their obvious ineffectiveness and such perverse side effects as large numbers of border-crosser deaths—that may persuade the United States to consider truly alternative ways of dealing with these first two issues.

It is our view that the U.S.-Canada and U.S.-Mexico borders and associated relationships are slowly moving along paths that are likely to bring a gradual change in the terms of the North American debate in the years ahead. If that becomes the case, the three NAFTA partners are likely to enjoy many more of the fruits that greater North American integration can offer for border communities and, more generally, for most of the citizens of the three partnering countries. Will we prove equal to the larger task? That is a question whose answer lies in the future. Without basic changes in our thinking, however, it is an answer that we may never reach.

Notes

1. Each president defeated the party that was in power when that paradigm was established.
2. In both areas, the EU is far ahead of the pack, having organized and funded an "assembly" of representatives of border areas and having granted it an institutionalized advisory role to the EU Commission and European Parliament. (See Schmidt and Salt, as well as Witt, this volume.)
3. The Illegal Immigration Reform and Immigrant Responsibility Act (IIRIRA) (Public Law 104-208; 110 Stat. 3009-1820).

Works Cited

Andreas, Peter. 2001. *Border Games: Policing the U.S.-Mexico Divide*. Ithaca: Cornell University Press.

Andreas, Peter, and Timothy Snyder, eds. 2000. *The Wall Around the West: State Borders and Immigration Controls in North America and Europe*. Lanham: Rowman & Littlefield.

Blatter, Joachim, and Norris Clement. 2000. "Cross-Border Cooperation in Europe: Historical Development, Institutionalization, and Contrasts with North America." *Journal of Borderlands Studies* vol. XV, no. 1.

Canada-U.S. Partnership (CUSP). 2000. *Building a Border for the 21st Century: CUSP Forum Report*. Department of Foreign Affairs and International Trade, Canada.

Cooper, Andrew F. 2000. "Waiting at the Perimeter: Making U.S. Policy in Canada." In *Vanishing Borders*, eds. Maureen Appel Molot and Fen Osler Hampson. Don Mills: Oxford University Press.

Eschbach, Karl, Jacqueline Hagan, and Nestor Rodriguez. 2001. *Causes and Trends of Migrant Deaths Along the U.S.-Mexico Border: 1985-1998*. Houston: University of Houston.

Flynn, Stephen E. 2000. "Beyond Border Control." *Foreign Affairs* vol. 79, no. 6.

Kuhn, Thomas. 1962. *The Structure of Scientific Revolutions*. Chicago: University of Chicago Press.

Policy Research Initiative. 2001. "Rethinking the Line: The Canada-US Border. A Conference Report." *Horizons* vol. 3, Special Issue.

President's Interagency Task Force. 2000. *First Annual Report of the President's Interagency Task Force*, Volumes I and II. Washington, D.C.: Government Printing Office.

Solis, Luis. 2000. "Trans-Border Cooperation in Central America: Lessons from a Project on the Southern Border of NAFTA." Paper presented at conference titled "Managing Common Borders: North American Border Communities in the 21st Century," in Washington, D.C.

Tomás Rivera Policy Institute and Universidad Autónoma de Tamaulipas. 2001. "Temas Prioritarios Para Residentes de la Frontera México/Estados Unidos." May.

U.S.-Mexico Migration Panel. 2001. *Mexico-U.S. Migration: A Shared Responsibility*. Washington, D.C.: Carnegie Endowment for International Peace.

Wirth, John D. 1996. "Advancing the North American Community." *American Review of Canadian Studies* vol. 26, no. 2.

Additional Resources

Carnegie Endowment for International Peace. 2000. "Managing Common Borders: North American Communities in the 21st Century, Conference Summary." <www.ceip.org/files/events/NAmerConfReport.asp?p=6>.

ISUMA. 2000. "North American Integration?" *Canadian Journal of Policy Research* vol. 1, no. 1.

Papademetriou, Demetrios G. and Deborah W. Meyers. 2000. "Of Poetry and Plumbing: The North American Integration Project." Paper presented at June 16 conference titled "Managing Common Borders: North American Communities in the 21st Century," in Washington, D.C.

Sparke, Matthew. 1998. "From Geopolitics to Geoeconomics: Transnational State Effects in the Borderlands." *Geopolitics* vol. 3, no. 2.

Zago, Moreno. 1999/2000. "The State of Cooperation Between Border Towns." ISIG *Magazine: Istituto di Sociologia Internazaionale.* December/February.

PART ONE

North America

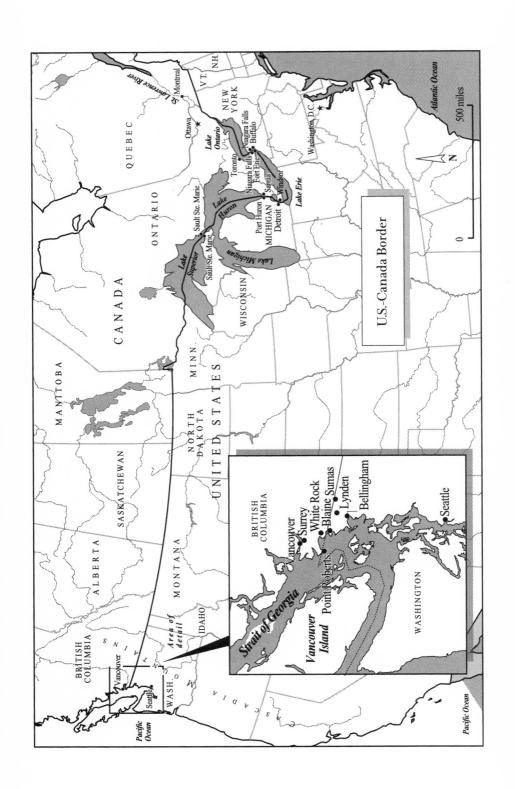

U.S.-Canada Border

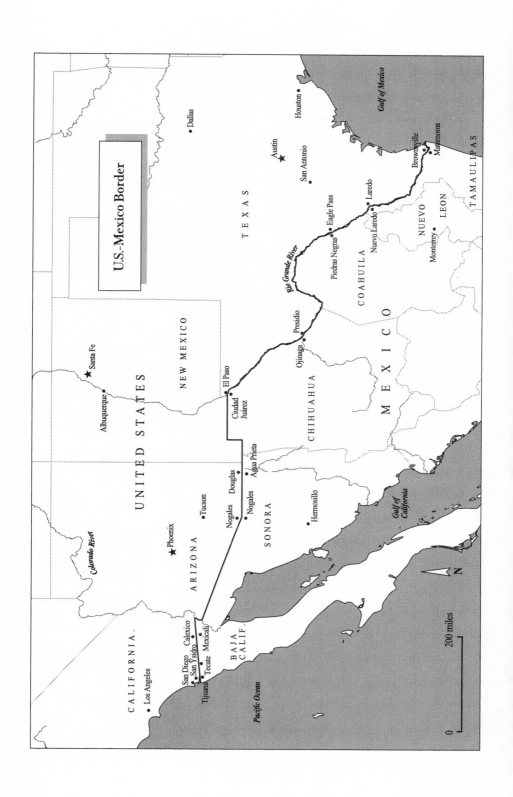

U.S.-Mexico Border

I

Self-Governance Along the U.S.-Canada Border: A View from Three Regions

Deborah Waller Meyers and Demetrios G. Papademetriou

CANADA AND THE UNITED STATES share a border that is 5,525 miles (8,895 kilometers) long, making it the longest undefended border in the world. They also share a language (mostly) and historical tradition, similarly deep commitments to the rule of law, the protection of civil and human rights at home and abroad, and a commitment to democratic principles and stable public institutions. In addition, the two countries have a history of cooperation in most regional and global issues, virtually identical immigration experiences, and similar levels of social and economic development, particularly in the border regions. Further, the relationship between the two countries is distinguished by a history of special bonds, the reality that access to each other's countries has been a long-established and accepted practice, and the geography and topography of the border itself. Yet these allies and neighbors are two independent, sovereign countries with often distinct legal regimes, social (and in some forms, political) systems that at times emphasize different priorities, and independent identities and cultures.

We express our appreciation to Nicole Green and Ana Carrion for their invaluable research assistance.

The traffic of goods and services for business between the United States and Canada is valued at about $1 billion per day, or approximately $365 billion of two-way merchandise trade in 1999. U.S. direct investment in Canada was just over $100 billion in 1998, with Canadian direct investment in the United States around $75 billion.[1] Further, there are over one hundred million crossings of people annually, for business as well as for pleasure (see Figures 1.1, 1.2). The United States' trade with Canada exceeds not only its trade with Japan and Mexico, but also that with the entire European Union (see Figures 1.3, 1.4).[2]

As the largest bilateral trading relationship in the world, the ever-increasing trade and commercial relationship between the United States and Canada has become extremely important to the economies of both countries. Well before the North American Free Trade Agreement (NAFTA) came into force in 1994, many industries along the border already related to both countries seamlessly and viewed their proximity to the border as a critical asset. NAFTA simply accelerated the pace and added depth to the level of such seamlessness; in fact, total trade between the United States and Canada has since increased by 50 percent (see Figure 1.5). Recent high-level agreements include the 1999 Canada-U.S. Partnership Forum (CUSP), the 1998 Pre-Clearance Agreement, the 1995 Shared Accord on Our Border, and the 1995 Open Skies Agreement. Other important agreements are long-standing, such as the 1965 Auto Pact, which integrated the two countries' automobile industries, and the International Joint Commission, which acts as an independent advisor to both governments, resolves disputes under the 1909 Boundary Waters Treaty, and helps protect the transboundary environment.

This chapter discusses fieldwork and other research conducted along the U.S.-Canadian border from the fall of 1998 through the spring of 1999 as part of the International Migration Policy Program's project on Self-Governance at the Border. This study's goal was to investigate how some of the individual communities along this border manage cross-border issues, particularly the movement of people. We hypothesized that at the local level, communities on both sides of a common border were thinking creatively and often collaboratively about common problems and interests and that they tried to develop processes and institutions that gave substance to the concept of devolution of power, particularly with regard to these cross-border rela-

FIGURE I.I

INS Inspections by Land Ports of Entry, FY 1999

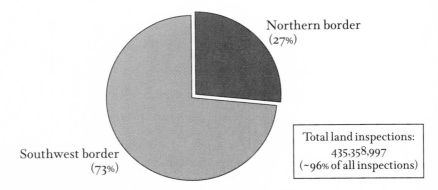

Northern border
(27%)

Southwest border
(73%)

Total land inspections:
435,358,997
(~96% of all inspections)

Note: Numbers are for land ports of entry only; they exclude data for air and sea entry points.
Source: U.S. Immigration and Naturalization Service Statistics Branch.

tionships. We aimed to catalogue existing local initiatives, understand similarities and differences and what accounted for each, and identify and highlight "best practices" in local self-management. We also aimed to draw some conclusions about the factors that make local initiatives more likely to succeed and to learn, understand, and share with others alternative visions of the future.

The project's point of departure was a deep concern that policy making and discussion about borders and their management occurs primarily in national capitals, without the benefit of input by local communities and interests or of their experiences in problem solving and living together. Such a process may have been of no particular consequence as long as the central governments paid only scant attention to borders. With concerns about borders on the rise, however, and central governments eager to be seen as activists on the security issue, attention to borders has grown—although without a commensurate effort (if any at all) either to consult with or substantively to take into account the views of local stakeholders.[3]

The chapter briefly describes each region visited, discusses the research findings, highlights some of the best initiatives, and outlines potential solutions to the challenges raised. Finally, it draws some broader conclusions about the effectiveness of border management,

FIGURE I.2
Breakdown of Total INS Inspections, 1999

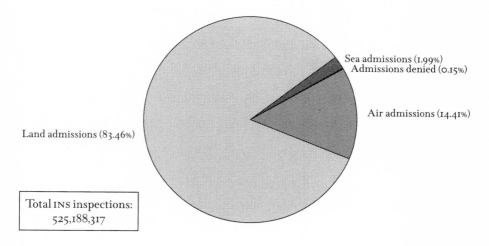

Sea admissions (1.99%)
Admissions denied (0.15%)

Air admissions (14.41%)

Land admissions (83.46%)

Total INS inspections:
525,188,317

Note: Admissions count multiple entries. Data for land admissions are estimates and may contain an unspecified margin of error.
Source: INS Monthly Statistical Report, September 2000 FY Year End Report. INS Office of Policy and Planning.

the nature of cross-border communities and initiatives, and the role of stakeholders in federal policy-making which can be compared and contrasted with those from the other international borders studied in this project.

Methodology

Between the fall of 1998 and the spring of 1999, our research team visited the three busiest regions along the northern border of the United States, one in the West, one in the Midwest, and one in the East. We also interviewed a number of public and private sector leaders in both national capitals. We visited over a dozen ports of entry, including three along the Michigan-Ontario border (the Detroit-Windsor Tunnel, the Ambassador Bridge, and the Blue Water Bridge), three along

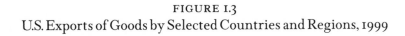

FIGURE I.3

U.S. Exports of Goods by Selected Countries and Regions, 1999

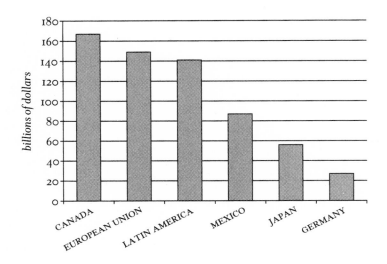

Source: "United States–Canada: The World's Largest Trading Relationship." Canada Department of Foreign Affairs and International Trade, August 2000. <www.canadian embassy.org/trade/wltr.html>.

the New York-Ontario border (the Peace Bridge, the Rainbow Bridge, and the Whirlpool Bridge), four along the Washington-British Columbia border (Peace Arch crossing, Pacific Highway crossing, Sumas/ Abbottsford, and Point Roberts), and two international airports (Detroit Metropolitan Airport and Vancouver International Airport).[4] We spent varying amounts of time in the cities/communities of Windsor, Detroit, Port Huron, Buffalo, Fort Erie, Niagara Falls, Bellingham, Blaine, Lynden, Sumas, Surrey, Point Roberts, Seattle, Vancouver, Washington, D.C., and Ottawa. In these cities and at these crossing points, we conducted approximately one hundred interviews in both countries with local government officials, business leaders, federal immigration, customs, and transportation officials, bridge operators, community-based nongovernmental organizations, researchers, and local residents.

FIGURE I.4
U.S. International Trade with Leading Partners, 1999

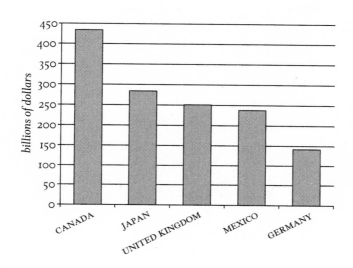

Source: "United States–Canada: The World's Largest Trading Relationship." Canada Department of Foreign Affairs and International Trade, August 2000. <www.canadian embassy.org/trade/wltr.html>.

Demographic Profile

The Detroit-Windsor Region

Detroit, Michigan, and Windsor, Ontario, are about 1.6 kilometers (one mile) apart, separated by the Detroit River but linked by history and a single economy. Geographical proximity to the Great Lakes and a strategic location on the U.S.-Canada border have facilitated economic development in both cities and helped to forge solid economic ties, cooperation, and integration. Home to the once-powerful Iroquois, Windsor and Detroit were settled by the French. Detroit was founded in 1701 as Ville d'Etroit (City of the Strait). Windsor, or Assumption, was founded in 1749. In 1763, French possessions were passed on to the British at the end of the Seven Years' War, and both settlements fell

FIGURE 1.5
U.S. Trade with Canada, 1988–1999:
Exports and Imports, Goods, Services, and Income

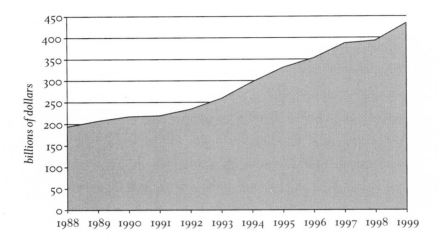

Source: "United States–Canada: The World's Largest Trading Relationship." Canada Department of Foreign Affairs and International Trade, August 2000. <www. canadian embassy.org/trade/wltr.html>.

under the control of British Canada. Detroit was in essence a part of Upper Canada until 1796, when American troops occupied the area.[5] It later became an important station on the Underground Railroad, which brought fugitive slaves north to freedom.

Detroit is approximately three times the size of Windsor, and its metropolitan area includes approximately 4.5 million inhabitants, more than twenty times the 200,000 population of the Windsor metropolitan area. Although a diverse immigrant population has settled in both cities, their social compositions are quite different. Detroit's population is three-quarters African-American, with an increasingly diverse ethnic composition that now includes Hispanics and Arabs/ Chaldeans, while the population of Windsor is primarily white, with small percentages of Arabs, West Indians, African-Americans, Chinese, and others.[6] These demographic differences may, in part, account for a lower level of social integration among the downtown populations than exists in other border communities, although there is a great amount of cross-border traffic between the metropolitan areas for social, cultural, and business purposes.

As the hubs of the automobile industry in their respective countries, economic links are the linchpin of the Michigan-Ontario cross-border relationship.[7] Marketing campaigns to attract business emphasize accessibility to the large metropolitan areas and the fact that over half of Canadians and half of Americans live within a day's drive of the Ontario-New York or Ontario-Michigan borders.[8] In addition to the automotive industry and auto-parts manufacturers, the Windsor-Essex region also has a strong manufacturing industry in plastics, aerospace equipment, surgical instruments, chemicals, pharmaceuticals, and robotics. Moreover, university and government partnerships have helped establish technology centers for research and development, and agricultural, food, and beverage processing industries, including wineries, also are strong. Other major players in the Detroit regional economy include the banking industry, international trade, machine tool accessories, metal fabrication, and plating industries. The newest Canadian and American industry is casinos. Casino Windsor, for instance, has created over 15,000 jobs since its 1994 opening, and it estimates that 80 percent of its visitors are from across the border. It received 6.8 million guests in its Fiscal Year 1999/2000 and almost $840 million in revenue.[9]

The Detroit-Windsor region has the highest volume of cross-border trade between Canada and the United States, with access across the border available through integrated highway and rail systems and a deepwater port. The three primary ports of entry in the region are the Ambassador Bridge, the Detroit-Windsor tunnel, and the Blue Water Bridge (see Figure 1.6).[10] These totaled 27.5 million crossings in FY 1999. The Ambassador Bridge, the longest international suspension bridge in the world, carries the largest volume, with 12.4 million crossings in 1999, up from almost 11 million in 1997. The Detroit-Windsor tunnel had 9.6 million crossings in 1999, while the Blue Water Bridge, one hour north connecting Port Huron, Michigan, and Sarnia, Ontario, had 5.5 million crossings in 1999. Its new span opened in 1997 and the refurbished original span re-opened in 1999.[11]

The Niagara Region

Buffalo, New York, and Fort Erie, Ontario, located across from each other on the shores of the Niagara River, also share a long history, with location and geography serving as a unifying force. Old Fort Erie was once a French trading post that later became an important battle site in the War of 1812 (between the then-British Canada and the recently independent American colonies). Like Detroit and Windsor, the area also was a stop on the Underground Railroad. In 1825, with the establishment of the Erie Canal, the region became a major transportation lifeline between the East and the Midwest, thus establishing the economic foundation for the region as a link or gateway. Today, its accessibility to 50 to 60 percent of the North American market is well advertised by both communities across the border and has been an asset to the regional economy. In fact, regional organizations such as the Niagara Economic and Tourism Corporation and the Buffalo-Niagara Partnership promote the region's binational assets and resources and encourage investment and resettlement through a series of economic development initiatives.

The Niagara region extends over nearly 9,700 square kilometers (6,000 square miles) and encompasses an 800-kilometer (500-mile) radius from western New York to Toronto, reaching over nine million consumers in the North American marketplace.[12] With a population of approximately 27,000, the town of Fort Erie is one-tenth the size of the city of Buffalo, which has approximately 300,000 residents. The two regions have similar ethnic compositions, with Erie County in western New York having a population almost 85 percent white and 3 percent black, with small Hispanic, Asian, and Native American Indian components.[13] Fort Erie's visible minority population is likewise relatively small, perhaps smaller.

The service sector is the largest component of Buffalo's economy, followed by trade and manufacturing. Other areas include construction and mining, finance and real estate, transportation, and agriculture. Despite a declining industrial base, Buffalo has diversified into high-tech industries and telecommunications and is trying to increase tourism, particularly by redesigning its waterfront, as well as to attract new businesses, financial resources, and jobs to the area. Across the river, industry and tourism have laid the foundation for Fort Erie's development, leading to high employment in the service sector and retail sales. The gaming industry and brokerage industries also are important sources of employment, although an aerospace corporation is the town's largest employer. Other manufacturing includes pharmaceuticals, plastics, food processing, transportation equipment, and fabricated metal products. Fort Erie is trying to become a transportation and communications hub, and is focusing on improving infrastructure, attracting investment and high-skilled labor, and revitalizing its waterfront and urban areas.[14]

Both Buffalo and Fort Erie claim to be the gateways to their respective countries. The region is the site of four important border-crossing points that connect American and Canadian highways used by tourists and cargo trucks along the U.S.-Canada border and account for approximately 17 million crossings annually (see Figure 1.6). The crossings are the Peace Bridge, the Whirlpool Bridge, the Rainbow Bridge, and the Lewiston-Queenston Bridge. The Welland Canal and the Port of Buffalo provide access to the St. Lawrence Seaway and international shipping routes. The Peace Bridge, with eight million crossings in 1999, is the primary port of entry for this region and a reminder of the friendship between Canada and the United States. Operated by the Buffalo and Fort Erie Peace Authority, it carries around $35 billion in trade each year.[15] Discussion is under way regarding a new span to significantly increase capacity and facilitate traffic flows. The Rainbow Bridge and Lewiston-Queenston Bridge each account for around 4.3 million crossings, with the Whirlpool Bridge having fewer than 800,000.

The Cascadia Corridor

Vancouver and Seattle, with one-half million residents each, are the major cities located along the nearly 650-kilometer (400-mile) cross-border region known as the Cascadia Corridor. This corridor extends from Eugene, Oregon, through Seattle, Washington, across the U.S.-Canada border to Vancouver, British Columbia, and its population is expected to reach 15 million by 2010. The corridor includes small border communities such as Bellingham, Blaine, and Lynden in Washington and Surrey, Langley, and White Rock in British Columbia.[16] These border communities are linked historically through the Native

FIGURE 1.6
Two-Way Traffic at Selected Ports of Entry
on the Eastern U.S.-Canada Border, 1999

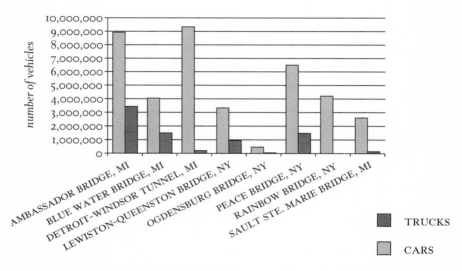

Source: United States-Canada Bridge and Tunnel Operators Association, statistical report for two-way traffic, 1999.

American tribes that once lived there and the explorations of Captain George Vancouver. In 1858, the Fraser River gold rush spurred massive immigration and growth in the area; later, coal mining, lumber, and the railroad brought in more settlers.

Border communities in Cascadia also share environmental and socio-cultural traits such as a similar natural resource base and comparable early settlement and industrial development patterns. Even more important may be the region's sense of independence and its political tradition of grass-roots democracy, taking matters into its own hands when necessary, whether it is on border issues, transportation planning, trade and tourism, or natural resource management.[17]

While not physically located on the border, Vancouver and Seattle are the key cities in the trade corridor. Both have major ports that anchor Pacific Rim and international trade, and they are more comparable to each other than the other cities we visited. The Greater Vancou-

FIGURE I.7
Incoming Traffic at Selected Ports of Entry
on the Western U.S.-Canada Border, 1999

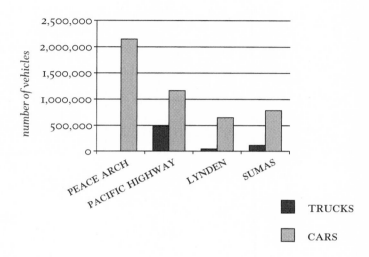

Source: U.S. Customs, Blaine, WA. Compiled by the Whatcom County Council of Governments for the International Mobility and Trade Corridor Project-IMTC.

ver area had a population of 1.8 million in 1996, while the Seattle Metropolitan area was estimated at 2.3 million in 1998.[18] Approximately 40 percent of Vancouver's population is Asian (mostly Chinese), while in 2000 Seattle's population was 70.1 percent white, 8.4 percent black, 1 percent American Indian, and 13.1 percent Asian.[19]

As the home of Boeing and Microsoft, the Seattle area continues to be an important hub of the advanced technology industries, housing 2,500 software development firms, according to the Seattle Office of Economic Development. It also has been a meeting place for regional and global development organizations. Other well-developed industries, most of which have spread across the border to Vancouver, include aerospace, biomedical and environmental engineering, research and development, transportation distribution, and electronics. The Vancouver area has also emerged as a manufacturing center for British Columbia, primarily in more traditional sectors such as forestry, mines and minerals, and fishing and fish products. Most of these items are exported through the port of Vancouver, one of North America's busiest. Tourism and the film industry also have grown in strength.[20]

Quality transportation and infrastructure have helped Vancouver and Seattle become the premier import-export gateways of the Pacific Northwest. Of the four major border-crossing points in the area (the Peace Arch, Pacific Highway, Lynden, and Sumas), the Peace Arch is the largest, with two million passenger crossings in 1998 (see Figure 1.7). The Peace Arch was built to commemorate the Treaty of Ghent, which ended the War of 1812, and is shared by the Peace Arch State Park on the U.S. side and the Peace Arch Provincial Park on the Canadian side.[21] Pacific Highway receives the majority of commercial traffic, with a half million trucks in 1998, an increase of almost 50 percent in five years.[22] An integrated transportation system with ports, air, and railway lines connects to the highway systems of both nations (I-5 and Interstate 90).

Findings

In all the localities visited, we found a variety of cross-border community connections in place. These cross-border connections exist not only regarding migration but also for environment, physical infrastructure, health, safety, and education issues. Some of these connections are formalized, but most tend to be more informal. Rather than listing the findings from each community separately, we discuss the findings thematically. While specific differences make generalizations about the Canadian-U.S. border difficult, these cross-border communities face numerous common challenges in terms of the relevant issues and means of resolving them.

Distinctions

The uniqueness of border communities along the U.S.-Canada border results from a variety of factors. These include the history of the regions, the economies of the border communities, the degree of economic and social integration, and the size and composition of the local populations. It also is shaped by the physical/geographic settings, the nature of the border itself (land, water, mountain), whether the border crossings are publicly or privately owned, the types of people and goods crossing the border, and even the personalities of federal agents stationed at the border.

Levels of Economic and Social Integration. Economic integration may be strongest between Michigan and Ontario. The regional economy is anchored by the automobile industry, whose seamlessness was enshrined in the 1965 Auto Pact. Components move back and forth across the Ambassador Bridge at various stages during the manufacturing process, and the local economies are deeply dependent on each other. In fact, although the overall traffic is greater along the southern U.S. border, commercial traffic is higher along its northern border; there are more trucks crossing the Ambassador Bridge than any other crossing along either the U.S.-Mexico or U.S.-Canada border (see Figures 1.8, 1.9). Of 12.4 million vehicles crossing the Ambassador Bridge in 1999, 3.5 million were trucks (an increase of a million in just two years). Another 1.5 million trucks crossed over the Blue Water Bridge. Alternatively, in the Pacific Northwest, agricultural products and lumber may regularly cross the border, but the industry is not integrated in the same way. The Niagara region perceives itself as more of a gateway and convenient point of distribution for both countries, rather than as a point of both origin and destination. Nonetheless, it has developed a corridor of high technology, fiber optics, and medical research, and there are numerous companies located in the region that do a great deal of cross-border business. Of the eight million crossings in 1999, almost 1.5 million were trucks at the Peace Bridge, along with another 950,000 at the Lewiston-Queenston Bridge. Estimates are that at least 70 percent of U.S.-Canada trade passes through the eastern border, with approximately 45 percent going through a Michigan-Ontario port of entry and 30 percent through the Buffalo/ Fort Erie-Niagara region.[23]

The unique aspects of each port of entry and region mean each has its own strengths and weaknesses, and cooperation co-exists with competition. Seattle and Vancouver, for instance, both vie to be the Northwest's principal port and the gateway to the Asian economies (although neither city is literally on the border, both see themselves as part of the border region), while the Ambassador and Blue Water Bridges compete for trucking business. This creates a unique challenge—how can

FIGURE I.8
Incoming Truck Traffic:
Comparison of Northern and Southern Border Ports of Entry, 1997

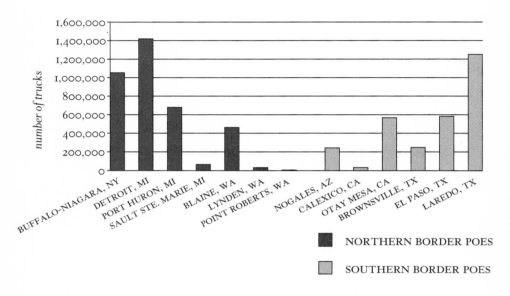

NORTHERN BORDER POES

SOUTHERN BORDER POES

Source: U.S. Customs Service, Mission Support Services, Office of Field Operations. Data extracted from the U.S. Department of Transportation, Bureau of Transportation Statistics. <www.bts.gov/programs/itt/cross/mex.html>.

one position oneself for a pie that is constantly increasing, rather than simply dividing up the existing one?[24]

Social integration tends to be strongest when it engages small-town border communities or neighboring communities of disparate sizes. Both situations typically lead to policies that avoid expensive duplication and favor economies of scale. Small towns are thus more likely to share limited public and private resources. For instance, Port Huron, Michigan, and Sarnia, Ontario, have an agreement to share emergency response equipment and personnel (the Blue Water Bridge connecting them is the top hazardous-materials crossing on the northern border), while Windsorites go to Henry Ford Hospital in Detroit for heart surgery (the closest Canadian facility is in London, Ontario, two hours away), demonstrating the wisdom of avoiding duplication and the ad-

FIGURE I.9
Incoming Crossings:
Comparison of Northern and Southern Border Ports of Entry, 1997

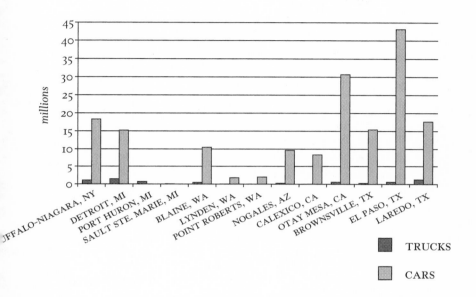

Source: U.S. Customs Service, Mission Support Services, Office of Field Operations. Data extracted from the U.S. Department of Transportation, Bureau of Transportation Statistics. <www.bts.gov/programs/itt/cross/mex.html>.

vantages of scale. As a focus group participant noted, the "mall in Port Huron wouldn't have been built if Canadians didn't come over to shop," because the American population alone was too small to sustain a mall. He recalled watching Sesame Street in French and being able to look into the backyards of houses on the other side of the narrow Saint Clair River, which divides the two communities. We experienced this sensation in Point Roberts, Washington, when driving along a local road, separated from houses in Canada only by a small ditch that easily could be jumped if one so desired.[25]

Similarly, a small city often avails itself of the social and cultural resources offered by a major metropolitan area. Windsor residents work in Detroit and fervently cheer for the Detroit Tigers and Red Wings (rather than the Toronto Blue Jays and Maple Leafs). The sharing can be bidirectional too; Detroit residents view Windsor as another suburb of the metropolitan area and routinely take trips to Windsor restaurants, Casino Windsor, and even Toronto theaters. Similarly, Buffalo residents frequent their summer cottages in Fort Erie, Ontario, and Canadians fill the parking lot at the Ellicottville, New York, ski resort. Many of these border cities (such as Bellingham, Washington, and Surrey, British Columbia) also feel they have more in common with their neighbors across the border than they do with their national capitals, far across the country. A Canadian whom we interviewed stated that he found popular culture very integrated, knowing about American media, movies, music, and so on.[26] On the other hand, despite this social integration and shared events such as joint independence day celebrations and the Freedom Festival fireworks along the Detroit River, focus group participants who had grown up in the Detroit area said they rarely, if ever, learned about their Canadian neighbors in school and could probably name countries in Eastern Europe more easily than the province in which Winnipeg is located.

Nature of Border Crossings. Physical characteristics also play an important role in distinguishing between border regions. In the East, the Detroit and Niagara Rivers form a natural boundary, while much of the Midwestern and Western border is on land, except for places like Point Roberts, Washington. Frequently, the crossing infrastructure (such as the Detroit-Windsor tunnel underneath the Detroit River) cannot be enhanced without enormous investments of additional funds. Due to the lack of sufficient physical space at the Ambassador Bridge, the Canadian Customs facility at the bridge actually is off-site, with trucks having to drive nearly five kilometers (three miles) on local roads to reach the facility and Customs being notified by computer if trucks fail to arrive.[27] Similarly when a crossing is an integral part of a well-established landscape (for example, the Peace Arch crossing surrounded by the Peace Arch Park), the opportunities for enlarging it are limited. Even if one were to use part of the park to build additional lanes, or if one were to build a new bridge over the Detroit River, the infrastructure on either end would be unable to accommodate additional traffic on the existing highways.

These topographical differences mean that in some localities authorities are dealing with pedestrian crossings, or even crossings by snowboard or skis in remote areas, while in other areas the only way to cross is by ferry across a waterway, such as when crossing to and from Victoria Island. In Detroit/Windsor, there are no pedestrian crossings, so an automobile, bus, or truck is required to cross the bridge or tunnel; the Blue Water Bridge does have a pedestrian crossing option, though the vast majority of crossings are passenger and commercial vehicles. We are left, then, to deal with myriad physical setups, as well as a variety of ways in which these crossings are run. Border operators range from the privately owned Ambassador Bridge, to the public Blue Water Bridge Authority, to the tunnel owned by the cities of Detroit and Windsor, to land border crossings owned by the federal government and run by the General Services Administration.

The Nature of Border Crossers and Border Officials. The types of people who cross the border also vary, not only by region but also by port of entry. Certain American Indians born in Canada may cross freely into the United States (for instance upstate New York),[28] while crossings at Point Roberts, Washington, consist almost exclusively of approximately 1,000 local residents plus tourists. As a result, with the exception of a few months in the summer, the same few inspectors see the same cars and passengers numerous times each day, every day, every week, every month. Residents of Point Roberts cross 37 kilometers (23 miles) through Canada, for instance, to return to American territory at the Blaine border crossing, for work or school or shopping or anything else that is not available on the Point.[29] The Buffalo region sees an extremely large number of international tourists, particularly at the Rainbow Bridge because of Niagara Falls, although commercial traffic is significant as well.[30] Truckers and local commuters use the Peace Bridge and the Lewiston/Queenston Bridge. Similarly, local passenger cars carrying workers, casino and restaurant patrons, and sports fans cross through the Detroit/Windsor tunnel, while trucks servicing the auto industry cross the Ambassador Bridge. Inspectors at the Detroit ports of entry also see many European and Asian visitors who initially entered the country through the international airport, which receives direct flights from Asia and Europe.

Moreover, the organizational culture of the agencies at the border and personalities of senior field or district officials in charge also exert great influence on how their employees think about the issues and treat the general public. For instance, those inspectors who work for a district director whose background is with the Border Patrol may be more likely to be looking for reasons to prevent entry or to focus on enforcement actions, while the adjudicators may be looking for reasons to deny, rather than approve, applications. Alternatively, some district directors and inspectors are more attuned to thinking about facilitating legal traffic, with adjudicators finding ways to help immigrants receive the benefits to which they legally are entitled. Of course, they are all operating under the same general rules and guidelines but interpretations of these rules and subsequent actions are not always consistent among ports of entry, much less among regions.

Similarities

The Canadian border is nearly two and a half times as long as the Mexican border, and approximately 90 percent of the Canadian population lives within 160 kilometers (100 miles) of it. (In contrast, only a small portion of the U.S. population lives that close to the Canadian border.) Many of these localities, on both sides of the border, face common challenges and try to exploit common opportunities. They all are trying to manage traffic and facilitate trade, commerce, tourism, and other legitimate crossings while at the same time effectively addressing public security, stopping unauthorized entries of persons and goods (a tiny percentage of the legitimate cross-border traffic), and collecting customs duties within the constraints of the available physical infrastructure.

Increased Traffic. Similar to the growth of commercial traffic discussed earlier, passenger traffic also has increased significantly, and all indications are that it will continue to do so (see Figures 1.10, 1.11). According to the Immigration and Naturalization Service (INS), in FY 1999 over 44 million people were inspected in the Detroit district, followed by nearly 33 million crossings in the Buffalo district, and over 16.5 million in the Seattle district.[31] The Seattle district alone includes 23 ports of entry and about 800 kilometers (500 miles) of border. A large portion of the inspections in this district are from the Seattle/Tacoma airport and pre-inspection at the Vancouver International Airport—over 17 million in 1998, not including inspections at the land border, at seaports for cruise ships and cargo ships, or of rail passengers. In the Detroit region, there were 8.9 million passenger cars that

FIGURE I.IO
Two-Way Traffic on the U.S.-Canada Border:
Comparison at Selected Eastern Ports of Entry, 1995, 1997, 1999

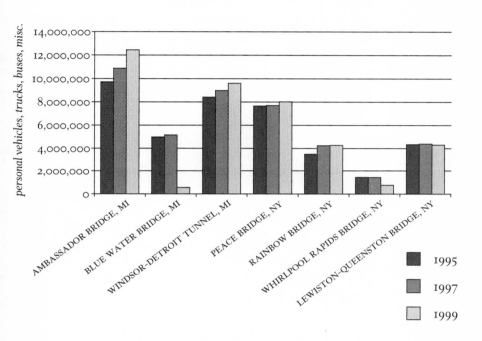

Note: In 1999 the original span of the Blue Water Bridge was closed for refurbishing, which accounts for its low traffic.
Source: United States-Canada Bridge and Tunnel Operators Association, statistical reports for two-way traffic, 1995–1999.

crossed the Ambassador Bridge in 1999, with 9.3 million crossing just down the river at the Detroit/Windsor Tunnel and another four million crossing the Blue Water Bridge, as well as 2.6 million in Sault Sainte Marie. Similarly in the Niagara region, there were 6.5 million passenger cars crossing at the Peace Bridge, 4.2 million at the Rainbow Bridge overlooking Niagara Falls, 3.3 million at the Lewiston/Queenston Bridge, and 750,000 at the Whirlpool Rapids Bridge.

Declines in Service Quality. These numbers have had a noticeable effect on service. For instance, one constant theme on our research visits was complaints about long lines at the border. We heard these

FIGURE I.II

Incoming Traffic on the U.S.-Canada Border:
Comparison at Selected Western Ports of Entry, 1995 and 1997

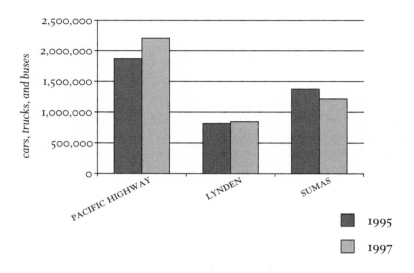

Source: U.S. Customs, Blaine, WA. Compiled by the Whatcom County Council of Governments for the International Mobility and Trade Corridor Project-IMTC.

complaints everywhere—in Michigan, Ontario, New York, British Columbia, and Washington. Local traffic reports in these cities often mention whether or not there is a wait at the various crossings, and if so how long. Often the complaints related to existing booths that were not open because of understaffing, but they also addressed dedicated commuter lanes that could not be accessed because there was no way to bypass all the other traffic to get there. Not only do these communities face the issue of insufficient inspections staff to open all existing lanes and meet the demand of cross-border traffic, but they also must deal with quality-of-service issues. Cuts in federal budgets have led districts to hire temporary workers, rather than permanent ones with appropriate training. Temporary hires seem quite common in the Seattle district, and they also are common in the summer months in tourist hot spots like Niagara Falls. On occasion, particularly in Whatcom County, Washington, we heard complaints about treatment by U.S. officials at the border and about arbitrary or inconsistent enforcement or interpretation of the laws, especially those regarding the entry of professionals under NAFTA. This relates to the earlier point regarding the impact of organizational culture on border agencies. (There seemed to be fewer complaints regarding entry into Canada.) Also expressed were complaints about having to register for separate pre-clearance programs in both countries. In addition, in almost every port of entry, the volume of crossings is affected by a factor over which the local residents have no control—the exchange rate.

Security Concerns. Border communities also are trying to protect their security, their culture, and their identities by keeping out undesirable people and activities. An underlying theme, if not a dominant one, was an acceptance of the proposition that borders have important symbolic value and a resistance to notions that crossing is simply an entitlement. Objectively speaking, every port of entry is vulnerable to penetration by undesirable elements,[32] but these events tend to be rather rare and isolated, particularly relative to the number of crossings. In fact, in town hall and focus group meetings in Point Roberts, Washington, and Detroit, Michigan, both of which included American and Canadian citizens and residents and one of which included police officers and a judge, not a single person raised serious security concerns about the entry of either Canadians or Americans into their neighbor countries. Nor did anyone argue that a more open or differently managed border would lead to less (or presumably more) security. In fact, they were strongly skeptical of "solutions" that might further inconvenience the legitimate traffic to try to catch an additional few violators.

Differing Perspectives on Policy Making. Another issue border communities have in common is variable amounts of tension over the role of the federal government in border management issues. Community residents shared their frustration at what they feel is a lack of input into the decision-making process that affects their daily lives. These may range from investments in physical infrastructure (believed to be grossly inadequate) to amounts and quality of staffing by federal agencies. Local residents specifically mentioned insufficient space to expand crossings such as the Peace Arch, crumbling highways such as I-94 and 401 in Michigan and Ontario, and bridges in need of repair or expansion, such as the Peace Bridge. They would like additional federal attention in the form of more inspectors to reduce waits (without compromising security) and funds to improve highways and border crossings. Yet at the same time, there is no desire for government involvement that would increase the difficulty of crossing or hinder trade because of a lack of understanding of the local circumstances. Thus the paradox is the simultaneous desire for more and less government attention.

A lack of federal understanding of local circumstances was best exemplified by the debate over the Section 110 provision of the 1996 Illegal Immigration Reform and Immigrant Responsibility Act (IIRIRA) which mandated the creation of a comprehensive entry-exit data system in the United States. Although the initial intent of the provision was to match entries and exits at airports for the purposes of tracking visa overstays, it came out of the conference committee as a much larger provision, encompassing all ports of entry. Once this was discovered, local businesses, local congressmen, state governments, and other stakeholders argued that the reality of this proposed system (including collecting information on Canadians and Mexicans, who are now exempt) would lead to a de facto shutdown of the border. They argued that the additional time required to record the entry and exit of every "alien" would have enormous consequences for service. Specifically, it was expected to lead to massive delays, causing significant harm to tourism and industry and significantly affecting the automobile industry with its just-in-time system that spans the North American continent, as well as damaging other businesses and enterprises dependent on relatively easy, predictable cross-border movement, such as universities, casinos, and agricultural producers. That would not even include the inconvenience imposed upon local residents who cross back and forth to shop, to eat, to work, or to visit family members.

In another example of how the views of local residents differ from those of Washington policy makers, two focus group participants noted some of the consequences of the increased use of the Ambassador Bridge due to growing commercial trade (which in and of itself is positive). The expansion of the bridge and its related activities has affected their minority neighborhood in southwest Detroit, leading to good business for a local restaurant but high truck traffic in the area, destruction of homes, and insufficient room for parks and schools, making residents feel they are being pushed out. As one said, "Our community is being ripped apart." It is not that they are opposed to increased trade, but its practical consequences affect their day-to-day lives in ways that few people, much less policy makers in Washington, D.C., and Ottawa, consider. Additionally, the increased traffic at the tunnel caused by casino patrons has made one respondent's job as a policeman more difficult (though not in terms of importing crime), while another said it lengthened the commute.

Causes of and Responses to Local/Federal Tensions. The tensions described above between federal agencies and local communities seem to result from two primary problems. The first is that the headquarters staff often is too distant from the field, out of touch with the realities better understood by their senior representatives on the ground. The second problem occurs when these senior field managers or even individual officers are too independent, using their own philosophy to guide their operations and decisions and interpreting regulations in ways that serve their agendas but are not always consistent with stated policy. In fact, if a single finding defines our work, it is that the different lenses, measures, and levels of sensitivity that exist make for an often different definition of what the problem is, and more importantly, of the best way to solve it. This seems to be true whether comparing federal agencies and legislatures with local public and private sector agencies, national governments with state governments, federal officials in the capitals with local representatives of federal agencies, or local level public or private sector agencies. The Section 110 entry-exit provision of IIRIRA discussed above exemplified this.

Similarly, the preferred methodology to resolving issues also is likely to differ, as is the degree of inclusiveness of whatever strategies are adopted and the sensitivity with which they are implemented. The Washington, D.C., conversation about a particular border crossing, for instance, is more likely to be about a negative item such as the December 1999 arrest of Ahmed Ressam along the British Columbia-Washington border than about effective transborder trade or organized transcommunity relationships along the same border, such as the Western Governors and Premiers Association which meets annually, the International Mobility Trade Corridor which will be discussed in the next section, or even the U.S.-Canada relationship more generally.

One way in which some local representatives of federal agencies and their headquarters have dealt with these tensions has been by following an informal policy of border management, what we have called a "don't ask, don't tell" policy. If local officials have a good, creative idea that can improve effectiveness or efficiency, they are reluctant to share it with their headquarters, much less ask permission to try it, for fear they will be told they are not allowed to do so or must make changes that make it worse.[33] This informal system prevents the testing of creative ideas and best practices in alternate locations, though we believe these are exactly the types of innovations and experiments that should be encouraged. Alternatively, there are times when headquarters staff is unaware of problems at the local level because citizen or business community complaints may have been stopped at the district level and never forwarded up the chain of command. To address this type of dilemma, the U.S. Customs Service instituted a program to improve customer service whereby complaints are sent via postcard directly to an ombudsman at headquarters who then investigates with the local office and is obliged to respond to the complainant. Such a system keeps headquarters adequately informed and alerted to any problems, which can then be handled in a timely manner.

Best Practices

Overall, our fieldwork confirmed the hypothesis that border communities often focus on and have to manage a different set of realities and priorities from those being discussed and decided in the countries' capitals. It is thus not surprising that border communities often are thinking more creatively and show a greater openness and collaborative approach to problem solving than either national legislatures or capital-based regulators and bureaucrats. We tried to focus on programs that were initiated in localities, rather than at the level of central governments, and we tried to understand why they succeeded.

Public-Private Partnerships

Many of the larger and more well-known projects we learned about also were some of the more successful. This is probably related to their ability to form a broad-based coalition of stakeholders who know how to articulate their interests and raise sufficient funding to do so. One example is the Canadian-American Border Trade Alliance, a border-wide public/private binational partnership that seeks to improve the efficient flow of goods and people across the U.S.-Canadian border. Created in 1993 and based in Buffalo, New York, it acts as a resource, provides a forum for discussion of border issues, and provides a unified voice for interactions with the most relevant government officials from both countries. CAN-AM BTA meets biannually, and its membership includes shippers, brokers, bridge and tunnel operators, banks, railroads, economic development and trade corridor coalitions, universities, chambers of commerce, and government agencies.

Similarly, the Eastern Border Transportation Coalition (EBTC), also based in the Niagara region, focuses on greater communication and cooperation among U.S. state and Canadian provincial transportation agencies and on cross-border issues. Membership includes state departments of transportation, provincial transport ministries, metropolitan planning organizations, and municipalities. Its 1997 and 1998 reports on trade and traffic provide comprehensive data, analysis, and projections about the eastern U.S.-Canada border, as well as recommendations. EBTC's final recommendation is to work toward an open border, setting the year 2012 as the goal since it will be the 200th anniversary of the War of 1812.

On the West Coast, the Cascadia Project is a coalition of government, businesses, and NGOs run by the non-profit Discovery Institute in Washington and the Cascadia Institute in British Columbia. Covering Washington, British Columbia, and Oregon, the project is dedicated to developing transborder strategies that emphasize sustainable communities, cross-border mobility, and improved regional transportation, trade, and tourism linkages. The Cascadia Project began in 1993, growing out of a concern that the region was ill-equipped to respond effectively to NAFTA. The fact that opportunities for federal funding began to arise at about the same time also was important to the project's launch. Cascadia has lobbied against border fees and for permanent pre-clearance lanes, has searched systematically for funding to improve border crossings and the approaches to them, has worked on technological innovations, and has created public education and finance plans.

Concerns about the region's ability to take advantage of opportunities led the British Columbia government in 1998 to ask the Cascadia

Institute to begin the British Columbia-Washington Corridor Task Force. The concept behind this initiative was to coordinate the multitude of existing cross-border initiatives and relationships and also to coordinate requests for cross-border funding under the Transportation Equity Act for the 21st Century (TEA-21) legislation.[34] Their theme of "cooperate regionally and compete globally" fairly encapsulates the initiative's goals.

Local county governments and planning organizations also provide examples of partnerships as they work together and with their counterparts across the border to secure funds for significant improvements to the infrastructure of trade corridors and to cross-border mobility more generally. In particular, the Whatcom County Council of Governments (WCCOG) and the Southeastern Michigan Council of Governments (SEMCOG) secured funds under TEA-21 for significant improvements to the infrastructure of the trade corridors in their regions (such as I-94 in Detroit and I-5 in the Pacific Northwest). More specifically, WCCOG and the Washington Department of Transportation received over $800,000 for coordination of binational planning, almost $240,000 for a study of freight and traveler origins and destinations, and $200,000 to market the local pre-clearance program. In addition to the more than $10 million received to improve the Ambassador Bridge gateway and reconstruct parts of the approaching highways, the state of Michigan received $1.2 million for improvements at the Blue Water Bridge and $100,000 to study cross-border transportation improvements in local counties.[35]

In addition, the Whatcom County Council of Governments has organized a binational regional planning group composed of stakeholders from both countries, including representatives of localities, federal government agencies, and chambers of commerce. The resulting International Mobility and Trade Corridor (IMTC) project, in which more than 80 organizations have participated, meets monthly, sharing information and discussing challenges and solutions, with the shared goals of facilitating trade, transportation, and tourism. At a meeting we attended, senior local representatives of federal agencies shared successes such as receiving additional staff for the Customs cargo facility, noted problems such as possible Y2K disruption of the small-boat pre-clearance program, and vetted ideas such as joint (binational) administration of the PACE program. In effect, IMTC has become a regional clearinghouse of ideas and information and was one of the most innovative programs we discovered in our field research.

Private Sector Initiatives

Though we identified and studied a number of successful private sector initiatives, those most successful seemed to have a number of commonalities. These include actors who have common needs or self-interests, have organized themselves effectively, have raised sufficient funding, and have developed creative yet practical ideas. The resultant networks of personal and institutional relations may hold the best promise for doing better on the ground, almost independently of the situation in the capitals. For instance, as a result of growing trade between Canada and the United States since the 1988 U.S.-Canada Free Trade Agreement, in 1992 businesses in western New York created the first cross-border chapter of the Canada-U.S. Business Association to link their businesses with Toronto's marketplace.

The Canada-U.S. BorderNet Alliance, a cross-border regional network of business organizations, was created to focus on the development of trade, tourism, and investment in the Niagara region. Conceptualized in 1994 by a private attorney and a Canadian consul general who were longtime residents of the region, the project is a non-profit institution incorporated in both Canada and the United States. Spanning Toronto, Hamilton, Buffalo, and Rochester, the Alliance's goal is to assist the region to become more globally competitive. BorderNet Alliance has published cross-border directories of medical industries, provided business matchmaking, and encouraged economic projects. Current projects include development of a web site and database as well as a CEO Economic Development Summit and trade events. Likewise, the Red River Trade Corridor, which includes Minnesota, North and South Dakota, and Manitoba, has published business information directories for the region, held trade summits, and organized trade missions. Based at the University of Minnesota in Crookston, it is a regional, rural development organization designed to strengthen the region's economic capacity and strengthen its competitive position globally.

The Tunnel Bus, based in Windsor, Ontario, is another creative idea that filled the needs of commuters, concert-goers, sports fans, and casino patrons to cross the Detroit River between downtown Windsor and downtown Detroit (where crossing by foot or by boat is not a possibility). Begun in 1981, it is run by Transit Windsor and connects with local bus services in both countries. The bus provides regular transportation and fares can be paid in American or Canadian currency. Details have been worked out with U.S. and Canadian border agencies to check passengers and their belongings, and Transit Windsor takes responsibility for returning those who are deemed ineligible to enter.

From a tourism perspective, the Convention and Visitors' Bureaus in Washington State and British Columbia have marketed the Two-Nation Vacation in Cascadia to increase both the number of tourists visiting the region and the length of time they spend there. The chambers of commerce in Niagara, Ontario, and Niagara, New York, and the Greater Niagara Partnership are doing the same for Niagara Falls through the Niagara—Attracting the World Campaign. In fact, the two chambers are thinking regionally in even more substantive ways by undertaking joint overseas trade missions and promoting the economic development of the entire region.

Nongovernmental Initiatives

Locally based initiatives also exist in the nonprofit sector. In fact, the success of these projects may be directly related to the fact that they are taking into account local circumstances and addressing local needs, rather than having them imposed from elsewhere. They typically result from individual leadership and creative thinking. As an example, the communities in Sault Sainte Marie, Ontario, and Sault Sainte Marie, Michigan, two sister communities that are more connected to each other than to other parts of their state or province, conceived the Binational Regional Initiative Developing Greater Education (BRIDGE), an education-led economic development joint venture designed to address joint needs. BRIDGE works with Algoma University College and Sault College in Ontario and Lake Superior State University in Michigan, as well as with Native American and Canadian First Nation communities.

Canadian students can attend Lake Superior State University for in-state tuition similar to the way in which American and Mexican students can attend the University of Windsor for a special NAFTA tuition rate over a third less than that paid by other international students and close to that paid by Canadians. Similarly, the Golden Horseshoe Educational Alliance, another educational coalition made up of academics at over twenty colleges and universities in the region ranging from Toronto to Rochester, encourages greater academic cooperation and focuses academic attention on regional issues. It began in 1994 and has hosted regional student conferences and engaged in a survey of cross-border academic interests.

In the environmental arena, a positive example of cross-border work on behalf of common interests is Great Lakes United, founded in 1982 by environmentalists, community groups, labor unions, sports organizations, and citizens. Headquartered in Buffalo, it is a binational coalition of over 170 member organizations dedicated to conserving and protecting the Great Lakes-St. Lawrence River ecosystem. Member-based task forces work on issues such as habitat protection and eliminating toxic pollution, and coordinate input to relevant government officials. Similarly, the Detroit River Greenways Partnership works with both the Windsor and Detroit governments to protect the natural and cultural resources along the shared river and border.

This type of partnership to protect the natural environment occurs along the western border as well. For instance, the Peace Arch Anniversary Project helps draw attention to the preservation of the park, which straddles the international border and sheds light on its cultural importance as the symbol of the long-standing U.S.-Canada friendship and the end of the War of 1812. Other cultural cooperative ventures include the World University Games held in Buffalo, New York, and Saint Catharines and Hamilton, Ontario, in 1993, and the first-ever binational marathon course in 1995 for the World Veterans Championships.

Finally, in the human rights realm, two American nonprofit organizations are taking advantage of their locations in border communities to act as shelters for those seeking asylum in both the United States and Canada. Freedom House began as the Detroit/Windsor Refugee Coalition in 1983, part of the sanctuary movement for Central Americans fleeing civil war. Located in downtown Detroit in the shadow of the Ambassador Bridge and on the edge of Mexicantown, it assisted almost 400 people from over 50 countries in 1999, providing food, shelter, clothing, and legal, medical, and psychological services to individuals applying for asylum or refugee status. It also assisted more than 1,000 other people in applying for asylum and dealing with other immigration matters. Buffalo's Vive La Casa also was founded as part of the sanctuary movement in 1984 and also has a strong reputation overseas via word of mouth for those who need it. Vive has helped refugees from more than 100 countries; individuals simply show up at their doorstep at an old Catholic school in a minority neighborhood in Buffalo, usually after arriving in the United States with visitor, student, or business visas or with fraudulent documents. Although it can shelter only approximately 100 people at a time, it provided assistance with asylum applications (primarily to Canada) for more than 2,500 individuals in 1999.

"Local" Government Initiatives

This section notes public agency initiatives that were undertaken either by local city officials or by local representatives of federal government agencies. Their mere existence, often in the face of bureaucratic challenge, seems to be attributable to personal contacts and informal relationships on the ground, a sense of partnership with one's counterparts across the border, a willingness to experiment, and an understanding of local needs and circumstances, as well as the presence of a supportive overarching framework (such as the 1988 U.S.-Canada Free Trade Agreement, 1993 NAFTA, the 1995 Shared Accord on Our Border, the 1997 Cross-Border Crime Forum, and most recently, the 1999 Canada-United States Partnership).

The Pacific Northwest offices of Customs and INS have experimented with some innovative ideas with regard to staffing and technology, including multi-agency international border enforcement teams working against organized crime, pre-clearance of certain types of cargo, the use of transponders, and the re-routing of late-night passenger traffic to truck lanes to permit staff from the lightly used car traffic lanes to staff truck lanes and thus reduce the long waits there. In addition, the dedicated commuter lane in the region is widely considered a resounding success. Conceived to deal with long backups of Canadians wanting to enter the United States to shop, the PACE lane (Peace Arch Crossing Entry) in Blaine, Washington is counted on by both users and implementers of the 1991 pilot project to keep traffic flowing. Now with over 140,000 enrollees, PACE accounts for 40 percent of all crossings in Blaine and 50 percent in Point Roberts.

Another innovative program to reduce traffic congestion and delays was developed jointly by American and Ontario trucking associations, Northern Border Customs Brokers, and the Association of International Border Agencies. Called the Commercial Vehicle Processing Center (CVPC), this U.S. Customs facility was first implemented on the Canadian plaza of the Peace Bridge in Buffalo/Fort Erie in November 1999. The CVPC reviews commercial paperwork for U.S.-bound goods while the cargo is still in Canada, rather than having the vehicle pull into a secondary inspection lane to correct or complete paperwork, releasing it to U.S. Customs only after the paperwork is in order and has been approved. The program has significantly reduced delays at the bridge for both commercial and non-commercial traffic. Also in Windsor, Revenue Canada has established the Customs Trade Administration Consultative Committee (CTACC) which meets quarterly with stakeholders and businesses to ask how to better facilitate trade while maintaining departmental goals. While most members are Canadian, American businesses participate as well.

In the same region, the successful 1998 breakup of a major international alien-smuggling ring in the St. Regis Mohawk-Akwasasne reservations bordering eastern New York and Cornwall, Ontario, was credited to the ability of the various agencies in both countries to work together under the 1997 Cross-Border Crime Forum created by the Canadian and American federal governments. The smuggling ring spanned five continents, beginning in China and ending up in New York via Canada. Agencies cooperating in this effort included the U.S. INS, the Royal Canadian Mounted Police, the Toronto Police, Citizenship and Immigration Canada, the U.S. Attorney's office in New York, the Federal Bureau of Investigation, the New York State Police, and the St. Regis Mohawk Tribal Police.

Local officials also have been active in undertaking joint cross-border ventures. For instance, municipal officials in Buffalo and Fort Erie took advantage of the opportunities created by TEA-21, the Shared Accord, and a plan to redesign the Peace Bridge to work toward connecting the area's assets and making their region a gateway that would attract more travelers and economic development, as well as improve the quality of life for the region's residents. Using the input of public workshops and outside consultants, they designed the Buffalo/Fort Erie International Waterfront Gateway Strategy. Moreover, the annual Great Lakes Mayors Conference, hosted by Windsor in 1998, attracted at least seven mayors from the region and also led to greater attention to common border issues, such as the environment, marine transport, economic development, and federal legislation. The Great Lakes mayors began meeting in the 1980s and have continued to meet annually on issues of common concern, with meetings rotating between Ontario, Quebec, and the United States.

Proposed Solutions

In the course of our fieldwork, we came across a variety of ideas about improvements both large and small for life along the border. These ranged from specific issues such as opening more lanes and adding more staff at a particular port of entry, to eliminating the border completely, to maintaining the border-related functions but performing them away from the border itself. We heard suggestions not only from those professionally involved in these issues but also from people who have only occasional interactions with the border and its realities. Ideas emanated both from those who have never had a problem crossing the border and those who face daily frustrations or challenges at it. Some recommendations were extremely sophisticated or nuanced, while others were quite simple and straightforward. However, a recurring commonality was that people were very open and willing to speak with us, and everyone had something to say on the issue—no one suggested leaving the border exactly as it is.

Technical

Personnel. Some of the problems described by residents of border communities were very straightforward, and we believe they can be resolved with additional federal funds and a bit of dedicated attention. For instance, when long lines and long waits are due to the fact that only two out of ten booths may be staffed, additional staffing can alleviate the problem. In fact, the need for an increased number of immigration and customs inspectors was a common theme of our interviews. It is clear that the Canada-U.S. border is understaffed relative to the demand and that it has been given short shrift by Congressional attention, which is focused almost exclusively on the U.S.-Mexico border. INS decisions to detail Border Patrol and Inspections staff to the U.S.-Mexico border have exacerbated the problem. More inspectors can translate into both greater facilitation and better enforcement while also addressing such collateral issues as the additional environmental pollution resulting from trucks idling their engines as they await inspection.

A related personnel issue, described to us by frustrated residents of the regions, is the inconsistent, and often seemingly arbitrary, behavior of the staff of the inspection agencies. Most residents with whom we spoke said they would be happy to comply with the rules if they knew what the rules were and if they did not seem to change all the time. Along these lines, they expressed widespread support for improving educational efforts regarding the rules about crossing and the laws of the two countries with regard both to commercial and passenger traffic. Such efforts could help reduce long waits by reducing the number of people pulled over for inadvertent violations.

Another personnel-related issue, easily, if mistakenly, overlooked when envisioning broad policy changes, relates to unionized employees. However, for those on the ground, this is a very practical issue, with real implications. In both Canada and the United States, inspectors at the border are union members. The existence of these different unions and different labor agreements poses a challenge for national policy makers and local managers considering operational changes. For example, under joint staffing of primary lanes, at times one agency may have enough staff to open additional lanes at the port of entry, but the other agency may not, so the lanes remain closed. Alternately, an agency might have enough employees available but they may have already worked the maximum number of hours or the district may lack sufficient funds to be able to pay the necessary overtime. Unions, then, add an additional layer of complexity to attempts at more unified port management, not only between the two countries but also between the various agencies at the border in each country. Any changes to port management will likely require renegotiations in both countries.

Infrastructure and Technology. A more straightforward, though very costly, issue to address, and one raised frequently in our interviews, was the need for infrastructure improvements. The infrastructure at the Canadian-U.S. border—which includes not only the land crossings, bridges, or tunnels themselves, but also the inspection space for both countries, the immediately surrounding roads, and the highways leading into and away from them—was not designed to handle the existing levels of commercial and passenger traffic, and it is already overloaded. A significant planning and financial investment would be necessary to allow the infrastructure to meet current demand, in addition to considering future demand.

A complementary means of addressing some of these infrastructure challenges and speeding legitimate crossings is through the use of existing technology and development of new ones. However, views on this issue were more mixed among respondents. Some border residents felt that these technological improvements would cost too much and would be no more effective than existing low-tech programs such as the PACE lane. Others expressed concern that these high-tech programs would collect too much personal information from those using dedicated commuter lanes. On the other hand, commercial crossers seemed to be much more enthusiastic regarding high-tech programs.

Thus, while we were convinced of the need for improved infrastructure along this border, we also suggest that given the levels of resources necessary to bring the physical infrastructure into the twenty-first century, we should first decide how we want borders to operate in the future and only then build the supporting infrastructure that will allow us to meet our objectives. Moreover, while we see the value of technology for solving some existing border problems, the relevant agencies should not become too dependent on technological improvements as the magic solution to all problems. Technology in and of itself, with no other systemic changes, is not a panacea. When combined with other forward-looking solutions, however, it does become a key component of the future of border management.

Border Inspections. In some areas, a particular law enforcement problem may make inspection agencies on either side of the border reluctant to experiment with perhaps more efficient but at least seemingly less robust inspection regimes. For instance, in ports of entry in the Pacific Northwest, U.S. border inspectors were focused on trying to prevent the entry of "B.C. Bud," a high-quality marijuana produced in British Columbia and apparently much valued among U.S. users (thought to be traded one-for-one with cocaine), while Canadian inspectors focused their efforts on deterring weapons and cocaine smuggling. In addition, the Customs officials of both countries had to work harder to prevent the entry of goods that are fraudulently labeled so as to make them tariff-free under NAFTA.

Some of these difficulties might benefit from increased cooperation and improved communication between the two governments. Cooperation and communication, both on the ground and between administrative agencies in Washington and Ottawa, are good and getting better. Such cooperation can, nonetheless, be expanded and institutionalized. It can include enlargement and integration of pre-clearance programs such as PACE (American) and CANPASS (Canadian), cross-training of inspectors, joint operations, and additional intelligence-gathering and sharing regarding third-country nationals and drug-, alien-, or weapons-smugglers. The Canadian government and its inspection agents are no less interested than their American counterparts in keeping out both undesirable people and goods.

An alternative means of addressing these challenges within the current system might be for Canadian and American inspectors to share a joint facility, or for the United States to copy the Canadian model in which one agency mans the primary inspection lane and both agencies are represented in secondary inspection. While the latter idea does not appear to be under discussion, the former one is, particularly for smaller, more remote ports of entry. Joint facilities existed in Danville, Washington/Carson, British Columbia, in 1988, in Noyan, Ontario/Alburg, Vermont, in 1988, and in Turner, Montana/Climax, Saskatchewan, in 1993. Discussion is under way for three additional shared stations: Poker Creek, Alaska/Little Gold, Yukon Territory, Oroville, Washington/Osoyoos, British Columbia, and Sweetgrass, Montana/Coutts, Alberta.[36] Benefits from these modes of operation would include a reduction of costs and duplication, increased efficiency, a single set of rules, and increased accountability.[37]

One could go even further, considering, on a case-by-case basis, allowing one country's agents to handle border inspections in a given location but with the responsibility for checking for violations of both countries' laws (for example, Canadian inspectors in Buffalo/Fort Erie and American inspectors in Detroit/Windsor). This may be particularly useful for ports of entry located in urban areas where space limitations leave few options for physical infrastructure improvements. The CVPC begins to move in this direction, with U.S. Customs inspectors doing their work on the Canadian side of the plaza. We also recommend consideration of the concept of an international zone in the border region with free movement, as well as engaging in experiments and pilot projects at various ports of entry (such as Point Roberts, Washington, one out of the four Niagara crossings, or a remote port).

Conceptual

The Purpose of a Border. Other questions raised by border residents were not so straightforward, beginning with the most basic one, "What purpose does the border serve?" A border denotes the existence of two sovereign countries, each physically and psychologically different from the other, with its own laws and values, and each determined to exclude "undesirables." As discussed earlier, border community residents were well aware of the symbolic value of the border as a dividing line between the two countries as well as the "protection" offered for one's physical security and cultural identity. Generally, respondents stated that Canadians value the border's protection of their social services, their health care system, and their national identity (while keeping out negative American influences such as guns), while Americans value the border as a means of preventing terrorism and unwanted outsiders.[38] They had no problem, though, with the other's nationals working in their countries, nor did they feel that the other's nationals posed any sort of security threat.

Even officials committed to the anti-alien-smuggling and anti-drug efforts acknowledged during interviews that the inspection system currently in place fails to intercept most would-be violators and that a random system could be just as effective. In fact, most good "busts," such as the breakup of the international alien-smuggling ring in Native American territory, occur as a result of tips, old-fashioned human intelligence work, and seamless on-the-ground cooperation. For these reasons, and almost regardless of (reasonable) additional resources invested in the current system, significant changes in inspections efficiency and enforcement effectiveness will come only from thinking differently about the inspection system itself.

The Process at the Border. Once there is agreement on the goals of the border, the next question becomes, "How do we want to see borders operate in the future, and what is the best way of getting there?" A number of changes would need to be part of such a "remaking" of borders. On one level, that could mean changing the current methodologies. Today inspectors ask every crosser the same few questions and check his or her documents. Engaging in random checks and relying more on intelligence may in fact lead to results that are no less robust and allow, gradually, for moving into a different modus operandi. Such a shift would imply that the two countries work jointly on a number of additional issues, whose resolution will prove thorny and thus require a significant investment of additional capital. Among them are harmonizing overseas visa policies, developing joint pre-clearance programs, cooperating deeply in law enforcement programs, and a common (or joint) focus on perimeter security.

On another level is the question of whether the functions currently undertaken at the border need to be done at all, and if so, whether they need to be done at the border. An example might be inspecting and sealing a truckload of manufactured items when they leave their factory, rather than doing so at the port of entry. Another example of creative thinking is the United States' pre-clearance locations at airports in Canada. U.S.-bound passengers undergo all necessary checks prior to boarding and on arrival are free to deplane as if it were a domestic rather than an international arrival.

When asked what they would propose to their capitals regarding the border, focus group participants gave suggestions ranging from concrete requests for new bridges to the elimination of land borders and a focus on international entries into North America (in places like New York City, Seattle, Toronto, and Vancouver). Others suggested allowing the border to become regionally managed, including ensuring that local residents have a say in what happens there. Overall, most people we interviewed were deeply interested in more seamless movement, but— with varying intensity and for varying reasons—they also believed that the border between the United States and Canada should not disappear.

Parity with NAFTA Partners. Finally, participants recognized that for U.S. policy makers, the appearance of equity is an important issue, with some of them likely to be concerned about an appearance of disparate treatment for the United States' two NAFTA partners when conceptualizing a new border approach. They noted the reality, however, that many aspects of the U.S.-Canada border relationship are far ahead of that of the U.S.-Mexico border relationship. These include intelligence cooperation, similar enforcement priorities, ability to deliver on commitments, similar levels of technological capability, a habit of working together on matters large and small, and other issues. Conversely, some aspects of the U.S.-Mexico border relationship seem to be more advanced than those on the U.S.-Canada border, such as the depth of engagement of a strong national network of Mexican consular representation in matters involving Mexican nationals, and a variety of control and facilitation methodologies at the border. That is why "lessons learned" and information sharing should take place in a multidirectional manner.

Thus, we suggest viewing border relationships as a continuum, within a single national policy framework, with progress along different borders, different ports of entry, and at different speeds in different regions. Experimenting with and then sharing best practices based on input from local residents, local businesses, local officials, and other community-based groups is likely to serve broad U.S. interests best while acknowledging both the different realities of each border (and each port of entry) and the need not to be seen as treating Canada and Mexico differently. However, while local flexibility and innovation should be encouraged and rewarded, it must be accomplished in a manner that makes arbitrary actions or the arbitrary interpretation of fundamental rules unacceptable.

Conclusions

Our research has led us to three primary conclusions. First, border regions are unique zones, each facing different challenges and concerns, and one policy does not fit all. Differences among ports of entry in terms of needs, challenges, and priorities make it difficult to generalize even about the entire length of a single border, much less about other borders. Second, despite the unique factors of the regions, these cross-border communities have much in common, facing similar challenges such as facilitating trade and tourism while trying to protect their security and their cultures. They also face similar frustrations, ranging from an outdated and overloaded infrastructure to a lack of input into the decision-making process. Third, numerous initiatives exist in these binational, cross-border communities, with lessons to be learned from forward-thinking local actors.

These "best practices" seemed to have a number of common factors, which may explain their success. They include the degree to which the actors involved have common self-interests, sufficient funding, and a broad coalition of stakeholders. In addition, the presence of individual creative thinkers is crucial, as are projects that take into account local circumstances and receive local input. In some cases, the presence of a supportive overarching federal framework has been an important factor in determining success or failure. Strong local-level relations, built upon personal relationships, trust, and informal contacts, exist between U.S. and Canadian counterparts at every level, with information sharing routinely taking place on matters large and small.

We have become convinced that border policy must be sensitive to the facts on the ground in each border area. Consciousness raising needs to happen both vertically (within each of the two governments) and horizontally (across the relevant public agencies and all the border communities). At present, too few coalitions span the country between Blaine and Buffalo or between the business community and nongovernmental organizations. The grassroots effort must be broad-based if it is going to reach Ottawa and Washington, D.C. After all, it is those who live in the communities, and who use a commonsense approach, who often know what is best for their communities, in terms of integrating while maintaining distinctions. These communities view the border as an asset, not as a disadvantage, and they believe they prosper because of the border, not in spite of it. Therefore, despite the challenge of balancing multiple interests on border issues—with its implications for security and national identity—local officials, in partnership with business interests, worker organizations, and community-based and other relevant groups, should play a much more significant role in the ongoing discussions about and the implementation of policies that affect their lives. This is, by necessity, an incremental process, with a slow building of trust and a responsibility for an enhanced level of communication, interaction, and consultation shared by both the federal government and border communities. We hope that our fieldwork and regional seminars helped expand existing and create new networks to prospectively address these border-related issues and to bring a greater awareness of the Canada-U.S. border to broad national policy audiences.

Notes

1. See <www.usembassycanada.gov> for information about trade between the two countries.
2. For additional statistical information, see <www.usembassycanada.gov>, <www.ins.gov>, <www.canadianembassy.org>, and <www.statcan.ca>.
3. Although this was the case at the time of the research, we note that the two governments have begun to engage border communities and others through two Canada-U.S. Partnership (CUSP) meetings held in 2000.
4. See Figures 1.6 and 1.7 to get a sense of the volume of cross-border traffic in these three regions.
5. Detroit Regional Chamber of Commerce Home Page. Research and Information. <www.detroitchamber.com>.
6. Statistics: Canada 1996 Census Community Profile for Windsor, and U.S. Bureau of the Census 1998 Estimates. <www.statcan.ca and www.census.gov>.
7. Ford and General Motors are headquartered in the region, and they, along with DaimlerChrysler, have an integrated production system that includes production and assembly in both countries. The Detroit Economic Growth Corporation estimated in August 1999 that more than half of all U.S.-Canada trade passed through the Detroit area.
8. A frequent graphic depicts one-hour increments of concentric circles from Detroit/Windsor or Buffalo/Fort Erie to visually demonstrate the major cities encompassed within this framework, including Toronto, Montreal, Ottawa, New York, Boston, Pittsburgh, Philadelphia, Washington, D.C., Cleveland, and Chicago.
9. See <www.occ.gov.on.ca> for additional information regarding the gambling industry in Ontario.
10. Another Michigan-Ontario crossing point is the International Bridge connecting the two Sault Sainte Maries, which had 2.6 million crossings in 1999.

11. Crossing data are from the December 1999 statistics of the U.S.-Canada Bridge and Tunnel Operators Association and do not include airport arrivals.
12. Information obtained from the Buffalo Niagara Partnership. <www.the partnership.org>.
13. U.S. Bureau of the Census. Population Estimates. <www.census.gov>.
14. Information obtained from a December 9, 1998 meeting of the Buffalo Niagara Partnership, from their "Prospect Package," their Assets List (<www.thepartnership.org>), and from the Fort Erie Economic Development Corporation website, <www/forterie.on.ca>.
15. "Economic Impact." The Buffalo and Fort Erie Peace Bridge Authority. <www.peacebridge.com>.
16. Bellingham, located some 140 kilometers (90 miles) north of Seattle and one hour south of Vancouver, is the largest U.S. city along this border, with 60,000 residents. Traditional industries include lumber, fishing, and agriculture, with high-tech, services, transportation, and communications becoming more prominent. Nearby Blaine, with 3,500 residents, shares the Peace Arch with Surrey, also home to over 40 parks and one of the fastest-growing cities in Canada, with 30 percent of its 300,000 residents under 19 and immigration accounting for 41 percent of its growth. Another small port of entry in the region is Point Roberts, Washington, located at the tip of a peninsula of British Columbia, across the Strait of Georgia from the U.S. mainland.
17. For information on this region and these border communities, see Alan Artibise, "Cascadian Adventures: Shared Visions, Strategic Alliances, and Ingrained Barriers in a Transborder Region." Vancouver, B.C.: University of British Columbia, 1997. Also see: <www.bwedc.org>, and <www.ci.blaine.wa.us>.
18. U.S. Census, 1998 estimates and British Columbia Ministry of Finance and Corporate Relations.
19. U.S. Bureau of the Census. Census 2000, Summary File 1 (SF-1), "100-Percent Data Profile of General Demographic Characteristics: 2000."
20. Community profiles for Seattle and Vancouver taken from the Greater Seattle Datasheet (www.cityofseattle.net) and BC Stats (www.city.vancouver.bc.ca).
21. See: United States-Canada Peace Anniversary, Inc. <www.peacearchpark.org>.
22. Cascade Gateway data were provided by the Whatcom County Council of Governments. For more information see <www.wccog.org/data.htm>.
23. Data from 1996 Transport Canada survey, as well as from *Trade and Traffic Across the Eastern US-Canada Border*, Vol. I (1997) and Vol. II (1998). Ottawa: Ontario Trucking Association and Eastern Border Transportation Coalition.

24. Such competition has significant payoffs both in increasing the quality of infrastructure and quantity of business to guarantee that a "larger pie" will indeed continue to materialize and by the emerging efforts to market an area/region, rather than a single location in one or the other country.

25. Point Roberts, Washington, is located on a peninsula below the 49th parallel. It has approximately 1,000 year-round residents and is bounded on three sides by water and on the fourth by Canada.

26. This was consistent with the views expressed by both Canadians and Americans throughout our trips that Americans are less aware of Canada than Canadians are of America.

27. Revenue Canada has a number of different programs in place to facilitate commercial traffic, including FIRS (Frequent Importer Release System) for companies bringing in bulk goods, PARS (Pre-Arrival Review System), which sends the information to the customs broker ten days to two hours before arriving at the border, and EDI (Electronic Data Interface), which is part of the Accelerated Commercial Release Operational Support System designed to allow brokers to send electronic requests to support a paperless environment.

28. According to the statute (Immigration and Nationality Act Sec. 289, 8 USC Sec. 1359), such "American Indians" must be at least 50 percent "American Indian." This provision results from Article III of the Jay Treaty between Great Britain and the U.S. in 1794 which recognized the Indians' existing right to move freely across what had become an international border by the 1783 Peace of Paris but which ran right through land long occupied by Northern American Indian tribes. The Jay Treaty does not govern entry of American Indians to Canada.

29. According to U.S. Customs, twelve thousand commuters crossed at Point Roberts in 1998, of whom 70 percent were Canadian.

30. Niagara Falls receives approximately twelve million visitors per year. See: <www.niagarafallslive.com>.

31. These figures do not include airport or seaport inspections, only those at land-border ports of entry.

32. The reference here is to meaningful violations (such as violations of gun and drug laws or alien smuggling) rather than technical ones. An example of the latter is the occasional confiscation of fruits and vegetables carried by children and adults from Point Roberts in their lunches.

33. Another informal practice is strong cooperation between Canadian and American officials at the local level generally, as exemplified by informal arrangements of immigration officials handling American minors returning from a night of drinking in Canada intoxicated and without identification, having given insufficient consideration to the fact that

they are crossing an international border. When the minors are stopped upon their return, instead of detaining them, the officials frequently call the parents directly to verify their ID and arrange for pickup.

34. The Transportation Equity Act for the 21st Century (TEA-21), signed by President Clinton in June 1998, was frequently cited as an impetus for cross-border organizing. This landmark transportation bill allocated up to $140 million in funds for National Corridor Planning and Development and Coordinated Border Infrastructure programs until FY 2003. In FY 1999, 32 states (55 projects) received about $124 million in grants under this legislation. TEA-21 is based on the 1991 Intermodal Surface Transportation and Efficiency Act (ISTEA).

35. For additional information regarding TEA-21 funding, see <www.fhwa.dot.gov>.

36. U.S. Customs initiated discussion on joint facilities in 1982 and the two countries' customs services signed an MOU after studying the European model of common border facilities.

37. Some remote ports of entry already have innovative arrangements, such as the Remote Area Border Crossings in northern Ontario, which allows local residents (Canadian or American) to get a permit for $30 biannually allowing them to cross the border elsewhere than at Canadian ports of entry. They have proven particularly useful for fishermen and snowboarders.

38. Interestingly, both then agreed that free trade and simple economics has overridden and will continue to override these types of perceptions, moving the countries closer together, potentially in the direction of the European Union. One participant even predicted that sometime in the (distant) future there will be no border between Canada and the United States.

2

Transborder Community Relations at the U.S.-Mexico Border: Laredo/Nuevo Laredo and El Paso/Ciudad Juárez

Nestor Rodriguez and Jacqueline Hagan

It seems that we are all finally understanding that Nuevo Laredo and Laredo, Texas, are a single city, divided by a river, independent of their nationalities. And that the border zone is a different world, apart from the rest of the two countries. The people of Laredo, Texas, understand this, and we [in Nuevo Laredo] understand it.

—Mexican Official, Nuevo Laredo

Having to deal with the federal government [is a disadvantage in a border city]. It is much easier to get things coordinated [locally]. . . . [If] there is a problem at the bridge, I can assure you that Mayor Betty Flores picks up the phone and calls Mayor Garza in Nuevo Laredo and in five minutes they can have an answer and solve the problem. But sometimes the problem becomes a major problem because federal

We would like to thank Ruben Hernñandez-Leon, Janna L. Shadduch, and Lorena Orozco for their research assistance.

governments in the United States and on the Mexican side have to notify Washington and Mexico City and so on. Big problem. If it was left up to us, we could probably figure it out pretty fast and solve it. That is one of the major problems, federal regulations. Because [they] are imposed by people that do not even understand the border.

—Business leader, Laredo

THIS IS A STUDY of the nature and extent of institutionalized relations between the adjacent border communities of Laredo and Nuevo Laredo and El Paso and Ciudad Juárez. In a larger sense, it is also about how transborder communities manage the international movement of goods and people at the local level. Communities throughout the world maintain varying levels of local, state, and national identities, but communities adjacent to one another but divided by international borders are particularly challenged, as the function of national boundary maintenance falls heavily on them. The challenge is even greater when communities on both sides of the border have established an historic web of cultural, social, and economic interdependency.

This is the story of four Texas-Mexico communities in our two research sites, four communities that originated from the history of Spanish-Mexican northern development and the formation of a U.S.-Mexico border in the mid-nineteenth century (Martínez 1994). Partly because of a common cultural history and partly because of their collective need to survive jointly in border areas, the communities of Laredo/Nuevo Laredo and El Paso/Ciudad Juárez have developed local strategies to cope, and even prosper, despite the international boundary that divides them. Other recent and seemingly paradoxical developments also influence the course of local practices between these communities. For example, our research shows that although recently strengthened INS enforcement activities in the western part of the Texas-Mexico border have enhanced the geographical divide between El Paso and Ciudad Juárez, the North American Free Trade Agreement (NAFTA) has escalated trade relations between the sister communities of Nuevo Laredo and Laredo.

To examine the nature of, and variations in, transborder relations along the U.S.-Mexico border in the fall of 1998 and spring of 1999, we conducted six months of field research in Laredo/Nuevo Laredo and

El Paso/Ciudad Juárez. In both border sites, we interviewed community leaders and residents from a number of formal and informal institutions about a wide array of issues of common concern, including government, business and commerce, education, media and other cultural affairs, public safety, sports and recreation, immigration and commuters, and health. Approximately 225 interviews were conducted. As the field work progressed, particular issues concerning transborder relations emerged as most salient in each of the two sites. In the Laredo/Nuevo Laredo site, the research increasingly focused on the areas of government, business and commerce, public health and safety, community, and education. In the El Paso/Ciudad Juárez site the research concentrated on the arenas of border crossers, maquiladoras, transportation, and education.

We begin this report by providing some background on the two border settings and then move on to present the study's findings, which are organized into three sections. The first section describes the salient arenas of transborder relations and activity; these include economic relations, migration, public health, public safety, law enforcement, education, environmental concerns, and relations at the community grassroots level. We then describe attitudes and perceptions of leaders regarding their cities' transborder relations, and the relationships between the federal governments and the border area. We end the findings section with a discussion of self-governance practices along the border, in which we address the conditions underlying the development of these practices and the limitations imposed by the two national governments. We conclude by emphasizing the similarities in findings from our two research sites.

Background

In recent years, the two research sites have gained increasing international prominence as critical points of activity along the U.S.-Mexico border. Since the passage of NAFTA, Laredo/Nuevo Laredo has achieved recognition as the largest trade conduit between Mexico and the United States. El Paso/Ciudad Juárez's prominent position results partly from being the origin of a U.S.-Mexico border industrialization program of maquiladoras and partly from having one of the most intensified locations of U.S. border enforcement activities. The twin cities in both sites have experienced high population growth since 1990. According to the most recent U.S. Census figures, El Paso grew by 19 percent, reaching 615,000 by 1998, and according to early releases of the Mexican 2000 Census, Ciudad Juárez grew by 53 percent, reaching a population of 1.2 million by 2000 (U.S. Bureau of the Census 2000; INEGI 2000). Laredo grew by 43 percent, climbing to 176,000 by 1998, and Nuevo Laredo grew by 41 percent, climbing to 310,000 by 2000 (U.S. Bureau of the Census 2000; INEGI 2000).

Laredo/Nuevo Laredo

Laredo/Nuevo Laredo is the land point with the greatest volume of U.S.-Mexico trade. In 1999, 38 percent of all the trade between the United States and Mexico passed through this corridor as well as 51 percent of the total trade through Texas (Laredo Development Foundation 2000). In dramatic contrast, the bustling San Diego/Tijuana border area handled only three percent of the U.S.-Mexico trade in 1999. Moreover, in the late 1990s the number of pedestrian crossings from Nuevo Laredo into Laredo through the two international bridges approached three million.

The two cities are linked by at least four levels of common economic activities. The most visible level is trade of manufactured goods, which accounts for a sizable volume of the 1.6 million loaded trucks that traversed the Laredo/Nuevo Laredo border in 1999 (Laredo Development Foundation 2000). A second level of economic interdependence is located in the area's maquiladora industry. As of April 2000, 30 of the 62 maquiladora plants located in Nuevo Laredo had office, distribution, or manufacturing facilities in Laredo (Laredo Development Foundation 2000). A third level of shared economic activity involves a large number of businesses in Laredo that import low-to-moderately priced merchandise (such as toys, small radios and stereos, and wristwatches) from Asian countries to sell to Mexican customers, including vendors who resell the merchandise in Mexico. A fourth level of economic interdependence consists of the wide range of informal economic activities between the two cities. These activities include the selling of used clothing by the pound to Mexican vendors in Laredo, the gathering in Laredo of disposed container materials by Mexicans to sell in Nuevo Laredo, and the daily crossing of Nuevo Laredo laborers into Laredo to work in the city's informal labor market, such as domestic and construction work.

Laredo and Nuevo Laredo have also institutionalized relations at the political level. Although the two cities function as separate political systems, city leaders and municipal institutions in the two cities gain political capital from their interaction when they strive to advance their cities' standing through transborder cooperation. Some examples of this interaction are meetings between the city councils of the two cities, joint planning between city departments of the two cities, and the recent signing of a Sister Cities Pact (*Pacto de Ciudades Hermanas*) to acknowledge the cities' economic interdependence, cultural interaction, and agreement on activities to promote joint local development. Yet, as some respondents pointed out, there is an awareness of the political asymmetry that exists between the two sites, reflecting U.S.-Mexican political relations, exemplified by the United States' measures to control the border, deciding whom to let into the country and whom to keep out.

The strong social relationship between Laredo and Nuevo Laredo is best captured by the common expression, voiced by residents in both cities, *los dos Laredos* (the two Laredos). The social unity binding the two cities is symbolized by the *Ceremonia del Abrazo* (Ceremony of the Embrace) on George Washington's birthday (22 February), when the mayors of the two cities embrace on one of the two international bridges connecting the cities. In addition to the vigorous business activity uniting the two cities, a large Mexican-American population in Laredo creates a strong Hispanic social bond between the two cities. In 1990, the census found that 94 percent of Laredo's population was Hispanic, and 97 percent of the city's Hispanic population was of Mexican origin (U.S. Bureau of the Census 1993, Table 7). Twenty-four percent of the city's overwhelmingly Mexican-origin Hispanic population is foreign-born (U.S. Bureau of the Census 1993, Table 12). Native and foreign-born Hispanics promote strong ties between families in the two cities. These "binational" families help to unite substantial parts of the two cities into one social unit. Perhaps exaggerating this familial connection, a respondent in Nuevo Laredo commented,

Here it is very particular; here it is different [as compared to other border sites]. The difference is that Laredo and Nuevo Laredo work very much hand-in-hand. Yes, a river divides them, but a culture unites them. Laredo is 90 percent Latino; 90 percent of them have families in Nuevo Laredo. There are many [shared] backgrounds. And here, as over there, there is not a person that does not have a relative in Laredo. Everyone here has cousins, aunts, or grandmothers [in Laredo].

Other comments also demonstrated the common social bond felt by many Hispanic residents in the two cities, for example, "[I]n the Laredo area there is no border," and "The bridges between our two cities, unite us rather than separate us." The constant crossings of the international bridges by relatives on both sides exemplified these sayings. Yet, not everyone in Laredo manifested this spirit of social unity. Some Laredo residents rarely crossed into Nuevo Laredo and considered the Mexican city a source of social problems for Laredo.

The social unity between many residents in Laredo and Nuevo Laredo also creates cultural unity. Most obvious is the cultural continuity of Mexican heritage and the use of the Spanish language. For example, the city of Laredo has in its central plaza a large statue of General Ignacio Zaragosa, who successfully led a Mexican army in Puebla against an invading French force on 5 May 1865 (*el Cinco de Mayo*). The use of the Spanish language in the Laredo area is widespread among the Hispanic population. According to the 1990 U.S. census (1993, Table 138), 92 percent of the population age five and older in Webb County, of which Laredo is the county seat, uses Spanish, with almost half (46 percent) of them bilingual speakers who can also speak English "very well." As one respondent commented in Laredo, "In terms of language there really is not a border." The Spanish-language culture is present throughout the city of Laredo, just as the English language is found in many areas of Nuevo Laredo, especially along the larger avenues. More recently, sports has added to the cultural commonality between the two cities in the form of the Tecolotes (Owls) baseball team. This team officially represents los dos Laredos in the Mexican professional baseball league, playing home games in both cities. It is believed to be the only professional sports team in the world representing adjacent home cities in two countries (Klein 1997). When the

"Tecos" won the Mexican World Series several years ago, team fans celebrated wildly, honking and screaming in their cars and passing unchecked through opened border checkpoints between the two cities.

El Paso/Ciudad Juárez

With a combined population of 1.8 million residents, the cities of the El Paso/Ciudad Juárez corridor represent the largest twin-city population on the U.S.-Mexico border. With a population of 1.2 million, Ciudad Juárez had the largest Mexican border population in the 2000 Mexican census (INEGI 2000), and with a population of about 615,000 El Paso had the largest U.S. population on the U.S.-Mexico border in 1998, according to the most recent U.S. census projections (U.S. Bureau of the Census 2000). The combined city population of San Diego/Tijuana of about 2.4 million residents (U.S. Bureau of the Census 2000; INEGI 2000) is sometimes cited as the largest U.S.-Mexico border concentration, but the small U.S. city of San Ysidro is actually opposite Tijuana; San Diego is some 19 kilometers (12 miles) away from the international boundary line.

During the 1990s, El Paso/Ciudad Juárez made national and international news for crime-related violence in Ciudad Juárez and for the intense U.S. efforts to bolster border enforcement in the El Paso area. A large number of persons have been killed in Ciudad Juárez as rival gang members battle for control of the area's lucrative illegal drug trade. This violence is also believed to be responsible for the disappearance of some residents of the city. By the late 1990s, these problems and a series of kidnappings and murders of Juárez women appeared to be reclaiming for Ciudad Juárez the title of "The Most Wickedest City in the World," which the Boston Herald bestowed on it in 1915 (Dwyer 1994). In El Paso, the launching of Operation Blockade (later renamed "Operation Hold the Line") in the mid-1990s by the U.S. Border Patrol gained national and international attention as the operation created a human barrier of Border Patrol agents to stop the entrance of undocumented migrants. While some El Paso residents welcomed the Border Patrol action, the construction of a fence stretching from downtown El Paso to the Lower Valley created images of a "Tortilla Curtain" for other area residents.

Border historian Oscar J. Martínez describes El Paso/Ciudad Juárez as "a major gateway from Mexico to the United States and long the 'heart' of the borderlands" (1994, 147). Martínez is certainly correct if he is referring to the heart of capitalism on the U.S.-Mexico border. As prominent as Laredo/Nuevo Laredo is as a major trading point between the United States and Mexico, El Paso/Ciudad Juárez is even more prominent as the original site of the U.S.-Mexico Border Industrialization Program (BIP), initiated in 1965, which created the border maquiladora industry of automated mass production involving U.S. and other foreign corporations. Described as "fordism" by some analysts (Peña 1994), the maquiladora industry produces a range of items for export to the U.S. market, especially electronics, textiles, electrical machinery, and auto parts, through assembly-line production. Firms like General Motors, Ford, General Electric, Toshiba, and AT&T are major players in maquiladora production, which depends primarily on the unskilled, low-wage labor of young Mexican women. With low-wage labor and the reduction of tariffs and import restrictions, maquiladora industries gained major advantages as they brought items to the U.S. side for final manufacturing and distribution. NAFTA created even bigger advantages for maquiladoras as it eliminated even more restrictions, including opening the Mexican consumer market to maquiladora products in the early years of the twenty-first century. By 1996, Mexico's 2,465 maquiladora industries accounted for almost 40 percent of the country's exports, using a total workforce of more than 500,000 workers. By mid-1999, the number of maquiladoras had mushroomed to over 3,000, employing more than a million workers (*Twin Plant News* 1999, 71–72).

Ciudad Juárez has the second-largest concentration (after Tijuana) of maquiladora plants in northern Mexico and ranks number one in terms of the number of maquiladora workers. By 1999, Ciudad Juárez had 273 maquiladora industries (all different economic enterprises), which employed over 219,000 workers (*Twin Plant News* 1999, 71–72). With a heavy involvement of U.S. firms in the Ciudad Juárez maquiladoras, El Paso became a prominent twin-plant site, as many U.S. firms opened facilities there. Moreover, El Paso also became an important site for the many businesses that provide support services for the maquiladora industries. In sum, El Paso/Ciudad Juárez has become a major location of the internationalization of U.S. capital, forging a strong structural relation between the two cities.

Many binational families reside in the adjacent border communities of Ciudad Juárez and El Paso. Children born on one side may be raised on the other, while adults travel back and forth to work and visit relatives. The strong binational presence in El Paso is reflected in its foreign-born population, which reached twenty-two percent in 1990 (U.S. Bureau of the Census 1993, Table 1). Not surprisingly, this immigrant population is almost all of Mexican origin. This generation and its U.S.-born children maintain a steady stream of visits and other social exchanges between the two cities. Mexicans entering from Ciudad Juárez to El Paso usually use a border commuter card (*la mica*) that allows visits (but not employment) in the U.S. side for up to 72 hours within a 40 kilometer (25 mile) radius. However, some enter without visas or micas and add to a transient, undocumented migrant population on the El Paso side. Both cities have responded with the development of community-based organizations to deal with the problems that arise from undocumented migration. In Ciudad Juárez religious workers, and in El Paso legal activists, struggle to support the undocumented migrant population that accumulates in the two cities. This population includes Central Americans and minors and is partly recycled as U.S. border agents remove about 300 migrants daily to the Mexican side of the border.

Much like Laredo, El Paso enjoys a substantial continuity of Mexican culture. The use of the Spanish language is widespread among the Hispanic population of El Paso County, where 65 percent of those five and older use Spanish; about half (53 percent) of them also speak English "very well" (U.S. Bureau of the Census 1993, Table 138). Cultural continuity is also found in places of worship, restaurants, and stores that sell items popular among Mexican-origin customers, while the El Paso newspaper has Spanish-language sections. Ethnic culture, however, is not the only culture that helps bond the two communities; there is a business culture that also helps to link the two cities. A business culture of corporate practices transcends the border, involving administrative charts and time schedules that synchronize maquiladora business administrators and managers across the border. This culture helps to create even a common time zone, as maquiladora industries in Ciudad Juárez run on El Paso time (Mountain Standard Time) rather than on Mexican time.

As in Laredo/Nuevo Laredo, El Paso/Ciudad Juárez share a common economic background at various levels. We have already pointed to the formal level of the maquiladora corporations, which we elaborate below, but other economic levels that involve a wider spectrum of the two cities' populations also exist. These levels include Korean-owned stores that sell low-cost clothing and other items to Mexican customers, downtown loan companies that lend from $25 to $500 to El Paso and Ciudad Juárez residents, and the Mexican consumers who comprise 20 percent of the customers in El Paso malls.

Finally, there are examples of political activity that draw El Paso and Ciudad Juárez into a common web. Although much less intense than what was found in Laredo/Nuevo Laredo, one example is meetings between public officials of the two cities. A more salient example at times is the joint activism around immigration and border issues, including recent activism concerning the U.S. interest in establishing a nuclear waste site near the border. All types of activism bring members of the two communities together; indeed, it is not uncommon to encounter a protest right on the international bridge connecting the two cities.

Findings: Transborder Relations and Activities

Project researchers in each site surveyed a variety of institutional sectors to determine which institutions were involved in transborder relations and activities. The focus was on institutions that fostered high levels of interaction between leaders and members in the two sets of cities and that involved substantial movement across the border. Our findings are presented below.

Laredo/Nuevo Laredo

In the Laredo/Nuevo Laredo site high levels of transborder relations and activities were found in the institutional arenas of local government, commerce and business, public health, public safety, community/ grassroots, and education.

Local Government. The city governments of Laredo and Nuevo Laredo have historically maintained high levels of interaction, dialogue, and cooperation. One transborder project has been a collaborative urban growth plan—Urban Plan of Los Dos Laredos—developed jointly by the planning departments of Laredo and Nuevo Laredo in 1994. As one official commented, "[T]here is a conscious attempt by the local government of both cities to influence the character of future development, and to make los dos Laredos grow as one metropolitan area to the year 2010 and beyond." The plan was developed to promote common, organized growth for both cities based on technical standards, land use, capital improvement, public services, private development decisions, and associated government regulations. Although the plan promotes cooperative efforts, it also maintains separate regulations and evaluations for each city. In another mutual cooperation agreement (see Pacto de Ciudades Hermanas, above) the mayors of the two cities agreed to collaborate on building a new international bridge, creating committees to promote joint economic development, integrating projects to renovate historical districts, and building a new railroad bridge between the two cities. The Laredo planning department and the municipal archive of Nuevo Laredo have developed an historic guide for both cities, and in 1997 they produced a joint environmental plan. All of these activities in the local government area involve constant movement across the border by officials and urban specialists.

Commerce and Business. Laredo/Nuevo Laredo maintains a high level of transborder relations and movement through the maquiladora industrial sector. The 90 maquiladora plants located in Nuevo Laredo employ 3,000 Laredo workers. The maquiladora industry also stimulates a constant flow of merchandise and truck trips back and forth across the border. To illustrate, over 400 customs brokers in Nuevo Laredo and 500 transportation lines handle the movement of merchandise across the border. Business leaders from both cities regularly interact through personal contacts and business organizations, for example the Laredo Development Foundation and *Comité para el Desarrollo Industrial de Nuevo Laredo* (Committee for the Industrial Development of Nuevo Laredo; CODEIN). In the words of the general manager of CODEIN, "the cities are promoted as a border region and not as two separate or independent cities." The general manager further illustrated this economic unity by emphasizing that every dollar earned in Nuevo Laredo's maquiladora sector sends 40 cents to Laredo's economy. Government officials and business leaders of the two cities regularly participate in business meetings and events in each other's cities. For example, Laredo mayor Betty Flores participates in Chamber of Commerce meetings in Nuevo Laredo, and the director of the Nuevo Laredo Chamber of Commerce participates in business meetings in Laredo. Commercial and other business leaders in both cities emphasized that NAFTA only further increases their cities' transborder economic relations.

Public Health. The institutional sector of public health was considered by interviewees in Laredo and Nuevo Laredo to have stimulated the longest and strongest transborder activities between the two cities. The area's very high poverty levels (reaching 45 percent for children under 18 in Laredo) and poor sanitation conditions, which have in the past triggered communicable disease epidemics, have led to joint recognition that public health is a transborder issue (Hagan, Rodriguez, and Capps 1999). This historic relationship centered on the issue of public health has been further developed by the many Mexican health professionals working as directors and staff in Laredo public health agencies. Examples of the transborder collaboration in public health include exchange programs in which nurses go to training seminars in the opposite city, and Nuevo Laredo public health workers regularly attend workshops sponsored by the Laredo Public Health Department. According to a public health official in Laredo, the idea for sharing training programs was simple: "[W]e both felt very strongly that our people *son los mismos, van y vienen* [are the same, they go and come]."

Hospitals in the two cities also share information and equipment. Hospitals in Laredo donate equipment to enable medical personnel to perform complex surgeries in Nuevo Laredo and treat persons with contagious diseases. Public hospitals in the two cities also share information necessary to continue the treatment of patients who have been deported to the Mexican side. The City of Laredo Health Department has a formal program with public health agencies and private practitioners in Nuevo Laredo to work toward eliminating tuberculosis. According to the Laredo-Webb County Health Department (1995), rates of tuberculosis, hepatitis, and other communicable diseases in the Laredo area are three times the general Texas rate. A joint program, *Programa Binacional de la Tuberculosis de Los Dos Laredos*, uses U.S. federal monies channeled through the Texas Health Department to

Laredo. The Mexican Ministry of Health coordinates the program in Nuevo Laredo.

With funding from the Environmental Protection Agency and other U.S. sources, the City of Laredo and the Ministry of Health also train Mexican health workers to teach safe drinking-water practices to 250 families on each side of the border through the program *Agua para Beber* (Water to Drink). The program's goal was reached faster on the Mexican side of the border, presumably because of greater outreach knowledge and coordination on that side. In this case, health care workers in Laredo learned from the experiences and expertise of their counterparts in Nuevo Laredo.

Public Safety. On a lesser scale, public safety is also considered a transborder issue; however, unlike the equal exchange of resources over the issue of public health, Nuevo Laredo is overwhelmingly dependent on its northern neighbor for technical resources in the area of public safety. Nonetheless, there is considerable interaction between institutions in the two cities in issues of public safety. For example, the *Consejo Municipal de Protección Civil* (Municipal Council for Civil Safety) in Nuevo Laredo includes a representative of the Laredo Fire Department, as well as a representative of the U.S. consulate. The Laredo and Nuevo Laredo fire departments have a 50-year agreement of mutual assistance in cases of severe fires and emergencies, although usually it is the Laredo Fire Department that lends equipment and donates supplies and safety literature to the Nuevo Laredo Fire Department. While Nuevo Laredo has almost twice as many people as Laredo, it has only two fire trucks, compared with Laredo's seven. The two fire departments also conduct joint training sessions on a biannual basis. Law enforcement agencies in the two cities regularly share information regarding crime suspects, wanted criminals, missing persons, stolen cars, and so forth. The Laredo Police Department provides SWAT training, suspect sketching, and scientific evidence analysis to the Nuevo Laredo police.

Community/Grassroots. The most visible and obvious transborder interaction is the constant, daily movement of residents back and forth across the border to visit families and to work. A segment of the populations of the two cities consists of families who have members living on both sides of the border and who maintain contact through regular visits, some daily, others weekly. A brother or sister may cross into Laredo, for example, to care for a sibling's children. Some, such as Mexican children attending school in Laredo, who used to cross daily have reduced their crossing frequency by staying longer in Laredo, due to the fear that U.S. border agents will confiscate their border commuter cards. On a daily basis, a stream of workers crosses the border from Nuevo Laredo to work in Laredo. The workers concentrate in a plaza a couple of blocks from Laredo's downtown international bridge and wait to be picked up by employers. In the evenings, the employers return the workers to the plaza, who then head back to Nuevo Laredo. Community-based organization personnel also go back and forth across the border to carry out their missions. The legal aid center of *Centro Aztlán* in Laredo, for example, will send social service providers (such as immigration counselors) to Nuevo Laredo when residents there who need help are not allowed to enter the U.S. side. Community organization personnel also cross the border to promote joint community events, such as art displays.

Education. Educational activities are a major source of transborder relations. These activities occur at several levels. One level is the attendance by Nuevo Laredo youth in public and private schools in Laredo. There is no official count of how many students commute daily from Nuevo Laredo, but when the Rio Grande flooded in 1998 and the international bridges were closed some schools in Laredo experienced a 45 to 50 percent drop in attendance. Some Laredo residents see the Nuevo Laredo commuting students as a burden, yet some of these students are U.S. citizens who reside with their binational families on the Mexican side. Nuevo Laredo residents also enroll in Laredo's Texas A&M International University and in a local community college, though some Nuevo Laredo employers stressed that the best technical training was to be found in Mexican technological institutes. Institutions of higher learning in Laredo frequently offer the use of their facilities (e.g., conference halls and labs) to their counterparts in Nuevo Laredo. (In another border setting in southern Texas, the State University of Tamaulipas [Mexico] offers a doctoral program in education through the University of Texas-Pan American at Edinburgh, Texas.) Finally, universities in Laredo and Nuevo Laredo sometimes collaborate, but also at times compete, to develop educational and training support services for maquiladora industries in the area, ranging from administrative training to English classes.

El Paso/Ciudad Juárez

At the El Paso/Ciudad Juárez site high levels of transborder relations and activities were found in the institutional arenas of the economy, education, environment, health, immigration, and law enforcement.

Economic Relations. We have already described the large concentration of maquiladora plants in Ciudad Juárez. These maquiladora companies maintain facilities and staff in El Paso, and the regular interaction between company staff on both sides of the border translates into strong transborder business relationships, which are further fostered by the many El Paso support services for maquiladoras in Ciudad Juárez. For example, the El Paso Community College and the University of Texas at El Paso provide technology transfer and training courses to maquiladora managers and workers. At times this local partnership between the "maquiladora colleges" and private industry in Mexico is supported by U.S. federal monies (Barry, Browne, and Sims 1994). The federally supported Advanced Technology Center (ATC) in El Paso Community College, for example, provides customized training for maquiladora companies in Ciudad Juárez, but only for those that are owned entirely by U.S. firms. In a description of this support service, Barry, Browne, and Sims (1994, 103) state, "When ATC promotional brochures state that its mission is to 'promote economic development' and respond to the needs of 'local industry,' by *local* they mean not only El Paso but also Juárez" (italics in the original).

Other transborder economic relations in El Paso/Ciudad Juárez involve the consumer activities of residents from both sides of the border, examples of which are plentiful. El Paso youths cross to Ciudad Juárez to buy beer and other alcoholic drinks they cannot buy in their own city; at the informal level, individuals buy products in Ciudad Juárez to sell in El Paso street markets. For example, a Ciudad Juárez resident can buy a pound of tortillas in Ciudad Juárez for ten cents and then sell them for a dollar in El Paso. This is also done with cigarettes, candy, and vegetables sold by vendors in El Paso streets. Some El Paso home workers buy supplies in Ciudad Juárez to make items to sell in El Paso. For example, an El Paso woman may buy cloth in Ciudad Juárez to make dresses to sell in her city. Consumer-driven movement flows north as well. When Ciudad Juárez gasoline prices rise, more residents buy gasoline in El Paso; when the Mexican peso is devalued, more El Paso residents shop in Ciudad Juárez. Some store owners in El Paso malls state that 30 percent of their customers are Mexicans. It is estimated that 40 percent of Ciudad Juárez residents do some of their Christmas shopping in El Paso. El Paso retailers advertise in Ciudad Juárez newspapers. Many Ciudad Juárez residents respond by buying in bulk, which gives the El Paso malls the highest retail sales figures in West Texas. Finally, an informal work force travels daily from Ciudad Juárez to look for low-paying work in El Paso.

Education. As in Laredo/Nuevo Laredo, children commute from Ciudad Juárez to attend schools in El Paso. Much like the case of Laredo/Nuevo Laredo, public school administrators in El Paso do not count the number of Mexican commuting students because they say it is against the law to ask the students their nationality. However, private schools do keep count, and a religious high school in downtown El Paso reports that 80 percent of their 300 students are from Ciudad Juárez; a religious high school for girls in El Paso reports that 70 percent of its student body is from Ciudad Juárez. Institutions of higher education also draw persons across the border. This almost always involves Mexican residents traveling north to attend institutions of higher education in El Paso, rather than U.S. residents traveling south to attend Mexican colleges and universities. This is largely because Mexican students receive priority in Ciudad Juárez colleges, and these institutions lack resources to attract U.S. professors. Mexican students, many commuting daily from Ciudad Juárez, account for about 8 percent of the enrollment at the University of Texas at El Paso. As described below in the section on Self-Governance, this institution works through a special program to attract Mexican students.

Environment. The U.S. decision to establish a nuclear waste site in Sierra Blanca, Texas, near the Rio Grande, and the slow Texas response to it, stimulated a vigorous Mexican environmental protest in Ciudad Juárez, whose residents painted Spanish- and English-language banners protesting the proposed waste site and draped them over the international bridges. Some Ciudad Juárez residents, wearing anti-waste-site T-shirts and other paraphernalia, blocked the bridges several times, and some, including a mayoral candidate, went on hunger strikes. Many also crossed the border to join El Paso residents in anti-waste-site rallies in front of the El Paso County courthouse. When the decision was made in Texas on 23 October 1998 not to accept the nuclear waste site, Juárez newspapers attributed the victory as much to the Juárez activism as it did to Mexican federal diplomacy. While this transborder environmental issue did not last very long, it did demonstrate how certain social issues can quickly mobilize large numbers of people on both sides of the border and create collective currents between the two cities.

Health. Like public school administrators, public hospital officials in El Paso do not keep counts of patients' nationalities, but nonetheless they estimate that Mexicans account for about 30 percent of their patients. Physicians, dentists, and other health care personnel in Ciudad Juárez also report having significant numbers of patients from El Paso. For example, some Juárez physicians who accept U.S. health insurance payments report that 15 percent of their patients come from El Paso; some Juárez pharmacists estimate that up to 40 percent of their business is with El Paso residents, while Mexican sources also report that some El Paso residents cross to Ciudad Juárez to seek iridologists and other doctors of "natural medicine." At another institutional level, public health agencies have collaborated in promoting and administering vaccinations for children in their areas. These agencies see the constant border crossings of families with children as a possible source for spreading diseases and risking children's health. Again, public health emerges as a key transborder issue.

Immigration. The El Paso region is a major area of undocumented immigration, and the U.S. Immigration and Naturalization Service (INS) in El Paso handles one of the largest numbers of removals among all the INS districts in the country. Of the 181,572 total removals reported by the INS for Fiscal Year 2000, the El Paso INS district accounted for 12,955 removals, which ranked third after the San Diego (63,424 removals) and Phoenix (23,983 removals) INS districts (Immigration and Naturalization Service 2000).

Although the removal/deportation process has been routine for adults, the handling of minors creates a different situation. The INS cannot simply "deposit" children on the streets of Ciudad Juárez, where they can quickly become victimized or get into other trouble. The Mexican consulate and INS personnel in El Paso meet and exchange information to cope with the problem of undocumented minors. In another immigration-related issue, El Paso residents created grassroots efforts (Operation Family Unity) to counter a new INS policy of deporting Mexican immigrants with three violations for driving while intoxicated. Grassroots efforts, with connections in Mexico, also have successfully opposed the joint patrolling by police and the INS in downtown El Paso. Joint patrolling was discontinued after downtown residents and Border Rights Coalition members in El Paso presented their concerns in a forum with the police and the Border Patrol.

Law Enforcement. Long-standing criminal activity in El Paso/Ciudad Juárez has fostered increased transborder cooperation between law enforcement agencies in the two cities. In March 1998, 300 federal and local law enforcement officials from the United States and Mexico met in El Paso to discuss ways to combat the common problem of drug smuggling. Gangs in the El Paso area are believed to be affiliated with drug cartels in Ciudad Juárez. New concerns have arisen that drug lords may be buying warehouses and trucks to house and transport their cargo under the cover of NAFTA. The El Paso Police Department has also provided training to the Ciudad Juárez Police Department through the Program for Domestic Readiness on how to handle terrorist attacks. Some El Paso police officers point to the increasing number of times that activists have blocked the international bridges as a sign that the terrorist threat is increasing in their area. The two police departments also share information when searching for wanted criminals in their areas.

Attitudes and Perceptions of Transborder City Relations

In both research sites, interviews with community leaders and residents found strong attitudes and perceptions concerning transborder city relations. The most salient of these views are those concerning inter-city solidarity and those concerning the primacy of the local setting.

Views Concerning Inter-City Solidarity

Interviewees in both research sites repeatedly emphasized the solidarity that exists between their own and their sister-city. In the El Paso/ Ciudad Juárez site, respondents pointed to the strong collaboration between economic institutions in the two cities. In the Laredo/ Nuevo Laredo site, interviewees pointed this out too, and also stressed the social and cultural affinity between their two cities. Laredo and Nuevo Laredo respondents were quick to express this view with statements such as "(I)n the Laredo area there is no border," and "The bridges that join our two cities unite us rather than separate us."

Business leaders in the Laredo/Nuevo Laredo site were principal proponents of the view that strong solidarity exists between their two cities. One business leader commented as follows:

> In all senses, the river unites us more than separates us.... Organizationally speaking, in terms of commercial, industrial, and service promotion, [eventually] there will only be ... one institution at the binational level to promote this. [It] will be formed by persons from both cities, but with the goal of promoting both sides [of the border].

What stood out in the comments of the Laredo/Nuevo Laredo respondents was that they were referring to more than an organic economic relationship between two cities; they were referring to a single entity. This view was not lacking in the El Paso/Ciudad Juárez site (where the Mexican consul called El Paso "our community"), but it was stated more often in the Laredo/Nuevo Laredo area.

The respondents in the sites were not, however, completely of a single mind that their two cities shared a prosperous, inseparable relationship. In Laredo, a segment of the population considered Nuevo Laredo, and all of Mexico for that matter, to be a deficient area of little value to U.S. interests. This attitude defined Mexico and Mexicans as a third-world social problem. On the Mexican side, when probed, some respondents who previously professed strongly positive attitudes toward Laredo eventually remarked on the power imbalances between the two settings. This view appeared to come from two perspectives. One stems from the frustration of dealing with increasing regulations on the U.S. side of the border. The second emerges from recognition of the political asymmetry between the two countries, the fact that the United States sets requirements that Mexico usually follows. It should be pointed out, however, that both perspectives dealt with federal-level issues and not with those originating from local policies. Finally, one respondent suggested that the perception of strong unity and one-ness between Laredo and Nuevo Laredo would eventually change as the two cities grew into much larger settings and developed their own separate identities.

While views of strong inter-city solidarity were also popular in the El Paso/Ciudad Juárez site, the comments of an El Paso university administrator who recently moved there from New York City provided a contrast. According to her, the relationship between the two cities was "not that good"; the cities "are two separate entities connected by a bridge," and it was only binational family relations that created a sense of unity. If it were not for family relations, she thought, the two cities would soon feel unbearable strain because of their disparities. She pointed out that the lack of a real integration between the two cities was illustrated by the numerous group identities used in the area. The frequent use of group terms like "Mexican," "Mexican-American," "Chicano," "Latino," "Hispanic," and "American" indicated that the El Paso/Ciudad Juárez area still lacked unity.

Views Concerning the Primacy of the Local Setting

Throughout the interviews in the Laredo/Nuevo Laredo and El Paso/Ciudad Juárez sites, it was clear that persons saw their inter-city solidarity to be a product of local relational styles and local problem-solving approaches, owing nothing to formal, federal agreements between the United States and Mexico. Especially in Laredo/Nuevo Laredo, many respondents commented that the high level of transborder relations between their two cities was, for the most part, based on informal relations and interpersonal contacts. The Laredo/Nuevo Laredo respondents felt they could not stress this point enough. Moreover, in both research sites the respondents felt that an increasing number of official border agreements between the federal governments of the United States and Mexico would interfere with their ability to maintain highly efficient transborder relations at the local level.

A Laredo business leader illustrated the problematic implications of federal interference in his comments concerning a pending U.S. Congressional initiative to verify the immigration status of Mexicans as they exit the United States. The business leader stated as follows:

Congressmen in Washington decided that the United States needed to find out when people who are leaving the United States with visas exited the country. Sounds great. How do we find out when a person is leaving the country with a visa? Well, we have to check.... That means you have to check everybody leaving the country.... You can imagine the kind of problem that creates for us when we have 300 trucks crossing daily going south. We are crossing about three million people a month going south and everyone has to be stopped and asked for documents. Even if it takes a hundredth of a second to process each person that multiplies into a big mess. That is what I mean about federal regulations causing big problems for us.

According to El Paso's Democrat Congressional representative Silvestre Reyes, "decisions that are made in Washington and Mexico City often are dramatically against the interest of people on the border" (*El Paso Times* 1998). Ciudad Juárez Mayor Gustavo Elizondo expressed a similar attitude when he stated that border cities need policies different from state and national ones because state and federal policies do not offer the most viable solutions to border problems.

Self-Governance Practices at the Border

In the United States and Mexico only the federal governments have the power to regulate border crossings into each country. Nonetheless, our study revealed that various individual and institutional actors in border cities undertake a variety of measures to facilitate the border-crossing movement of people into their communities. These "self-governance" practices are undertaken for different reasons. One reason is simply to reduce transborder traffic and long lines on the international bridges; a second is to expedite business transactions; a third is to carry out health or medical transactions in an expedited fashion; and a fourth is to facilitate the recruitment of transborder clients and customers, who have become increasingly significant for the reproduction of a local institution. Often self-governance practices operate through the actions of both local and federal actors. In this section we present our findings on self-governance practices in our two research sites.

Laredo/Nuevo Laredo

Perhaps the most striking example of a self-governance practice in Laredo/Nuevo Laredo was when the Mexican Immigration Service (*Instituto Nacional de Migración*) set up a border checkpoint for returning Mexican migrants 22.5 kilometers (14 miles) into U.S. territory. The Mexican border checkpoint was set up on a main highway to Laredo in December 1998 to handle the high volume of Mexican migrants returning to visit their hometowns during the Christmas and New Year's holidays, and was established in conjunction with plans by the City of Laredo to promote tourism among south-bound Mexican migrants. The Mexican checkpoint, which was approved by the U.S. government, issued 1,800 permits in two days and reduced to minutes what in previous years had been hours of waiting in long lines at the Nuevo Laredo immigration checkpoint to enter Mexico. Reducing the time delay to enter Mexico benefited the city of Laredo by reducing traffic congestion on the highways passing through the city to the international bridges. Often, the sections of the highways nearest the international bridges become "parking lots" of cargo trucks waiting to cross into Nuevo Laredo. When the lines of waiting trucks back onto the Laredo highways, they pose serious accident risks for speeding motorists: Laredo motorists have died after crashing into the lines of waiting trucks. The large number of Mexican migrants waiting at the international bridges to re-enter Mexico added to the traffic congestion and dangers in Laredo.

Interviews in Laredo/Nuevo Laredo also revealed that local business associations meet with customs and immigration officials to deal with issues that might impede commerce. A case concerning a Mexican association of export transporters in Nuevo Laredo illustrates this. When the association (*Asociación Solidaria de Transportistas de Exportación*) attempted to bring U.S.-manufactured tractor trailers into Nuevo Laredo for use in transporting cargo, they were faced with hefty Mexican import fees. As explained by the association president, these fees were circumvented informally by getting Mexican customs officials to allow the association to put Mexican plates over the U.S. plates on the trucks when they crossed the international bridge into Nuevo Laredo.

Interviews in Laredo also revealed techniques for facilitating the movement of health and medical personnel carrying medical equipment and specimens across the border. In cases when medical supplies need to cross into Nuevo Laredo with some degree of urgency, but are delayed by import restrictions, one common practice is to send the supplies across in small quantities in private cars. An approach to avoiding import fees on medical equipment is to "lend" the equipment to the Mexican agency. "Lending" the equipment from Laredo to Nuevo Laredo avoids the importation fee because its ownership is considered to remain in Laredo. Nuevo Laredo public health agencies that need to promptly transport medical specimens for complicated analysis in Laredo have been able to navigate around lines of waiting import trucks at the U.S. checkpoints by faxing ahead the nature of the specimens that nurses will be transporting through the U.S. checkpoint.

The Laredo interviews also show that a Laredo university acts to facilitate the border crossing of Mexican students for enrollment on its campus. What the university does is to persuade the INS to allow these "international" students to enter the United States as part-time students. The university accomplishes this by writing letters that the students present to the INS explaining that a part-time student with a border commuter card is legally able to attend classes without a student visa. To additionally facilitate the recruitment of Mexican students, the university allows them to list more than one sponsor so as to meet the requirements of economic solvency. Some Texas universities are motivated to recruit Mexican students to increase their enrollment. As will be explained in more detail below, a Texas law permits state universities to admit Mexican students as Texas residents for tuition purposes.

Finally, the project found a host of self-governance practices implemented by residents in Nuevo Laredo to facilitate crossing into Laredo. These practices often involve persons who have binational family members in Laredo or have jobs or attend schools in the city, but who usually have only a border commuter card to cross into the U.S. side. The critical concern for them is how to enter the United States repeatedly without raising the suspicion of U.S. border inspectors, who can take away a border-crossing card or replace a valued legal resident-alien card with the temporary commuter card. Respondents reported trying to avoid the attention of U.S. border inspectors by crossing through different bridges, crossing during different inspector shifts, and even crossing in different vehicles.

The Laredo interviews indicated a couple of factors regarding the effectiveness of these self-governance border practices. One factor is simply the popular wisdom that these practices work best when they are arranged informally through personal contacts, which are sometimes made first with municipal officials of either or both sides and then with federal border agents. A second factor involves the role played, and the identity taken, by federal agents. Technically, all transborder movement is inspected by a federal agent, but the ability to influence this movement (whether of people or goods) can vary according to the degree to which a federal border agent assumes a "federal" or "local" identity. Border federal officials regularly participate in joint committees through which they find solutions to border problems through local strategies (such as how to handle apprehended illegal migrant children). Because federal agents live in the locale, it should not be surprising to find that they can develop strong identities with their local setting, including the binational metropolitan area.

El Paso/Ciudad Juárez

In El Paso U.S. federal officials have collaborated with local officials in attempts to help facilitate the movement of border traffic. One attempt is the Dedicated Commuter Lane (DCL), designed to expedite commuter traffic in the El Paso/Ciudad Juárez area and built by the El Paso Chamber of Commerce, which opened for traffic in the summer of 1999. To use the DCL, area residents pay a yearly fee of $329. This fee purchases an ID card with a laser strip which is fed through a computerized reader at the bridge to verify authorized drivers and other vehicle information. Drivers with the ID use the dedicated lane as long as only authorized riders are in the car and undeclared commodities are not being crossed. This plan is designed to speed up the northbound travel of people, especially workers and students, who cross on a daily basis. Maquiladora companies, the Chamber of Commerce, and the El Paso Foreign Trade Association were important promoters of the DCL plan, which they saw as a means to considerably reduce the crossing times of maquiladora employees. A secondary function of DCL is to help reduce auto emissions as the congestion and waiting time to cross the border is reduced.

A second attempt is a pilot program called Color Coded Processing (CCP), intended to reduce the time required for primary customs inspections. A primary inspection takes about 20 to 30 seconds, but under the pilot program, if a customs officer feels that a closer inspection of a vehicle is warranted, then the driver will be handed a folder of a specific color and told to proceed to another inspection station. The second and closer inspection will be determined by the color of the folder, and in this way primary inspection and the traffic flow should proceed more smoothly. Federal border officials in El Paso take pride in both attempts to facilitate border crossings and see the attempts as local, creative contributions to the El Paso community.

Business interests in both El Paso and Ciudad Juárez have been behind ideas and plans to facilitate vehicular border crossings. In El Paso, business leaders and city officials have promoted the idea of a transportation hub and road development to speed up the movement of people from the international bridges to workplaces and shopping malls in the suburbs. Congressional Representative Reyes has also proposed a study to examine the feasibility of establishing light-rail transportation to connect the downtowns of both cities. Already, an El Paso bus line, Sun Metro, has eliminated its fare, thereby attracting a larger number of Juárez residents to use the bus line. Business leaders in Ciudad Juárez are also thinking through their own idea of a transportation hub, especially for rerouting truck traffic to the border. Some Juárez business owners with stores near the international bridge have proposed to the Mexican federal government that it create an "open zone" that U.S. tourists could enter to shop without passing through any Mexican border inspection.

Unlike Laredo/Nuevo Laredo, where city planners from both cities developed a joint urban development plan, planners from El Paso and Ciudad Juárez have not interacted through a formal arrangement, nor do they meet on any formal basis. Nonetheless, planners in El Paso feel that they can communicate effectively with their counterparts in Ciudad Juárez about area development plans, such as the planning for transportation hubs.

In addition to promoting the DCL to reduce employee commuting time, maquiladora companies also help their Mexican workers obtain border commuting cards, by providing Mexican employees with reference letters to present to INS agents. The employers believe that proof of employment and residence in Ciudad Juárez makes it easier for their Mexican employees to acquire the cards. Other ways in which local businesses have attempted to promote border crossings include the following. When the El Paso police set up checkpoints to inspect for vehicle insurance, downtown business owners lobbied against these inspections, claiming that they reduced their business by 40 percent; the checkpoints were moved closer to the downtown international bridge. When the Mexican government limited the value of U.S. retail merchandise that Mexicans could bring back into Mexico to $50 per trip, El Paso retailers lobbied the Mexican government to increase the amount.

The University of Texas at El Paso (UTEP) has also become a significant source of practices that influence the transborder movement of people (mostly students) in the El Paso/Ciudad Juárez area. Almost all of the colleges, departments, centers, and institutes at UTEP have transborder interests or activities. As mentioned above, some research units at the institution act as "maquiladora colleges," providing customized support for maquiladoras owned by U.S. firms. Other units of UTEP are more inclusive in their transborder affairs. One example of this is the PRAXIS program, which combines student volunteerism with classroom training. PRAXIS has been providing student volunteers for El Paso agencies, but the program's director is at this writing planning to send volunteers into Ciudad Juárez. Expanding the program into Ciudad Juárez will give U.S. students an international experience and the Mexican students an opportunity to volunteer in their own community. About 10 percent of the 311 students in the program are from Ciudad Juárez. As the director explained, it might take a while for the program to take hold in Ciudad Juárez, given that volunteerism is not part of Mexican culture. When approached about the program, some agency supervisors in Ciudad Juárez were surprised to hear that someone would work for no money. Once the program is implemented it will send and regulate a steady flow of student volunteers back and forth across the El Paso/Ciudad Juárez boundary.

UTEP also operates a program to recruit Mexican students through the "Mexican Tuition Waiver Program" of the State of Texas (Texas Education Code Ch. 54.06 ¶B), intended to allow state universities to attract more Mexican students, increase enrollments, and charge Mexican students in-state tuition based on documented need. According to the most recent statistics, 1,810 Mexican students were enrolled in Texas institutions of higher education under this program in the fall of 1998. The majority of them (1,228 students) are enrolled at UTEP, where the program is known as "El Programa de Asistencia Estudiantil" and is referred to as PASE, an acronym which in Spanish means "Come in." UTEP administrators see PASE as a means to help recapture enrollment lost when a New Mexico state university started admitting El Paso students as New Mexico residents.

At UTEP, Mexican students enrolled through PASE are in English preparatory classes and thus do not have to take the English skills test required of international students. The students take classes taught in Spanish for several semesters and then take classes in English. Program recruiters emphasize this when they visit Juárez high schools to promote it. PASE students also qualify for financial aid if they maintain at least a 2.0 grade point average. This assistance is based on documented need, and the funds come from the Texas Public Education Grant for International Students. The PASE office on the UTEP campus provides an inviting atmosphere in which Mexican students in the program can congregate. For some PASE students, their experience in the program is similar to participating in a student club.

However, PASE has significant limitations that must be solved before the program can expand and recruit a significantly larger number of students. One limitation is that there are not enough Spanish-speaking professors to teach the number of classes needed for the PASE students. Another problem is that the textbooks selected for the courses are in English. Some faculty and teaching assistants also complain that some of the PASE students are not adequately prepared to take college classes, even when the classes are taught in Spanish.

There is a clear contrast between the PASE program in UTEP and its counterpart in the Laredo university. While PASE has its own office and director and provides a friendly atmosphere for its students, in the Laredo university the Mexican Tuition Waiver Program is administered by the Financial Aid Office. The promotional materials provided by the two universities also stand in contrast. UTEP 's materials have the inviting PASE acronym, while the Laredo university materials are titled "Program for Assistance to Mexican Students." UTEP provides easy-to-read application materials for students to enroll in PASE, while the Laredo university provides a complicated set of regulations and forms that appear cumbersome to fill out.

Conclusion

In each of the two study sites the research reveals a variety of formal and informal local practices that create what are effectively transborder communities. These communities reproduce themselves on a daily basis despite national regulations, such as U.S. enforcement campaigns to regulate migration, that attempt to divide them. Local governments, public agencies, private institutions, families, and individuals conduct a myriad of formal and informal exchanges. These exchanges result from the workings of integrated transborder economies, especially in the post-NAFTA period, and focus on issues concerning trade services and manufacturing. In addition, transborder metropolitan areas cooperate on issues of public safety and health, education, family organization, and government. Interactions also arise from the political and economic asymmetries that exist between Mexico and the United States. For example, there is a wide variety of private and public institutions in both research sites that engage in transborder exchanges to gain access to the superior technology and knowledge on the U.S. side of the border, especially in areas of mutual interest such as health, education, public safety, and commercial expertise. These interactions, exchanges, and relationships strengthen the ongoing processes of integration between Laredo and Nuevo Laredo and between Ciudad Juárez and El Paso. The informality of transborder exchanges is even more pronounced in Laredo/Nuevo Laredo than in El Paso/Ciudad Juárez, probably because the former community is smaller and has historically maintained strong social and cultural relationships. Nonetheless, what is most striking about both of these research sites is the many mechanisms the four cities have developed to create two well-integrated transborder communities.

Works Cited

Barry, Tom, Harry Browne, and Beth Sims. 1994. *The Great Divide: The Challenge of U.S.-Mexico Relations in the 1990s.* New York: Grove Press.

Dwyer, Augusta. 1994. *On the Line: Life on the U.S.-Mexican Border.* Nottingham: Russell Press.

El Paso Times, 1998. 9 March.

Hagan, Jacqueline, Nestor Rodriguez, and Randy Capps. 1999. "Effects of the 1996 Immigration Acts on Communities in Texas and Mexico." Working Paper Series 99-5. Houston: Center for Immigration Research.

Immigration and Naturalization Service. 2000. "FY 2000 INS Removals Show Slight Increase." News Release. December 20. <www.ins. gov/graphics/publicaffairs/newsrels/removals.pdf>.

INEGI (Instituto Nacional de Estadistica, Geografía e Informatica). 2000. *XII Censo General de Población y Vivienda 2000 (Resultados Preliminares).* <www.inegi.gob.mx>.

Klein, Alan. 1997. *Baseball on the Border: A Tale of Two Laredos.* Princeton: Princeton University Press.

Laredo Development Foundation. 2000. "U.S. Exports thru Texas Border Ports." <www.laredo-ldf.com>.

Laredo-Webb County Health Department. 1995. "Needs Assessment Survey of Health Risk Factors." Laredo, Texas.

Martínez, Oscar J. 1994. *Border People: Life and Society in the U.S.-Mexico Borderlands.* Tucson: The University of Arizona Press.

Peña, Devon G. 1994. *The Terror of the Machine: Technology, Work, Gender, and Ecology on the U.S.-Mexico Border.* Austin: Center for Mexican American Studies Books.

Twin Plant News. 1999 (July). "Maquila Scoreboard."

U.S. Bureau of the Census. 1993. *1990 Census of Population: Social and Economic Characteristics, Texas*, 1990CP-2-45. Washington, D.C.: U.S. Government Printing Office.

———. 2000. "Frequently Requested Population Tables." <www.census.gov/statab/www/pop.html>.

Additional Resources

Dirección General de Estadistica. 1990. <www.inegi.gob.mx>.

Inlandport: The Laredo Chamber of Business and Trade Magazine. 1998. October.

3

Between Order and Chaos:
Management of the Westernmost Border
Between Mexico and the United States

Gustavo del Castillo V.

SELF-GOVERNANCE at the U.S.-Mexico border, a region of contrasting cultures, beliefs, and economic systems, is a complicated endeavor. This is a zone where underdevelopment meets development and all its unintended consequences. This research took place in two very differing contexts. The first was the westernmost region encompassing the cities of Tijuana and San Diego, an area characterized by its fast economic growth, where great wealth and extreme poverty combine to form an urban zone extending in a transborder fashion for some 80 kilometers (50 miles) north to south, in a region where the hand of man has radically changed the desert environment. The second region studied is centered in the twin cities of Nogales, Arizona, and Nogales, Sonora, a place where a visitor gets the feeling that if he is not careful, the western desert will have the better of him. These are small cities trying to cope with economic transformations. In both, the presence of the Mexican culture is overwhelming, something not found in sophisticated San Diego. Also in the twin Nogales, the newly reinstated presence of national authority, a presence which has disturbed traditional exchanges and binational life, is resented by governing actors, complicating and bifurcating their lives.

I wish to thank Germán Vega of the COLEF for his help in describing some of the Tijuana NGOs.

The principal goal of this research was to gain an understanding of how governance takes place in these two different regions of the U.S. southern border. This is to say that agents in these transborder regions have had to devise ways to relate with one another to address a myriad of problems, some clearly bilateral in nature and others with "intermestic" (both international and domestic) origins, while minimizing conflicts. These relational aspects involve all dimensions of social, economic, and political life. In this context, both civil society and governmental actors are involved, mobilizing actors at all levels of government despite varying degrees of access to human and capital resources.

This chapter attempts to deal with this complexity of interactions in these contrasting bilateral regions. It begins with the development of a conceptual framework dealing with how transborder "understandings," achieved by a multiplicity of actors under asymmetric power conditions, aid in the governance effort along the border. After profiling the regions, the chapter first reports findings for the San Diego/ Tijuana region, followed by those for the twin Nogales. As these two principal sections were developed, preliminary conclusions appeared, which will be reinterpreted later in a final section of conclusions.

Ultimately, this work arrives at the conclusion that economic change in both the regions studied has led to a condition in which policy initiatives and problem solving are usually overtaken by changing events, leading to the participation of nongovernmental organizations (NGOs) who believe they can do better than their public-sector counterparts. There is, then, a constant deficit in policy making where actions are behind the curve of the objective realities; there is always a gap between the time a problem is recognized and the time a solution can be arrived at. This policy gap is a function of the complexity of a problem and the resources marshaled to address it, and it is increasing over time (at some point the costs of addressing problems will increase to where they will quickly be overtaken by diminishing returns).

The old bureaucratic structures and processes in place today to develop creative solutions to the many problems confronting border communities are clearly inadequate to the task. In order to address these problems, dynamic, adaptable, and flexible structures and processes are needed which can respond to immediate and medium-term problems with both policies and human and capital resources. More specifically, I call for supranational institutions with the capacity to make decisions on a regional and transborder basis, to coordinate existing institutions, and to override their policy suggestions when needed. These institutions must be flexible in order to confront the high rates of socioeconomic and political change occurring in the border region. Furthermore, they must be supranational in order to conceptualize this area as one distinct and specific region, where intermesticity is the order of the day.

Methodology

Research for this study incorporated a number of techniques, the primary one being identification and interviewing of "critical" public and private actors (those considered to be important in their own social dimension by other social actors). The interviews were guided by the theoretical perspective presented in these pages; consequently, the interviews were "directed" rather than completely free-flowing, emphasizing those concerns of transborder relations in which "understandings" might be possible or are known to occur. Other research techniques included use of primary and secondary evidence, primarily concerning demographics and population flows, to corroborate the findings derived from the interview process. Two small data banks were also created with data on border crossings and international trade flows, and newspaper information supports some of the arguments made throughout this chapter. The trade data bank was particularly interesting because its data tend to confirm the existence of a complex transborder production structure with many peculiarities, linking economic actors who are outside of normal interest group structures and outside of the much-studied maquiladora industry.

Most often this research was aided by the openness of those interviewed, who often invited this researcher to rummage through their files if necessary, and for that I am grateful. Other NGOs and institutions, especially in Tijuana, were reluctant to provide information, cautiously asking why they had been selected. Some seemed to believe that such information might fall into the hands of government or competing institutions; their relative newness and their constant struggle for resources might explain this reticence. Nevertheless, I am thankful to all those informants who graciously allowed themselves to be interviewed while remaining anonymous, with the hope that my account approximates the reality they have to confront on a daily basis.

Peeling the Onion of the Border: A Theoretical Approach

"Life's just too fast here; there are too many people, from too many places. There are no common rules; and then there are ... the gringos from across the line." (T.R.)[1]

Asymmetry and Understandings

When discussing the possible understandings existing at the U.S.-Mexico border, the notion of asymmetry in both power relations and access to material and human resources has to be taken into consideration as one of the principal determinants of the bilateral relationship. Although much has been said about the rapid economic growth of the Tijuana region over the last 20 years, this growth has had questionable developmental impacts.[2] In this context, one has to reflect as to what kinds of "understandings" might develop at the border, and what their fundamental, underlying nature can be, given the existing asymmetry between potential partners.

An initial definition of what is meant by an "understanding" is first necessary. "Understandings" can be of two distinct types: (1) those where values and norms are shared by two transborder actors that determine the necessity of common action (full norm convergence) and (2) those where there are no shared values of a common culture but where the understanding comes about because the investment of resources by either or both actors promises some type of return, even if intangible (functional-norm understandings with bilateral or unilateral action). In the first case, the investment of resources is seen as a necessity even when the outcome does not necessarily imply gains for either actor. Efforts may simply propel a common transborder value system, assuming a continuity of actors. The presence of an institutional infrastructure may assist in this. In the second case this type of understanding can come about because an action of a "practical" kind is seen as necessary to make life easier for the actors involved. The actors concentrate principally on "getting something done," since solving a problem is the fundamental reason for the understanding. A basic working premise in this work is that once understandings are arrived at, there will be resistance to changing them. In this respect, how and why they change is as important as knowing how they first were arrived at. Given this discussion, the question becomes, how does power asymmetry affect or shape these types of understandings?

Asymmetric partners recognize or accept that the dominant player will usually obtain most of the gains arising out of a relationship.[3] Undoubtedly, some transborder relations involve gains which, apart from the obvious commercial and trade relationships, are difficult to categorize and measure given that values and norms between partners underscore existing understandings. Yet, one fundamental factor that forms a key premise of this work is that the existence of innumerable transborder relations in the context of asymmetry means that most understandings at the U.S.-Mexico border will not result in a loss of resources for either of the actors involved. Even if the northern Mexican border has been characterized as having an "enclave" type of economic structure in which maquila operations dominate the panorama, most other socioeconomic relations cannot result in a loss of capital or other resources for the subordinate partner. In this context, the northern Mexican border cannot be conceptualized as a colonial entity of the United States from which to extract resources.[4]

I propose a three-dimensional conceptual model to define the meaning and characteristics of an "understanding." The Y axis defines whether or not there are "gains" involved for the actor while the horizontal axis (X) concerns the social dimension under consideration in which understandings may take place, such as environmental issues, population movements, and so forth. In the third plane, the nature of the understanding will also be defined by the type of actors involved in achieving it. When these three dimensions combine or interact, they will pinpoint a single point in analytical space that defines the type of understanding under consideration. Once defined, though, it will not necessarily be permanently fixed in space, but instead may change within the parameters imposed by this three-dimensional space according to a change in any one of the variables.

The Rise of Understandings

One of the principal propositions made here is that "understandings" are an essential component of social and economic life at the border and are a strategy for managing the border's complexities. This strategy arises because of the weak institutional structure for binational border management and the overall weakness of most public and private Mexican institutions, particularly when compared with the diverse, complex, and bountiful institutional structure north of the border. The centralized nature of the Mexican political system has traditionally inhibited both state and local public institutions from finding mechanisms with which to relate to their U.S. counterparts; whenever these levels of government took even small steps to relate to U.S. public institutions, they were forcefully reminded that only the federal government had the constitutional right to carry on foreign policy. As the democratization of the Mexican political system evolves, both of these levels of government have begun to develop contacts and the beginnings of an institutional structure to link themselves with U.S. institutions.

These problems vary somewhat from those experienced by U.S. structures; in their case, the institutional infrastructure is more or less present, but problems arise with the emphasis that the political leadership gives to bilateral relations and to problems at the U.S.-Mexico border. Since the mid-1980s there have been considerable shifts in state and local public policy toward Mexico and the binational region. Sometimes, socially proactive policies at the local level conflict with a generally anti-Mexico or anti-Mexican sentiment in Sacramento—à la Pete Wilson—or the emphasis shifts from border problem solving and management to issues of control imposed by Washington. Even in a region that boasts of its understanding of and close connection with Mexico, San Diego's former congressional representative Liz Shenk voted against the North American Free Trade Agreement (NAFTA) and then tried to lure NADBank and the Border Environment Cooperation Commission (BECC) to San Diego once it passed.

Either way, few transborder understandings attempt to deal with the structural nature of relationships existing in the border region. As such, this border region and most specifically, the subordinate partner, is immediately and constantly confronted by power asymmetries.

How understandings can succeed under these conditions is a tribute to imagination and persistence, not to mention to shifting quantities of political capital on both sides of the border.

Profile of the San Diego/Tijuana Region

Demographics

Mexico's northwestern border is unlike the rest of the country's border with the United States. It is characterized by what can best be described as rapid change—some would call it chaos.[5] The existing bilateral relationship is clearly asymmetrical in economic terms with respect to the size of the economies involved, but these same economies are also complementary in terms of goods and services exchanged; the existing system of production in this binational region also makes it increasingly integrated. The region includes approximately four million people distributed in the municipality of Tijuana, the city of San Diego, and a number of satellite cities such as San Ysidro, Chula Vista, and National City. The region has a highly urbanized population distributed along the coastal area—from the municipality of Rosarito, 32 kilometers (20 miles) south of the international line to the cities of Oceanside and Carlsbad, some 64 kilometers (40 miles) north.[6] In terms of the ethnic composition of San Diego's population, San Diego's Mexican-origin population was only 14.9 percent in 1980, but by 1990 had risen to more than 20 percent and was expected to further increase (to 25 percent) by 2000, increasing the social and cultural ties between these two cities (U.S. Department of Commerce 1983).

The dynamism-chaos mentioned above can be partially attributed to the very high demographic growth in the region which results from both international and domestic migration (see Table 3.1).[7]

Population Movements

The population growth along the Tijuana/San Diego border mentioned above is of enormous proportions. It is considered the most active border

TABLE 3.1

Population Growth Rates in Tijuana/San Diego, 1930–1995
(percent)

City	1930–40	1940–50	1950–60	1960–70	1970–80	1980–90	1990–2000
San Diego	3.3	6.7	6.4	2.8	3.2	3.0	1.3
Tijuana	7.2	11.4	9.8	7.5	3.1	4.9	6.8

Sources: California Statistical Abstract, 1979, 1994; San Diego Association of Governments (1995 data); Instituto Nacional de Estadística, Geografía e Informática, XI Censo General de Población y Vivienda. Datos por Localidad, Baja California, 1995.

in the world, with almost ten million legal pedestrians crossing along the ports of San Ysidro and Otay Mesa in 1997 and approximately 40 million private automobile crossings in these two ports (see Figures 3.1 and 3.2).[8] These are compared with Nogales, Arizona, where pedestrian crossings amount to less than 50 percent of those taking place in Tijuana, and vehicle crossings are but one-fourth of those taking place at San Diego/Tijuana. These population flows and their respective workplaces and types of employment place great pressures on border crossing infrastructure in the domain of all levels of government, from the corresponding federal governments to actions by city municipalities on both sides of the border. They affect various dimensions of transborder life, specifically legal and undocumented crossings along an increasingly controlled and patrolled border, and this population utilizes services and products originating on either side of this border. Workers residing in Tijuana now comprise a significant part of the workforce of San Diego; these are known as commuters or "borderlanders"[9] who every morning commence the trek to work in the United States (Martínez 1994).

Economic Interactions

The area's economic growth is also of tremendous proportions. Tijuana is characterized by three types of economic activity: the maquiladora industry, other manufacturing enterprises, and a very large service sector catering to U.S. tourists but also providing specialized

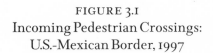

FIGURE 3.1
Incoming Pedestrian Crossings:
U.S.-Mexican Border, 1997

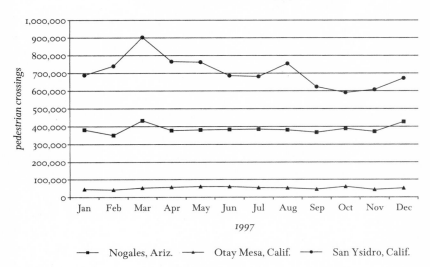

services ranging from computer programmers to medical and dental activities. Tijuana's maquiladora industry contributes 57.4 percent of total manufacturing value added in the state of Baja California, while employing 54.5 percent of total manufacturing employment. Yet Tijuana's maquiladora enterprises comprise only 12.9 percent of total manufacturing units, meaning that employment and value added in manufacturing are the result of the activities of very few units (Instituto Nacional 1993).

The industrial base meeting these requirements must be diversified and extensive since it must employ, at a minimum, some 65,000 workers (Instituto Nacional 1993), a workforce with few or no formal links with the United States except as market forces; the flow of goods and capital links the two transborder markets of Tijuana and San Diego (del Castillo 1996, 1998a). These workers amount to twice as many as those who commute daily from Tijuana toward San Diego and who are addressed by policy makers on both sides of the border, because they make up an important part of the San Diego labor force. Also their incomes, spent largely in Tijuana, contribute to that city's product.

FIGURE 3.2
Incoming Passengers in Personal Vehicles:
U.S.-Mexican Border, 1997

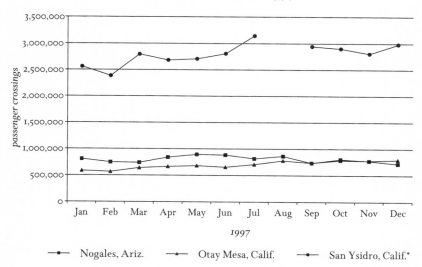

—■— Nogales, Ariz.   —▲— Otay Mesa, Calif.   —●— San Ysidro, Calif.*

*August data for San Ysidro, Calif., not available.

Although these commuters compose such a significant force, few empirical studies exist to measure their true impact along the border.

Not surprisingly, given demographic growth combined with the enormous growth of maquiladora operations in Tijuana since 1982, deficiencies exist in both the industrial infrastructure and in those construction needs and social services required for the working population. Some of these shortages parallel those that define the quality of life for San Diego residents, where specialists conclude that improvements occurred in the last decade in air quality, infant mortality, and transit ridership, while deterioration has characterized income distribution, highway congestion, housing affordability, and public high school graduation rates (Clement and Zepeda 1993, 92). Similarly in Tijuana, where over the last fifteen years economic growth has certainly outpaced economic development, "Tijuana residents have become increasingly aware of the region's development problems and growing disparities between economic growth and socioeconomic development. There are signs that this awareness is spreading throughout the public and private sectors, grass roots community organizations, and academics" (Clement and Zepeda 1993, 96).

Part of this gap between economic growth and socioeconomic development in Tijuana results from newly arrived internal migrants entering Tijuana's service sector. Its dynamism is intimately linked with economic cycles in the United States, increasing the degree of economic integration, economic convergence, and Mexican dependency (del Castillo 1998b). Further, this enormous service sector contributes approximately 50 percent of the gross product of Tijuana, although wages are lower than in the manufacturing sector, and it focuses not only on hospitality (meeting the needs of visiting tourists) but also on financial services, computer programming, and health care (del Castillo 1998a). All of these services can be provided in Tijuana at approximately 50 percent of the cost in San Diego; the demand for these services is complementary to the needs of many in San Diego, especially important given the declining income of certain sectors (Chávez and Zepeda 1996).

The relationship between Tijuana and San Diego cannot be described, though, solely in terms of complementarity. In effect, the flow of goods and services, labor and capital (factors of production which change over time) relate to the ever-increasing interdependency of both economies, with specialization occurring in those areas in which one side manages a comparative advantage. Trade theory dictates that wealth and wages will increase as cheaper products are created with the most efficiency. Yet the Tijuana/San Diego region indicates that although this reallocation of resources for comparative advantage is taking place, many of the flows are occurring because of inequitable distribution of wealth. It is in this context that one must appreciate the multiplicity of border contacts occurring between these two cities. If one accepts the premise that borders are places where something stops (a culture, a political system, one social order) and another begins, the transaction costs tend to rise. The purpose, then, of transborder cooperation—for example, on ecological problems or border crossings of fire brigades—is to reduce transaction costs. In this sense, when transborder "understandings" are reached, few or none of them will involve any transaction costs.

Research Findings from San Diego/Tijuana

Growth of Nongovernment Actors

As was posited earlier, the number of actors involved in transborder actions in the Tijuana/San Diego region has been growing by leaps and bounds in recent years. Tijuana municipal officials have identified approximately 650 NGOs and other types of organizations operating in the city; of course, not all of these are involved in transborder actions. I hypothesized that as public policy originating at a federal and state level has "hardened," imposing control measures as a primary aim, local-level actors on both sides of the border have searched for organizational ways to develop policies which "softened" relations, such as non-confrontational, binational approaches to problem solving, including the proliferation of NGOs in Tijuana.

The many NGOs in Tijuana do not constitute a phenomenon independent of the presence and actions of the United States. They exist because San Diego actors need a corresponding institutional structure to take various actions where, because of an international border, they themselves cannot. Moreover, they exist as a response to the need for transborder "management" and the failure of the public sector to satisfy the needs and demands of civil society (due to the lack of formal agreements by public-sector actors or their inability to carry out certain functions). For instance, Tijuana authorities need NGOs to act as the middlemen between San Diego NGOs and other public-sector authorities and other Tijuana NGOs. Few of these multiple Tijuana NGOs, though, are engaged in transborder relations, and when they are it is in sporadic cooperation to gain resources (stopping once they have been obtained) and to engage in functions the public sector cannot perform. One informant stated, "We always need money, and when we do, we go across the border to look for it." Few organizations experience a predictable, constant flow of resources from North to South.

Informants who have worked for Tijuana NGOs and the municipal government attributed this growth to the sense that the public sector has severe limitations in problem solving (principally because of insufficient public funds and human resources) and to the demonstration effect from the across the border in the North. Regarding the former, economic growth has outpaced the policy and problem-solving capacities of the public sector, especially that of the municipal government. On the latter, there is the perception in Tijuana that problem solving in San Diego is accomplished through the successful cooperation of private-sector actors and governmental institutions and that this cooperation permits private-sector organizations to succeed organizationally and gives them long life and community standing.

Factors That Affect Cross-Border Cooperation

When asked if there was a sense of real understanding between actors at a transnational level in the region, one of San Diego's principal decision makers with respect to border issues, also an advisor to the current mayor, whom we shall call G.L., replied, "No existe." Thus, current efforts are aimed at both developing public-sector institutional linkages and encouraging the rise of NGOs on both sides of the border. San Diego authorities, not wanting to appear dominant, are sometimes "afraid to propose solutions," says G.L., feeling more comfortable to "let [the others] propose." Additionally, he says, the importance of Mexico for state and local policy constantly shifts, meaning that "very often there is no continuity in policy, so new administrations continually reinvent binational relations." The actors seem to be responding, in part, to the existing asymmetry between them, he states, and this is reinforced further when U.S. actors—specifically those involved in regional planning efforts—are "unable to transfer resources to their Mexican counterparts." This "reinvention" by new administrations is a problem only for those who follow the issues closely. Such analysts see political actors "gaining" from what they "sell" to their unknowing political clientele as "new policies" but which actually are a repetition of policies and strategies from one administration to another.

Nevertheless, cross-border cooperation occurs despite problems such as those described by M.d.R., a former official of the Tijuana municipal government. He stated, "If we listen to one actor or group of actors, someone will always feel alienated and make life difficult for us." This holds true for intra-Tijuana relationships and those relations that link Tijuana with San Diego. Moreover, says M.d.R., there is the question of "which set of rules to use—those existing in the U.S., or the Mexican rules." According to this former official, "Crossing the border for government officials and private actors is like falling into a black hole of ignorance." As an example, Habitat for Humanity wanted to construct homes for the needy in Tijuana, but when "they [the Americans] come in here, they have not bothered to ask for the required permits; those working have not asked about health, insurance, and work permits. They suffer from the Superman Syndrome." This syndrome is one of supremacy, of invincibility, where the Americans "tell the Mexicans what to do." In the process of bilateral relations, he adds, "there is a very slow learning process."[10]

Complicating this dynamic panorama of institutional participation is the existence of a great number of interest groups that form "rolling coalitions," amalgamating common interests at one moment and others at another point in time. These coalitions raise the importance of some issues while advocating solutions of one type or another, but not taking direct action on the resolution being proposed (this function is handled by secondary actors at later times). Because these coalitions form and disappear (at varying rates), they provide border residents—and policy makers—with a dynamic panorama in which policy making can take on undefinable qualities. For instance, when an environmental problem crops up and the Environment Committee of San Diego/Tijuana region becomes involved, it may deal with a coalition made up of "some or all of the following groups: The Audubon Society, Planned Parenthood, The Sierra Club, Pro-Esteros, Ecosol, Gaviotas, and Proyecto Fronterizo de Educación Ambiental," according to another inteviewee (K.R.). Coordination of all of these groups is a monumental task, and policy proposals may vary widely among them. Thus, although it is nearly impossible for policy makers to adopt policy guidelines without alienating one or more actors, cross-border cooperation occurs despite these fundamentally different views among actors. Very often, the result of these conditions is that public policy making focuses only on "hot-button" issues and becomes characterized by hesitancy and, as mentioned earlier, by the constant rediscovery or reinvention of border solutions.

A primary reason for frequent changes in coalitions is that many of these groups come into existence for the specific reason of participating on issue-specific questions or problems, such as the San Diego/Tijuana Border Waste-Wise project, a recycling and pollution-prevention initiative. Once a problem is resolved, the groups are disbanded and are heard from no more. Moreover, there is the impact of Mexican law on their permanence, since groups threatened with having to pay a tax or comply with other aspects of the Civil Code (and most groups are in constant need of funding) simply disband or take on a new name. In this respect, L.D., an active participant on environmental issues, stated, "I cannot make a yearly budget; we live on soft money, but we have been taught enormously by our American friends." A further development in the "natural" selection process of the different groups is that the Tijuana municipal government now grants money awards to a number of these groups, and as D.R., one of the members of the private sector involved in the selection board, stated, "The competition has become fierce; many groups will not survive." Although it may reduce the number of significant actors involved in the various activities in Tijuana, and thus those groups that have a binational relationship, the new interaction between the public sector and private actors may lead to stability in the operations of groups in Tijuana and may facilitate the identification of viable partners for U.S. groups. [11]

Why and how U.S. actors initially decide to find partners on the Mexican side comes close to being a hit-or-miss process. The primary element seems to be a Mexican entity in search of an American partner. Very often, an American organization from one region on the U.S. border advises another in a different region about a Mexican searching for a U.S. partner in a very informal process that has been likened to "blind dating." It sometimes leads to successful union, but is often destined to fail. In a successful match, the American participation with Proyecto Fronterizo, described below, taught this Mexican group about the search for grants or incorporated the Mexican group in American grants in a cooperative fashion.

Nongovernmental Cross-Border Coalitions

While interest groups many appear and disappear with great ease, those with a medium-term presence (some going on twenty years) are always linked, operating with the support of a more permanent structure. Examples include groups with trade or commercial interests, those who work under the San Diego and Tijuana Chambers of Commerce or the Asociación de Maquiladoras de Baja California, and the Environment Committee of San Diego/Tijuana (formed in the late 1980s) working under the auspices of the United Nations Association of San Diego and the nonprofit Sister City Society. Organizations of this type are now acting with the BECC and the Commission for Environmental Cooperation as legitimate advocates of actions needed to improve life at the border. Simultaneously, this binational infrastructure is beginning to rely on these special interest groups for information and to learn the specifics of how actions can best be carried out at the border. The principal factor explaining the importance of these actors on the regional scene is their specialized knowledge and in-house experience.

The relationship of border interest groups with established structures also applies to actors on the Tijuana side. For instance, the Proyecto Fronterizo de Educación Ambiental is frequently referred to by Tijuana municipal authorities because of its expertise and binational linkages. Like its U.S. counterparts, it is also consulted by the newly established authorities of NAFTA when environmental (and labor) questions are concerned. It is, in fact, difficult to imagine what the development of the Proyecto Fronterizo would have been without the aid of its San Diego partners.

From small beginnings,[12] the Proyecto Fronterizo has become an important regional actor to "facilitate interagency and transborder collaborative strategies toward upgrading public education, policy, and actions to prevent urban pollution and natural resource degradation in the border region."[13] Proyecto Fronterizo has promoted multiple local conferences on environmental issues and engaged in binational environmental efforts; it has been a participant in environmental efforts and conferences at a world level, taking on agendas promoted at the global level and translating them into local demands and actions. The Proyecto has adopted the Rio de Janeiro Agenda and the OECD's standards of the "public right to know" in order to pressure relevant actors and help to develop local protection against environmental degradation.[14] In this process, the Proyecto has learned the process for obtaining resources independently of U.S. actors. This has been an active and necessary effort, because as the Proyecto's director stated, "The Americans know what to do, but ... Mexicans also know what to do. And very often it is not the same thing, and we are severely criticized for not following in their steps. When this happens we have to go our own way."

Americans would like the Proyecto to be more proactive than it has been, given the serious state of environmental affairs at the border, but Proyecto members explain that the U.S. actors do not understand the constraints imposed upon local actors by the Mexican political system, which requires caution for an actor to be perceived as "responsible" and deserving of a place at the table. Nonetheless, there is little doubt that the Proyecto has been successful in its educational activities and promotional efforts in the Tijuana/San Diego region (publishing a newsletter called *Ecos de Frontera*) and linking itself with numerous binational groups with a variety of interests, such as the Daedalus Alliance for Environmental Education, the San Diego County Water Authority, the Department of Education, the San Diego Natural History Museum, the U.S. Environmental Protection Agency, and the U.S. Fish and Wildlife Service.

Yet even with this successful record and its almost decade-old existence, the Proyecto's director feels that its tasks, as well as its definition of purpose, shift depending on who is working for the organization at a particular moment and what the issues of the day are. Life at the border is so dynamic that the institution itself has to be prepared to change—almost at a moment's notice—if it wants to remain a relevant actor on the border. The pressures for change come from both local and international conditions, more specifically from San Diego. In this context, the Proyecto feels that U.S. environmental actors are usually ahead of the curve in identifying environmental concerns that are obviously important, but which are perhaps technically and socially unaddressable in Tijuana. This problem of definition is sure to be of major concern for many border actors as border interactions increase, touching all the various dimensions of socioeconomic life. However, one common thread among "borderlanders" is their capacity to adapt to rapidly changing conditions.[15] This is perhaps why every analyst as a newcomer to the border seems to discover a wholly new place, and the process of rediscovery begins anew. This process attaches itself, not only to actors within civil society, but also to the public sector.

Public Sector Cross-Border Cooperation

Public society is confronted not only by the dynamic qualities of the border discussed so far, but also by the ever-changing administrations and political conditions of two neighboring countries. In addition, the Mexican side has to face the ever-present mistrust of U.S. officials, who believe that their system and operations are better than anything Mexicans can devise. In this context, public-sector actors in both nations suffer from a certain degree of schizophrenia, and their consultations and understandings must always work around this problem. Clearly, the same rapidly changing conditions that affect private-sector participants also challenge the public sector. These include the tendency to rediscover the border following a change in any level of government (meaning that the electoral process determines continuity or change in border public policy), the question of whether border-related issues can compete with other public-sector issues to merit budgetary concern and inclusion, and the question of whether public-sector officials feel that border issues merit their time and effort. In this context, concern over border problems becomes dependent on individual vision, which means that problem solving is an ever-changing process. Yet, in general terms, binational problem solving along the border by the public sector has been on the increase since the mid-1980s, when the growth of San Diego and Tijuana forced public-sector actors to examine the problems with varying degrees of success. A knowledgeable observer of the border region has written:

> Local governments for many years have had some involvement with their counterparts in Tijuana. These efforts were often the result of the vision and motivation of one or two individuals. At times, the enhanced interactions with Mexico grew out of the interests of staff persons at the department level; frequently the interaction grew out of the need to deal with a real problem such as renegade sewage flows, a public health concern, or shared emergency services. In other cases, they were the result of decisions by elected leaders who recognized that over the medium and long term, San Diego would have to maintain a closer working relationship in order to adequately deal with a range of San Diego problems with a border component. (Ganster 1993)

Cross-border cooperation by public-sector actors has occurred over a variety of issues, including trade, migration, municipal planning, and nonprofit activities. Examples of best practices and models are included in the discussion.

Economic Cooperation. In the Tijuana/San Diego region there is an obvious concern over international trade, because it and its associated services are sources of employment and give the region a certain degree of competitive advantage. Considerable misinformation over the issue, though, both at the private and public levels, leads to miscalculations and bilateral stress. For instance, during the 1982 peso devaluation, public and private officials in San Diego believed that retail sales in the county would drop by more than 50 percent, forcing the city to cut school services and staff in San Diego schools. They were ready to believe that San Diego's connection with Mexico was negative despite the lack of even one study of the Mexican consumers' effective demand on the San Diego economy (del Castillo 1983). This type of behavior or event is not uncommon between San Diego and Tijuana, as public-sector leaders are forced to deal with increasingly integrated economic systems without much common information on the workings of the regional economy. Complicating this situation is the independent private sector, driven by market rules and unhindered by public-sector planning or guidelines. In this context, transborder cooperation between manufacturers is a function of understandings and commitments among firms, many of them transnational industries (such as the San Diego Chamber of Commerce and its equivalent in Tijuana, and the Cámara Nacional de la Industria Maquiladora).[16]

Given the trade dependency that exists on both sides of the border, both of these institutions function with the principal aim that no instance of government hinder bilateral trade; local representatives lobby before their respective capitals on facilitating infrastructure development and harmonizing customs procedures that accelerate the exchange of production inputs and finished goods. This cooperation resulted in the creation by the federal governments of a new customs area with fast no-check procedures and traffic lanes during the early 1990s in Otay Mesa, when the port of San Ysidro became inadequate to handle the bilateral flow of goods.

Thousands of individual economic transactions occur across the border without any interlocutors coming between their agents. These multiple interactions, which affect thousands of workers and their families on both sides of the border, take place following market mechanisms and personal interventions. In an economic sense, these interactions supersede the value of wages paid to the maquiladoras, and are second only to the product generated by the tourism industry.

Trade and commercial relations break down when macroeconomic conditions in Mexico become unstable and repeating cycles of devaluation and capital flight take place, and even then the articulation between economic agents continues. The manager of a bank at the border describes the process as follows:

> When severe devaluation begin, things go all to hell. Everything breaks loose for a month or two, and we'll have meetings every ten minutes trying to solve mostly credit problems....We usually don't encounter any problems. Because of previous experience we carry larger reserves than federal law requires. Hey, most of our Mexican customers have their saving accounts with us. When the crunch comes we try and help them out; we need them as much as they need us. How can it be any different? We live together. (W.F.B.)

All informants commented on the effects of NAFTA on binational relations in the border region, including the production structure of Tijuana and an increasing impact on San Diego. This is an example of federal measures having a much more important role in defining bilateral relations at the border than could be effected by local actors. As one San Diego official (G.L.) stated, "Mexico has always been there, but NAFTA has brought it home that we're neighbors with specific international commitments." Yet policy attention is so focused on serving the needs of the maquiladora sector that it distorts public policy in both cities. While the industry is undeniably of great importance, both public policy and researchers have failed to see the other side of the coin, the importance of the rest of the manufacturing sector and its links with the regional economy, links which perhaps are as important, perhaps even more important, than any formal agreement. This entire segment of the economy has been unrepresented in interest-group structure and in public policy. Market mechanisms and industry decisions at a local, regional, or international level are ahead of any public policy that could dictate the nature of transborder linkages.

Migration. While the flow of capital, goods, and people across the international border often occurs in an unregulated fashion, the one area where control overtakes the issue of management is in U.S. attempts to stamp out the flow of undocumented Mexican labor. In this process, the actors who are most damaged are the workers themselves, and along the border many institutions arise to ameliorate U.S. police actions. It is not surprising that the issue of undocumented labor flows appears in the forefront of public discussions by varying actors and for different and multiple purposes (such as public safety or public services).[17] Although this issue dominates public discussion, transborder efforts at managing this flow take on the same characteristics as many of the other issues discussed earlier. In other words, discussion and management are for the most part intermittent, although federal immigration controls and the various efforts at "controlling" the border have begun to have consequences with respect to the presence and actions of the different institutions dealing with migrant issues.

Migration or migrant-related issues are important enough that the Tijuana municipal government has created a Department for Migrant Issues (Departamento de Atención al Migrante), and has a small, specialized directory of institutions and services for migrants. The main characteristic of all these associations is their readiness to incorporate new institutions whenever a problem arises and additional expertise is needed. In this sense, institutions related to migrant issues also form "running coalitions," described earlier, associating with one group at one time and another the next, depending on the requirements of the moment. These coalitions may involve organizations and local and federal entities on both sides of the border, although some work only nationally.

Perhaps the most influential organization working on migrant issues is the Centro de Apoyo al Migrante, which was set up by the political party Partido de la Revolución Democrática (PRD) and receives no outside funding.[18] Many of its positions on migration issues are dictated in Mexico City by the national PRD or by PRD congressional representatives who work in congressional committees in charge of migration issues at the national level. Coalitions in which the Centro participates are, in effect, political links with definite partisan ends. The Centro provides legal aid whenever this is required and also acts as a broker aiding migrants during their stay in Tijuana, directing them toward organizations that can provide housing and health services. In carrying out these functions, the Centro makes innumerable contacts with organizations in Tijuana and San Diego, but all of these involve the proverbial phone call to resolve a problem. Thus it carries out state and federal party mandates and policies at the local level while also distributing the migratory workload to other interested organizations.

In contrast to the many associations related to migrant issues that work only in Tijuana with no international links and advocate for such issues as human rights and charitable treatment of migrants, the Centro is intimately related to U.S. actors, carrying out joint actions with them in Tijuana and San Diego.[19] There are two principal San Diego organizations with which the Centro is associated: the Rural Legal Defense Fund (Liga Legal Rural de California) and the American Friends Service Committee. Because the Centro is a political party instrument, it has severe constraints in whatever actions are taken to aid international migrants within the United States. These constraints are both legal and self-imposed; on the other side, both of these U.S. organizations link themselves with the Centro via public forums, manifestations, and declarations pointing out the innumerable problems that migrants face on their arrival at the border.

A more typical NGO in Tijuana that aids migrants is the Casa del Migrante, which also has extensive contacts with the San Diego community. This organization, together with the Salvation Army of Tijuana, the Casa de la Madre Assunta, and the Casa del Menor Migrante (YMCA) form part of a network of associations known as Asociaciónes Unidas para el Desarrollo Social (AUDAS) and obtain their resources principally through national and international charitable donations. These organizations participate as interest groups (AUDAS) within the municipal NGO structure and have an extensive network of support in San Diego consisting of the Catholic Religious Services, Caritas, the Friends of the Poor, the Rural Legal Defense Fund, and others. One benefit of San Diego support is administrative technologies that efficiently use their limited resources. NAFTA controls have had a significant negative impact on charitable donations from San Diego (upon which they are dependent) in cash, first aid items, and food, among other things, which prior to NAFTA crossed the border with few or no controls. The conversion of goods into imports with specific values with a cost associated with their transfer has made them unaffordable for many of the former recipients, who try to find new ways to get them across.

The effectiveness of these organizations in dealing with the multiple migration issues is demonstrated not only by their multiple international linkages, but also by the way in which AUDAS has been able to frame the debate over immigration in the Tijuana/San Diego region. These organizations have pressured the Tijuana municipal government to create a Municipal Institute for Migration (Instituto Municipal

de Migración) which would act as the principal clearinghouse and support institution to migrants arriving in Tijuana—either on their way
north toward the United States, or south as returning migrants or
forced returnees. In addition to the organizations that make up AUDAS,
the municipal Social Development Agency (Dirección de Desarrollo
Social), the municipal DIF (Desarrollo Integral de la Familia), the Border Commission (Comisión de Asuntos Fronterizos), and the Ministry
of Public Safety (Secretaría de Seguridad Pública) participate as well.
One innovative aspect of this new institute is that it has set up offices in
San Diego to better operate with the differing institutions handling
migration issues there. Since at the time of our interviews the Institute
was but a month old, it is hard to predict its possible success, but what is
certain is that with respect to this most important bilateral issue, a local
Mexican institution is intent on becoming a transnational actor.

Municipal Planning. Local experience with binational structures
has similar agendas and runs parallel to the federal course of conception and extinction already discussed. Local actors involved in transborder affairs have tended to be associated with the San Diego City
Council and other executive agencies of local government. In 1983
there was an Assistant to the Mayor on Binational Border Development and Latino Community issues, a coordinating position for local
actors dealing with Tijuana; following this was the City Council's establishment in 1986 of a Department of Binational Affairs, which by
1988 had fallen under the direct control of the mayor and was used
only for protocol purposes because of funding difficulties.

Because of the relative geographical proximity of San Diego and
Tijuana, it is not surprising that governmental contacts occur with
frequency, although the efficacy of such relations can be questioned.
Perhaps the best example of regional transborder effectiveness is demonstrated by the San Diego Association of Governments (SANDAG),
formed by all local governments in the region to coordinate regional
planning efforts.[20] By 1989, SANDAG had created a Border-Related
Issues Task Force identifying issues and problems associated with the
border. One of the principal conclusions of this Task Force was that
instruments were needed to better articulate with Mexico, and expertise was needed if better bilateral relations were to be established
(San Diego Association of Governments 1998). Since then, these
efforts have accelerated to include SANDAG publications related to the

border, such as the "Baja Regional Development and Industrial Guide" and the "INFO Bulletin on Baja California Demographics." From 1989 though 1992 Mexican participation in these activities was minimal although the municipal president of Tijuana has been a member of the SANDAG board since 1974.

One result of the intense transborder relationship fostered by SANDAG has been "15 joint projects involving San Diego and Tijuana-area officials and researchers dealing with various aspects of border life. Such cooperation, almost unheard of a decade ago, is now increasingly routine. . . ." (*San Diego Union Tribune* 1999b). Examples include disaster response plans, coordinated traffic flow, and cross-border sports and cultural events. Yet, even in this positive context, "'There are some attitudes and old ideas that are hard to break down,' said Gonzalo Lopez, San Diego city coordinator for international programs. . . .' There is a lack of knowledge. We're both very ignorant of each other'" (*San Diego Union Tribune* 1999b).

Nonprofit/Educational. Bilateral efforts to address and solve regional transborder issues include not only government, public, and private-sector actors but also groups and institutions that advocate for closer cooperation within the Tijuana/San Diego region to manage joint undertakings. The San Diego Dialogue began in this context, although it was originally initiated by the University of California, San Diego (UCSD) to better relate to the local community, from which the university was perceived to be completely alienated. In 1995 to 1996, the Dialogue "discovered" the border, and its transborder advocacy role began. Other important actors in joining San Diego and Tijuana have been San Diego State University (SDSU) and El Colegio de la Frontera Norte (COLEF). The Dialogue differs from the Chamber of Commerce advocacy in that the Dialogue, set up on UCSD grounds, carried out research to identify areas or niches where businesses could be developed, expanded, or helped. Dialogue members participate in SDSU and UCSD seminars addressing regional issues, such as the "Californias in Transition" series (SDSU) and the SDSU/COLEF "Economic Modeling Project," and recently signed a formal agreement on research collaboration with COLEF. Although it has received good press coverage, it is difficult to evaluate the impact of the Dialogue's advocacy efforts, since its research is not taken seriously in regional academic circles. Most criticism around Dialogue research is that it finds what it wants to find, although a new research director has been appointed. For instance, one of its publications emphasized demographic similarities in Tijuana and San Diego, leading to conclusions that both were middle-class cities (San Diego Dialogue 1995).

The close working relationship between San Diego State University and scholarly institutions in Tijuana evolved as Tijuana began its rapid economic and demographic growth during the early 1980s. The Centro de Estudios Fronterizos del Norte de México (CEFNOMEX, now COLEF) began operations in Tijuana in 1982 and signed a formal cooperation agreement under which researchers of this institution could attend SDSU with an out-of-state tuition waiver. SDSU faculty also began to teach at CEFNOMEX's newly instituted Master's degree program on regional development, and San Diego State students could also attend courses at CEFNOMEX (though none ever did). More recently, COLEF faculty have also been asked to teach Economics, Latin American Studies, and Urban Planning at San Diego State at the graduate level. Research collaboration has evolved to where there are continuous joint research projects—some of which have received federal U.S. funding. SDSU/COLEF's successful collaboration has led them to develop further contacts, including a joint degree in International Business (Bachelor of Arts) now offered jointly between SDSU and the Universidad Autónoma de Baja California and the Centro de Enseñanza Técnica y Superior (CETYS) of Tijuana.

Another cross-border collaboration is the insITE program of joint transborder installation of site-specific art involving plastic artists from Tijuana, San Diego, and Los Angeles. Begun in 1992, insITE places exhibitions in public spaces in Tijuana and San Diego, often focusing on the issues raised by an artificial international dividing line. One of the most interesting exhibitions was the placing of a two-headed Trojan horse on the international border crossing between San Diego and Tijuana; the attention of those waiting to cross was drawn to the 30-foot wooden sculpture facing both Tijuana and San Diego, implying a question of which direction the challenges were coming from. The insITE project is unique among border projects for its wide amalgam of participants, as well as the ample number of sponsors, including private sources, foundations, governments, and corporate sources from both sides of the border. Few enterprises along this region of the border manage to bring together so many actors in a discussion of the meaning of the border and its implications for its inhabitants. Although the many artists who participate in insITE deal with overtly political subjects, their expression in the artform is nonthreatening, and it is perhaps this last fact that permits such diverse interests to sponsor these projects.

Formal Agreements (Federal and Regional). Clearly, there are significant areas of consultation and cooperation between public-sector actors in these two border cities. Local actors, however, are limited as to what they can do to influence or modify policy toward the region (especially in trade or immigration), because their efforts to facilitate the international passage of commuters and international trade goods inevitably involve federal customs and immigration authorities and public policy originating at the federal level. As a result of federal border-control measures, transborder authorities have focused their attention on two public safety issues. The first relates to the increasing—and generalized—violence resulting from the narcotics flow between San Diego and Tijuana (a major trafficking family has made Tijuana its headquarters), and the second relates to the many killings of Mexican undocumented workers at the hands of the U.S. Border Patrol (la Migra). A Mexican consular official (L.H.L.) states, "Over the last year, more Mexicans have died at the border than were killed at the Berlin Wall; protecting Mexicans in the hands of the U.S. authorities is our major concern." Separately, regarding the border he stated, "That is one area where it is unsafe for you to do research; it is dangerous, and there isn't much I could tell you about the ongoing cooperation that exists between us and the U.S. authorities."

To confront the issue of violence and other bilateral issues, a formal mechanism was created known as the Border Liaison Mechanism (BLM). It involves consular coordination and consultations with a number of advisory committees on immigration, public safety, water resources, and educational activities. Two distinct orders of actors operate within the BLM—law enforcement agencies from all levels of government and cultural agents dealing with non-police functions. The BLM also promotes other activities such as the Binational Public Safety Conference.[21] The San Diego Union Tribune described this event:

> They will spend the next two days exchanging business cards and swapping tactics for dealing with everything from illegal

border crossers and underage drinking to fire fighting and other emergency response practices. . . . Manuel Diego, a supervising agent with the U.S. Border Patrol, said the sessions allow officials from all levels of government to get to know one another and slice through red tape when needed. "We can iron out problems and concerns that affect both countries," he said. "Through better connections, we can resolve problems with a lot less hassle." (*San Diego Union Tribune* 1999a)

The appearance and disappearance of such task forces is an ongoing process of border life, as commented on earlier in this work. Yet the way in which the interactions between local and other state or federal actors have developed over time has a direct effect on the types of accords that develop at the border, as the parameters outside of the border region and the activities of regional actors determine which border issues become relevant. Undoubtedly, one of the oldest regional actors is the International Boundary and Water Commission (IBWC), first established in 1889 as the International Boundary Commission. This commission is divided into a U.S. and a Mexican section which cooperate closely and report to their foreign affairs secretariats (U.S. State Department and Secretaría de Relaciones Exteriores). This cooperation extends to working with local actors with respect to water issues. Another border-wide federal understanding is the 1979 U.S.-Mexico Agreement for Cooperation in the Field of Housing and Urban Development, meant to deal with the issue of rapid population and urban growth in border cities in the context of regional planning. In 1980, San Diego hosted the Third Border City reunion dealing with concerns over water, demographic growth, economic development, border infrastructure, and sewage contamination for twin border cities. These meetings ended in 1983, just as the Southwest Border Regional Commission (SBRC) became operational. Most notable among these undertakings has been the Border Governors Conference, which has met every year since 1980 with varied agendas.[22]

Preliminary Conclusions

Contemporary life along the Tijuana/San Diego border has been characterized by its dynamic quality and by the newness of the actors involved in a developing civil society. The latter relates to the collapse of the dominant role of the Partido Revolucionario Institucional (PRI) in Baja California and the takeover at the state and municipal levels by the opposition PAN party (Partido Acción Nacional). This party has incorporated new civil actors (NGOs) into the sociopolitical life of the city. In this context, these new civil-society actors, together with the public sector, have steep learning curves and have had to develop new working relationships, which—given the rapidity of change at the border and the limited resources available—makes them cautious. The resulting policy process is, by necessity, incremental in nature. The moving coalitions aim to incorporate as many of these new actors as possible until actor stability and resources can be developed and until alliances with the United States promise such stability and access to resources.

Nevertheless, transborder understandings do not come easily to the region; most actors mention cultural differences and mistrust as the principal reasons for the difficulties that arise between them. Given this environment, the understandings that develop are completely functional in content and last only as long as it takes to resolve a particular issue. When transnational understandings approach win-win scenarios, though, and are cumulative in time, then the relationship between them is reinforced. Because of the very informal nature of the understandings that exist between organizations in San Diego and Tijuana, it is difficult to identify a baseline from which to measure binational cooperation and evaluate the redefinitions of and progress made with a specific understanding. Actors quickly move to obtain new partners or redefine the objectives originally sought if they do not see a promising future in a relationship, so there is never an outright failure—just multiple changes in direction and possible partners.

This situation changes as these understandings take on more formal characteristics. If an understanding does not seem to be working it is allowed to die a quiet death; if the prospects for an understanding are not what the actors expected, often the agreement is not implemented or only partially implemented. This behavior partially explains the long history of binational agreements by different administrations which constantly rediscover or reinvent the border. In either case, formal or informal understandings are of a functional nature oriented toward immediate problem solving rather than an attempt to create a binational system of norms to facilitate regional interactions. Again, the reasons are the clear and distinct cultural differences which remain despite close and long-lasting collaboration between actors, and underlying mistrust among actors regarding potential gains or losses from collaborative efforts. For Mexicans in the public sector, collaboration with their American neighbors always carries political risks, and for U.S. actors, their willingness to work with Mexicans is seen as "going native."

In spite of the collaboration and intricate relationships which exist on a transborder basis, there is a great institutional vacuum at a regional level. There are no regional binational institutions derived from local efforts; the closest approximations to this are the joint degree programs that are developing between San Diego State University and some of the local institutions of higher learning in Tijuana. Yet this successful experience has not been transferred to policy-making circles on either side of the border. The binational institutions operating in the region are all the result of federal policies and actions, from the old International Boundary and Water Commission to the new institutions derived from NAFTA such as the NADBank and the BECC.

This regional vacuum is undoubtedly the result of past divisions of competence (political domains), where binational institution building has been the prerogative of federal-level actors. In this sense, political actors on both sides of the border are characterized by their timidity. Related to this is a clear lack of imagination at the regional level, where transborder institution building is still approached as an enterprise with very high opportunity costs, given the scarce and shifting resources budgeted for border management at the regional level. It will take an event of enormous proportions, affecting great numbers of the population on both sides of the border, to change the style of solutions sought for the region. With this perspective and in the short run, policy making either by public or private actors will continue to have the experimental and changing nature that it has had in the past and still has today.

A Comparative Perspective:
The Experience of the Twin Nogales

Introduction to the Region

When traveling outside the westernmost region of San Diego/ Tijuana, outside of the immeasurable richness of one of the world's major economies, where the manicured beaches and public parks end, one enters a more realistic world, that of the two Nogales. If one disregards the neon signs of the Pizza Hut or the Denny's Restaurant in Nogales, Arizona, it is easy to imagine being in a town at the turn of the twentieth century. It is a town rising from the desert, with hilly terrain and many trees, exploiting the little water accumulated in underground aquifers over the centuries. The scant supply of water both unites and separates Mexico's Nogales and Nogales, Arizona, forcing cooperation between these two border cities. The topography of Nogales, Sonora, appears even more broken than that of the U.S. side. Private homes extend to the north of the town, where back yards abut the international boundary. But when scanning the horizon from the northern, U.S. side, the great separator is clearly visible—the steel fence that divides Mexico from the United States. This divider becomes even more artificial when one realizes that most of the population in Nogales, Arizona, speaks Spanish, that kilometers have replaced miles in posted signs, and so on.[23] Many observers of border life in the two Nogales comment on this artificiality, noting that the two Nogales are joined not only by the obvious commercial and trade concerns but also by familial links. People in both communities calculate that some 85 percent of native Nogalenses are related.

The division between the communities of Tijuana and San Diego (or San Ysidro) is much more complete than at this border. Moreover, Nogales, Sonora, with a population variously stated as 130,000–250,000, is one-tenth the size of Tijuana, and Nogales, Arizona (37,000), has approximately one-twentieth the population of the San Diego region. This relatively smaller population signifies most of all that the expertise to be found in the Tijuana/San Diego region is not present in the Nogales region. From this information comes the primary working hypothesis that border management will present difficult issues here.

As R.R., a participant in the affairs of the Nogales, stated, "The border issues in the Nogales region are becoming increasingly complex and there are deficiencies of all kinds. This border is heading for major conflicts."

Nogales, Arizona

The Green Valley is some 32–40 kilometers (20–25 miles) from the U.S.-Mexico border; here the hills and canyons which characterize the border give way to flat lands where middle-class urban growth is taking place. Nogales, Arizona, adjacent to the international boundary, is 97.6 percent Hispanic, with a per capita income of $9,397 in 1996 and a median family income of $23,948. From 1989 to 1996, family income has risen 12.4 percent. Only 24.3 percent hold a high school diploma, with high unemployment rates, varying from 14 percent in 1990 to some 20 percent at this writing.[24]

Non-agricultural employment is centered in trade-related industries, where "Santa Cruz County has a larger percentage of its labor force engaged in manufacturing than any other Arizona County. Most of this work is characterized by low wages and low skill requirements and directly attributable to the explosive growth of the maquiladora program during the last eighteen years" (Nogales-Santa Cruz County Economic Development Foundation n.d., 14). The largest employers in Nogales and Santa Cruz county are the Nogales school district and the Santa Cruz county administration; in this sense, when combined with federal-level employment (INS, Customs, and the Border Patrol), it is the public sector that provides a great proportion of all employment in the city. Yet these figures tell us little of the economic life of Nogales, Arizona. This small town has become globalized, and only a few residents have come to realize it; this is shown by the fact that the local high school graduates 85 percent of its students without the ability to speak English proficiently, combined with the fact that only 50 percent of a freshman entering class actually graduates from high school.

This is a city which facilitates the flow of 60 to 70 percent of all winter produce imported into the United States and Canada, which added during 1995/1996 "an estimated $376.4 million in the Arizona economy. Through a multiplier effect, these marketing services generated more than 6,000 jobs (direct, indirect, and induced) in Arizona's economy, and close to $600 million in sales, which included $159 million in wages and $21.4 million in state revenues" (Pavlakovich et al. 1997, viii).

The economy has been internationalized not only by this transborder agribusiness production but also by the presence of the maquiladora industry in Nogales, Sonora (107 plants). This has furthered the ability of Nogales, Arizona to become a foreign trade zone (USEFTZ #60),[25] and to benefit from the State of Arizona Enterprise Zone. Yet local businesses find it hard to cope with an unsuitable labor force which, in the words of one interviewee (K.V.), "cannot answer the phone in English or type business correspondence in English. It gives the community a bad image when our customers can't order from our companies because workers aren't fully bilingual."

The community is also ill-served by the performance of local government, a disregard for the border region compared with other cities in Arizona, and an inability to achieve the economic potential of the maquiladora industry. The government is considered to be nonprofessional and rife with "nepotism and all sorts of political appointees," according to K.V. and one of his associates, B.D. With this style of local government, says B.D., "there can be no planning, everything is reactive."[26] Further, regarding economic development, there is "a great lack of knowledge" among important participants who, according to D.S., have failed to counteract "the passionate misinformation about the processes of internationalization and their impact on local communities." These views were constantly repeated by many local officials, who themselves were severely criticized by other community business leaders. These divisions among the local elite extend to criticisms regarding the role played by the local newspaper in not "informing the community of important issues" (B.D.). Apparently, some people buy the *Nogales International* only to find out which day of the week it is, though Mexican actors attribute this newspaper's lack of influence to the fact that the paper is in English. An interviewee (E.C.) commented, "Who would want to read that paper? It's in English; that's why Nogales [Arizona] residents buy the Mexico papers, which are in Spanish." In this context, Nogales, Arizona is a community divided, with little direction, especially when it comes to dealing with its internationalization.

These community divisions, again, are reflected in the community response to the Nogales Focused Future Strategic Plan for Economic

Development, made public in 1997. This plan "contains an analysis of the local economy and a comprehensive set of goals and strategies which guide and manage the economic activity of Nogales into the 21st century" (Arizona Public Service Company 1997). Goals included community and economic development, combined with a diversified and expanded economic base that would promote prosperity and preserve the quality of life (Arizona Public Service Company 1997). Despite these aims and a supposed collaboration between local government actors (the Nogales/Santa Cruz County Economic Development Foundation, the Nogales Chamber of Commerce, and the City of Nogales), no action was ever taken on the recommendations of the plan.[27] This plan apparently became so irrelevant that one of the principal institutional actors did not know where to find a hard paper copy of it.[28] Surprisingly, the plan lacked any discussion of the impact on economic development that might be due to the symbiotic relationship existing between the two Nogales. It is as if Nogales, Arizona, were an island unto itself—separated from Mexico, and alienated from Phoenix and Tucson. This experience is not new to the border communities, as has been discussed in the case of San Diego, and relates to mistrust between the actors charged with the implementation of the plan. Clearly, a gap exists between the implementation of desired actions and the rhetoric used in these border communities.

Nogales, Sonora

This community is approximately ten times the size of its sister community on the American side. Official government statistics indicate some 133,000 people reside within the municipality of Nogales (and 98 percent actually reside in the city), while government officials claim that the real number is 250,000. The enormous difference in the numbers may be real or being bandied about for political and economic reasons, since cities in Mexico receive both federal and state funds depending on their population numbers—the larger the population, the greater these funds will be. Nonetheless, there has been significant growth related to the internationalization of production and the presence of some 94 maquiladora operations within the city, employing 32,500 workers, according to an interview with H.M., of SECOFI. This growth has been so rapid that the region now lacks the human capital resources to adequately face its challenges. A well-known social activist in the city (J.G.) stated: "The leadership of the city has reached the limits of knowing how to manage a small ranch; now it has to learn how to govern a growing urban agglomerate, pretending to industrialize, but without any economic development, and they are lost." Besides the limited human resources existing in Nogales, the city has a very limited budget, $16 million dollars. Accepting the large population figures given by the municipal authorities, this is $64 per capita, according to another informant (S.A.). These parameters inhibit whatever plans the city might make to improve its services and infrastructure. Regional topography exacerbates the situation, since Nogales' location at the convergence of several deep canyons escalates the costs of providing public services.

In discussions with public and private officials in the city, three main concerns came to the fore; all were somehow related to infrastructure development and international trade. First, because Nogales, Sonora, is the principal port through which Mexican produce is exported to the United States, its streets and the sole southern highway coming from the interior are heavily used during specific seasons by some 1,500 trucks per day. To this traffic one must add the manufactured goods transported by the maquiladora industry. Thus, from September through April, the city experiences a collective neurosis because traffic becomes snarled by the trucks.[29] Second, Nogales is also the principal port through which Ford vehicles (manufactured in Hermosillo) are exported to the United States by rail. Not surprisingly, the rail line runs through the main canyon (downtown) into Nogales, Arizona, where shipments are then inspected by U.S. Customs, the Immigration and Naturalization Service, and the Border Patrol, halting all east-west traffic in Nogales, Sonora, for some three hours per train! Unfortunately, the daily train begins its crossing into the United States at midday, when Nogalenses are leaving for lunch—creating another traffic problem. The third problem addressed by most leaders in Nogales, Sonora, is the limited and jointly shared water resources in the region and the treatment by the United States of wastewater originating in the city. Under normal circumstances, such seemingly problematic issues would be the cause for an active bilateral dialogue between these two border cities, but this is not the case.

Cross-Border Cooperation in the Public Sector

All persons interviewed during the fieldwork period agreed on one thing: the border had hardened, and it was due to the narcotics problem, tied sometimes to undocumented workers. With the exception of the water management issues mentioned above, the issues of trucking delays, train delays, and commuter traffic at the border were becoming difficult because drug traffickers had chosen the Nogales region to cross their illicit goods. The hardening of this particular border, which used to be a "White Border" (*una frontera blanca*), according to an influential local actor, is not independent of the different problems confronting other regions of the border. Another long-time resident, A.R., indicated, "The drug traffickers have ended our good customs" such as "the festival of the Flowers [Festival de las Flores], in May. The dancing floors were put on both sides of the border; people went across the border without any controls. People from both sides of the border crossed to visit family, do some shopping—all those good customs are finished."

If these long-standing practices have begun to collapse, what has taken their place? C. M., an official of the Mexican consulate in Nogales, stated that "[t]here is no clarity about the different bilateral agreements which govern us here at the border. Most of these agreements really never touch on what is relevant to city government or regional issues." He continued, "There is no agency in Mexico City to coordinate interagency affairs with respect to border issues. Each ministry [department] is jealous of the other—little cooperation." If Mexico City appears that far away, so disjointed from what is happening at the border, one might expect a high degree of cooperation instigated at the regional or local level to resolve bilateral problems. Unfortunately this has not been the case.

At the regional level, says S.M., the Arizona-Sonora Commission will "get together; they take pictures and make agreements. Sometimes we're invited to sit among the public. Yet, they never take us into account; we're actually never told how the city fits into all their plans." Similarly, when municipal officials such as S.M. were interviewed, and the specific question was posed to them about how much time of their daily work day they spent on bilateral issues, they answered, "not even a few minutes." The Director of Social Development in the city, D.D., answered, "We don't think of them [the United States] at all." That does not mean that public officials would not like a different situation to exist. S.M. stated, "We live in an absolute informality; the telephone saves us when we have a problem; that is our most important link." One example was the mayor's office in Nogales, Arizona, notifying Nogales, Sonora, when the city dump would catch fire, even sending firefighters. Unfortunately, this link seems to occur only in extraordinary circumstances.

The major preoccupation in this region concerns the orderly flow of produce and goods for export. When the traffic flow is impeded for some reason, collaboration is sought on both sides. Yet Mexican officials find these occasions difficult to deal with, because the personnel involved are not local; they are dealing with both state and federal officials. At any one time, the flow of produce trucks may be detained by U.S. Customs, U.S. Immigration, the U.S. Department of Agriculture, the Arizona Department of Agriculture, the Federal Drug Administration, the Commerce Department, or others. It is thus difficult to identify which actors are responsible for the delays, and they are unaware of the administrative procedures, rules, and other factors these agencies use to justify their detention of goods.

Even in that all-important area of transborder water management (only 39 percent of the community receives water on a continuous basis), local actors are disassociated from the projects that affect their city, as the principal actors continue to be extra-local agents such as the Comisión del Agua Potable y Alcantarillado del Estado de Sonora (COAPAES) and the Comisión Nacional de Agua (CAN). To deal with the problems of wastewater and its treatment in the United States, a plan was designed by the Secretaría de Infraestructura Urbana y Ecología and the COAPAES. To accomplish the aims of the wastewater treatment plan, the involvement of new actors has risen, with the NADBank and the BECC involved with 50 percent of the funding, while the Mexican and U.S. governments fund 40 percent of the costs, and the remaining 10 percent is covered by private actors (Presidencia Municipal de Nogales, Sonora n.d.). Similarly, in the new projects involving air quality in Nogales, J.G. reports that the monitoring stations located on Mexican territory are read by technicians from the Environmental Protection Agency (EPA). If the public sectors on both sides of this border seem to disregard one another, there are no other societal actors such as nongovernmental organizations to fill the vacuum and conduct a dialogue with both of these border communities.

Cross-Border Cooperation by Private Sector Actors

Unlike the Tijuana/San Diego region, there are no locally-based operational nongovernmental organizations with bilateral ties or agendas in the Nogales region. Yet there is recognition that such organizations are necessary, as J.G. put it, "to fill those spaces left unfulfilled by the government, spaces which are growing." The most renowned local activist, J.G., now heading a shelter for abused women (Centro Contra la Violencia), began by doing a research project for the Colegio de Mexico's gender studies program in 1985 and became an activist "because I can't adjust to the underdevelopment of my city." Her multidimensional interests followed a logical path. She stated,

> I began caring over urban issues when there was no gas to heat the houses in winter. Once they were warm, there was no water —so that had to be solved; the violence against women also has to do with the rapid urbanization of this region, adding pressure to every context where people relate to one another. This same rapid rate of the city's growth has had negative aspects on our environment. So, now I have environmental and health concerns.

J.G. is now a Mexican representative to the Commission for Environmental Cooperation, where "for the first time I've had to deal with Americans; before this I didn't like them; I've matured." She goes on to say, "some of them have gained my respect." Perhaps these are the beginnings of a new bilateralism in the Nogales.

Governance at the Border: Final Commentary

The very tentative and exploratory nature of the cross-border relationships described contrast severely with the economic and social developments in this same border region. The region has experienced enormous, unrestricted economic growth as a result of very little planning and encouragement by national policies catering to international interests. This has resulted in growth through a low-wage policy in the industrial sector. Of the many social effects derived from these policies, two are of special importance. First, there has been an acute rise in the border population, resulting from internal migration. Secondly, this population growth has led to rapid growth in urban settlements, placing enormous pressures on infrastructure and resources and surpassing the ability of city planners and other public officials to cope with these events. In this context, cities along the border operate under "deficit policy-making" procedures. They are, in other words, always behind the curve.

This "operating behind the curve" arises from a lack of three principal resources: human, bureaucratic, and financial. First, the growth of these cities under the conditions described above requires human resources that the cities lack, especially on the Mexican side of the border. Secondly, while rapidly changing conditions characterize economic and social developments, policy makers are confronted by bureaucratic organizations unaccustomed to and incapable of dealing with these rapidly changing cities. Lastly, the "new federalism" developing in Mexico has left many cities without the financial resources to effectively deal with northern-border growth.

This combination of factors has led to discontinuous (and inconsistent) policy making, with the border region constantly being "rediscovered" and policies portrayed as being "new" and "innovative" leading to a never-ending cycle of repeated policy making, and many-times-repeated failures. Because financial resources have been slow in coming, the public sector has effectively shifted the burden of action to civil society actors in the form of nongovernmental organizations (NGOs). This shift occurs not only because of the failures of the public sector, but also because NGOs believe that the private sector is more efficient than the government in delivery of social services, and also because of the belief (primarily by opposition parties) that participation by civil-society actors is highly congruent with their democratic beliefs.

Socioeconomic events over roughly the last twenty years have resulted in a disjointed public policy process, with little continuity. Moreover, as time passes, the problems facing the region grow more complex and multiply, creating a gap between problem "emergence" and problem solving. This gap has some profound consequences (besides the problems created by a lack of resolution). One is that unsolved problems grow more complex with the passage of time, making resolution proportionally costlier. Additionally, with the growing complexity of the problems, the learning curve for policy makers becomes increasingly steeper. This disjointed policy-making process by public-sector actors is complicated by having to deal with transborder actors and by the rapidly growing numbers of NGOs involved, raising the challenge of effective coordination among this multiplicity of actors. Since many of the problems associated with border cities are in fact regional issues, the lack of transborder planning structures is a major failure of binational policy.

In order to confront an increasingly difficult situation, faced primarily by Mexican border cities where quality of life issues are at the center of the discussion, the region needs what might be called a "rapid response structure," operated on a binational basis and organized along functional lines, able to address short- and medium-term problems. As a first priority, this new bilateral agent should be able to mediate between existing institutions on both sides of the border, serving as a clearinghouse for binational planning. To be effective, it should have ready access to existing structures and have the ability to supersede national actions and plans. This supraregional organization should address strategically important issues that have the greatest impact on the quality of life along the border.

There are four strategically important issues in desperate need of bilateral attention and coordination on which short- and medium-term planning can meet with success: (1) population growth; (2) access to natural resources, especially water; (3) environmental degradation; and (4) indiscriminate industrial growth. The purpose of this supranational institution would be not only to address concrete problems being faced by the border region but also to help in the development of a transborder system of values. In this system, inhabitants of the region as well as public-sector actors would begin to see themselves not only as citizens of the cities in which they live, but also as citizens of a transborder region, where the actions on one side of the border will most likely affect a person or persons on the other side. This is conscience building, and in this context, the inhabitants will be ready to demand that solutions being considered by one side be discussed with and agreed to by the other side. Unless such a unified system of values can be created at the border, solutions will continue to be characterized by a unilateral nature and disjointed approach to critical problems. Further, without broad-based consensus building, resolution of the complex problems facing the region will require great support, which might not be forthcoming from a dejected and cynical population, accustomed to public failure and inaction.

Notes

1. To respect anonymity, interviewees are cited only by their initials.
2. San Diego also confronts special problems of economic development. For an explanation of these problems, see Marcelli and Jossart (1998).
3. Neoclassical international trade theory predicts essentially the reverse position, with the less-developed partner obtaining most of the gains as conditions of free trade develop, due to comparative advantage and factor price equalization. Among the many books on economics, see Krugman and Obstfeld (1995).
4. Most colonial cases reflect understandings between partners where resources flow to the North with the complicity of colonial elites. This theoretical perspective in no sense disregards the theoretical work involving dependence.
5. This term is an analytical one, referring to certain conditions of criticality (conditions under which complex systems tend to disintegrate), rather than the connotations of its everyday use. Yet before critical conditions are reached by a system, recurring patterns can be discerned within the system, making statistical predictions of system behavior possible. See del Castillo (1996).
6. This coastal corridor involves north-south interstate highways 5, 805, and 15 and east-west highways 8, 52, 94, and 76. The Mexican side of the border consists of coastal Highway 1—extending 1609 kilometers (1,000 miles) from Tijuana to Cabo San Lucas—and Highway 2, east from Tijuana connecting with Mexicali.
7. For a detailed study of the region's demographics see John R. Weeks (1993) and Canales (1993).
8. These numbers do not include commercial crossings.
9. The actual number of commuters crossing from their residence in Tijuana to work in San Diego has long been the subject of speculation and debate among public authorities and academics. Published studies from a decade ago estimated this number to be some 23,000 workers, undoubtedly increasing over time (Alegría 1990). Reasons for this situation are of some theoretical importance, especially when analyzing the manufacturing trends in San Diego, where decreasing wages in San Diego have forced workers to find cheaper living alternatives in Tijuana (Gerber 1993).

10. This same official compared the American participation in Tijuana to a situation in which Mexicans "... would go into La Jolla and tell the residents, hey, you guys don't know how to party, you don't know how to live life ... come here, shut down that business, get some drink, close the street, put on the loud music! You know what they would do ... ? Throw us in jail in a jiffy, and then they would deport us ... with good reason. Sometimes Americans think that there are no laws in Mexico, for them it is still the wild West!"

11. According to another interviewee (G.V.), some groups have refused to participate in this process, fearing interference by the public sector or being used for political purposes and thereby losing their independence and nonpolitical nature.

12. For example, the director of the Proyecto Fronterizo de Educación Ambiental of Tijuana first became acquainted with border environmental issues in Arizona through the Border Ecology Project, and after becoming a resident of the city was put in touch by these Arizona environmentalists with the Environmental Health Coalition of San Diego, which has become somewhat of a *padrino* to this Tijuana group.

13. Proyecto Fronterizo, presentation brochure.

14. In one of its informational leaflets, it refers to NAFTA and its side agreement on environmental cooperation in informing the public: "Tu tienes acceso a esta información; exígela, conócela y ejerce tu derecho a una comunidad limpia. (La contaminación no desaparece, solo se transfiere y su registro es tu protección.)"

15. This is a typology proposed by Oscar J. Martínez. See Martínez (1994).

16. The Cámara Nacional de la Industria de la Transformación (CANACINTRA) represents some eight hundred manufacturing firms, of which two hundred are maquiladoras.

17. California's Proposition 187, passed in 1994 with the support of its then governor, Republican Pete Wilson, is one of the more recent examples of the ongoing discussion about undocumented labor. Proposition 187 aimed to save money by denying education and certain medical services to undocumented migrants.

18. This peculiarity makes it interesting because of its close working relationship with the PAN-run municipal government and with the other organizations previously set up during PRI governments.

19. There are many San Diego organizations dealing with the plight of migrants in San Diego County. For a comprehensive review of these organizations and their functioning, see Vargas (1993).

20. There are 18 city governments in San Diego County, 200 special assessment districts, 43 elementary/secondary school districts, 5 community college districts, and numerous regional agencies or quasi-governmental service-providing agencies. This complex and diversified public-sector

structure is rapidly being copied in Tijuana, although for historical-political reasons a good deal of centralization is still prevalent. See del Castillo (1998b).

21. One concrete result of this conference was the creation of a "task force to unify U.S. and Mexican authorities in their efforts to find missing children, stop drug trafficking and combat other shared troubles" (*San Diego Union Tribune* 1999a).

22. As early as 1964 some states had border offices, including the Governor's Office of California-Mexico Affairs, located in San Diego, but its effects must be questioned because it closed in 1993 during the California recession.

23. The posting of kilometer signs instead of mile indicators is, according to a longtime resident, one of the many flukes within the Arizona public administration. It appears that Arizona was ahead of the curve in the 1980s when it seemed that the United States would change from the English system of measurement to a metric system; under this scenario, Arizona would have been ahead of the rest of the country, but, of course, nothing changed.

24. See: Arizona Department of Economic Security, Research Administration (1998).

25. Foreign Trade Zones benefit industries by allowing the importation of goods with many benefits with respect to the payment of duties, excise taxes, and freight duties, testing and assembly of new products, and storage of goods while markets are developed. These benefits create jobs and revenues for local communities and give them an international presence.

26. In response, these leaders are proposing a ballot measure to replace the mayor with a city manager, thereby professionalizing government.

27. This is also despite the fact that there were participants who did understand the close relationship existing between these two border communities, and who actively encouraged the economic and commercial relationship which exists de facto.

28. Although there is a new mayor and a new administration within the Chamber of Commerce since the plan was first written, the principal participant—the Economic Development Foundation—remains the same.

29. Now there is a belt line which moves traffic away from the city directly to a crossing point just west of the city. Previously, the city basically came to a stop when all of this truck traffic moved through the main downtown avenue on its way north.

Works Cited

Alegría, Tito. 1990. "Ciudad y transmigración en la frontera de México con Estados Unidos." *Frontera Norte* vol. 2, no. 4. Tijuana, Baja California: El Colegio de la Frontera Norte.

Arizona Department of Economic Security, Research Administration. 1998. "Arizona's Workforce." Tucson, Ariz.

Arizona Public Service Company. 1997. "Nogales Focused Future. Strategic Plan for Economic Development." Nogales, Ariz.

Canales, Alejandro. 1993. "Population Structure and Trends in Tijuana." In *San Diego-Tijuana in Transition: A Regional Analysis*, eds. Norris C. Clement and Eduardo Zepeda M. San Diego: Institute for Regional Studies of the Californias, San Diego State University.

Chávez, Fernando Gutierrez, and Eduardo Zepeda M. 1996. *El sector servicios: Desarrollo regional y empleo*. Mexico City: Friedrich Ebert Foundation.

Clement, Norris C., and Eduardo Zepeda, eds. 1993. *San Diego-Tijuana in Transition: A Regional Analysis*. San Diego: Institute for Regional Studies of the Californias, San Diego State University.

del Castillo, Gustavo. 1998a. "Non-Maquila Manufacturing in Tijuana and Its International Linkages." Paper presented at meeting of the Latin American Studies Association, Chicago, September 24–26, 1998.

———. 1998b. "Economic Linkages Across the U.S.-Mexico Border; Tijuana-San Diego and the World Economy." Paper presented at the meeting of the Latin American Studies Association, Chicago. September 24–26.

———. 1996. "Increasing Complexity. Border Interactions and the Conformation of a Region. The Case of San Diego-Tijuana." Paper presented at International Symposium, COLEF IV, October, Tijuana, Baja California.

———. 1983. "La crisis mexicana y su reflejo en el estado de California, U.S.A." Tijuana, Baja California: Centro de Estudios Fronterizos del Norte de México.

Ganster, Paul. 1993. "Transborder Linkages in San Diego-Tijuana." In *San Diego-Tijuana in Transition: A Regional Analysis*, eds. Norris C. Clement and Eduardo Zepeda. San Diego: Institute for Regional Studies of the Californias, San Diego State University.

Gerber, James. 1993. "Cycles and Trends in San Diego and California." In *San Diego-Tijuana in Transition: A Regional Analysis*, eds. Norris C. Clement and Eduardo Zepeda. San Diego: Institute for Regional Studies of the Californias. San Diego State University.

Instituto Nacional de Estadística Geografía e Informática. 1993. *Censo Manufacturero de 1993*. Baja California.

Krugman, Paul, and Maurice Obstfeld. 1995. *International Economics: Theory and Policy*. New York: HarperCollins, Inc.

Marcelli, Enrico A., and Pascale M. Jossart. 1998. "Prosperity and Poverty in the New Economy. A Report on the Social and Economic Status of Working People in San Diego County." San Diego, California: Center on Policy Alternatives.

Martínez, Oscar J. 1994. *Border People: Life and Society in the U.S.-Mexico Borderlands.* Tucson: The University of Arizona Press.

Nogales-Santa Cruz County Economic Development Foundation. n.d. *Industrial Investment Guide.* Nogales, Arizona.

Pavlakovich, Vera K., et al. 1997. "Fresh Produce Industry in Nogales, Arizona; Impacts of a Transborder Production Complex on the Arizona Economy." Borderlands Economic Development Program, Office of Economic Development. Tucson: The University of Arizona.

Presidencia Municipal de Nogales, Sonora. n.d. *Plan Municipal de Desarrollo, 1995-1997.* Nogales, Sonora.

San Diego Association of Governments. 1998. *Agenda Report, No. E, Final Recommendations of the Border-Related Issues Task Force.* February 23.

San Diego Dialogue. 1995. *Demographic Atlas San Diego/Tijuana.* La Jolla, Calif.: University of California, San Diego.

San Diego Union Tribune. 1999a. 4 September. p. B 3.

San Diego Union Tribune. 1999b. 1 December. p. B 4.

U.S. Department of Commerce. 1983. *Population Projections by Race/Ethnicity for California and its Counties, 1990-2040.* Washington, DC: Government Printing Office.

Vargas, Mauro. 1993. "La población de origen mexicano en el condado de San Diego, CA. Un análisis general de sus grupos y organizaciones." Bachelor's thesis. Universidad Nacional Autónoma de México, Facultad de Ciencias Políticas y Sociales, Mexico City.

Weeks, John R. 1993. "The Changing Demographic Structure of the San Diego Region." In *San Diego-Tijuana in Transition: A Regional Analysis,* eds. Norris C. Clement and Eduardo Zepeda M. San Diego: Institute for Regional Studies of the Californias, San Diego State University.

Additional Resources

Barry, Tom, and Beth Sims. 1994. *The Challenge of Cross-Border Environmentalism: The U.S.-Mexico Case.* Albuquerque: Resource Center Press.

Blatter, Joachim. 1997. "Explaining Cross-Border Cooperation: A Border-Focused and Border-External Approach." *Journal of Borderlands Studies* vol. 12, nos. 1 and 2 (Spring and Fall).

Cornelius, Wayne A., et al. 1994. *Controlling Immigration: A Global Perspec-*

tive. San Diego and Stanford, Calif.: Center for U.S.-Mexican Studies, University of California, San Diego, and Stanford University Press.

Heyman, Josiah McC. 1991. *Life and Labor on the Border.* Tucson: The University of Arizona Press.

Instituto Nacional de Estadística, Geografía e Informática. 1998. *Cuaderno Estadistico Municipal. Nogales, Estado de Sonora.* Aguascalientes, Guanajuato.

Lowenthal, Abraham F,. and Katrina Burgess. 1993. *The California-Mexico Connection.* Stanford: Stanford University Press.

Martínez, Oscar J. 1992. "Border People and Transnational Interaction." In *The U.S.-Mexico Border Region and the Free Trade Agreement*, eds. Paul Ganster and Eugenio O. Venanciano. San Diego: Institute for Regional Studies of the Californias, San Diego State University.

Nolasco, Margarita, et al. 1992. *Brevario de los municipios fronterizos de Mexico.* Centro de Ecodesarrollo. Centro Nacional de Desarrollo Municipal. Mexico City: Editorial Paran, S.A.

"The San Diego-Tijuana Region." In *Integrating Cities and Regions:* NAFTA *and the Caribbean Face Globalization*, eds. W. Wilkie and Clint E. Smith. Los Angeles, Guanajuato, Mexico: A.C. Guadalajara, Centro Internacional Lucas Alamán para el Cecimiento Económico.

Staudt, Kathleen. 1998. *Free Trade? Informal Economies at the U.S.-Mexico Border.* Philadelphia: Temple University Press.

Zabin, Carol. 1997. "Nongovernmental Organizations in Mexico's Northern Border." *Journal of Borderlands Studies* vol. 12, nos. 1 and 2 (Spring and Fall). San Diego: Institute for Regional Studies of the Californias, San Diego State University.

PART TWO

Europe

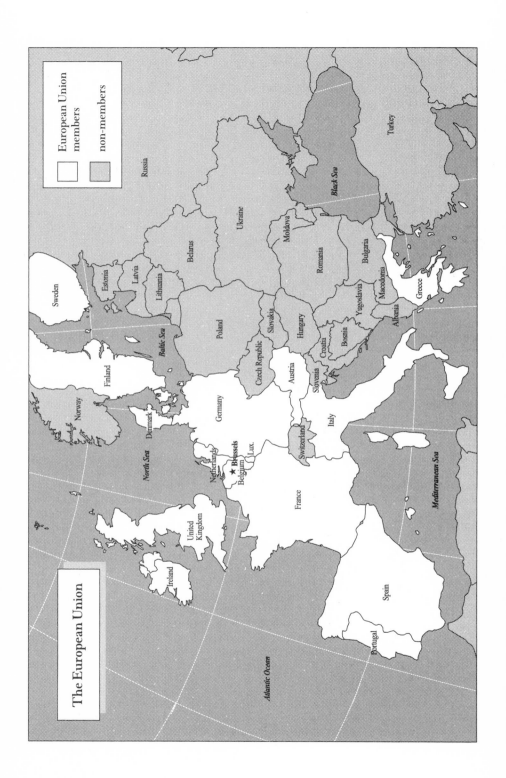

The European Union

European Union
members

non-members

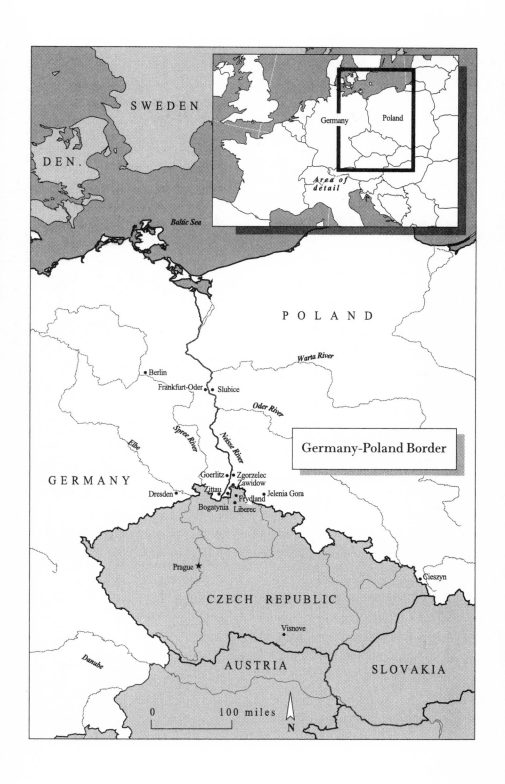

SWEDEN

DEN.

Baltic Sea

POLAND

Germany   Poland

Area of detail

Warta River

• Berlin

Frankfurt-Oder • • Slubice

Oder River

Spree River   Neisse River

Elbe

Germany-Poland Border

GERMANY

Goerlitz • • Zgorzelec
• Zawidow
Zittau
Dresden •   • Frydland   • Jelenia Gora
Bogatynia   Liberec

Prague ★   • Cieszyn

CZECH REPUBLIC

Visnove •

Danube   AUSTRIA   SLOVAKIA

0   100 miles

N

4

National Borders: Images, Functions, and Their Effects on Cross-Border Cooperation in North America and Europe

Andrea Witt

BORDER COMMUNITIES in North America and Europe are facing the same challenge—they must cooperate across international boundaries. While many of the problems evident on each continent are somewhat similar, the present mechanisms for transnational interaction vary greatly. Subnational cross-border cooperation as an instrument for tension management can develop from within the region (bottom-up), motivated by local concerns (House 1981, 180). Transboundary contacts also can be initiated from the federal or supranational level (top-down) to pursue long-time political goals. While many factors influence the structures and issues of local binational contacts, the capability of local actors to interact with each other has the main effect. Here, developments both within and outside the communities on both sides of a national border are relevant, for "national communities by no means exclusively make and determine decisions and policies for themselves, and governments by no means determine what is appropriate exclusively for their own citizens" (Held 1995, 17).

Local and regional cross-border cooperation as "local foreign policy" (Heberlein 1989, 1) does, however, concern federal governments. In that regard, national borders play a major role, for they are linked to questions of national sovereignty. The physical appearance and the tasks a border has can either support or hinder local and regional cross-border cooperation. The functions a government applies to the border depend on the image it wants its border to project. Border images are shaped by federal foreign policies and determined by the overlying concepts of continental integration. In that sense transboundary cooperation is a reflection of present border problems, border functions, and border images.

Local and regional cooperation along the U.S.-Mexican border has traditionally been characterized by predominately informal contacts (Ganster 1996, 187). In Europe, however, a process of institution building has taken place (Scott and Collins 1997, 97). This paper will share observations from fieldwork along the U.S.-Mexican and German-Polish borders. By comparing the situations between these borders, this article examines some of the factors that support or hinder cross-border cooperation and highlights some of the dominant influences responsible for the differences between the two.[1] It also gives special emphasis to federal border policies—comparing approaches toward security-related and non-security-related issues. While the main focus lies on the U.S.-Mexican border, a comparative examination of the European region, and of the relevance of international borders more generally, helps to specify certain dynamics and ultimately to draw some conclusions about how to embrace a more integrated approach toward transboundary cooperation. The research paid special attention to criticism and suggestions coming from border actors. Those voices reinforce the belief that in most countries the majority of the involved federal and subnational agencies and organizations are ill-coordinated (Asiwaju 1986, 174) to support transboundary contacts and that, regardless of the border issue to be addressed and the nation-states involved, one important point needing emphasis is that "border people themselves must play a more active role" (Martínez 1986, 202).

Relevance of International Borders

Based on the European principle of the nation-state, borders are limitations, defining three major characteristics associated with statehood: territory, citizenship, and public authority. It is the border that defines the international status (Ajomo 1989, 37) and marks the state as a political entity with territorial sovereignty and final legal power over a particular area (Seidl-Hohenveldern 1994, 143). National borders formalize citizens by perceiving them exclusively according to characteristics of international law (Fiedler 1993, 31). Other identities (such as belonging to a shared cultural, ethnic, or language community) do not matter. Borders also represent the line of physical contact between states and "afford opportunities for cooperation and discord" (Prescott 1987, 5). Integration concepts generally are shaped by multi- or supranational organizations such as NAFTA and the European Union (EU).

As a general rule, representatives of the federal governments act on questions of borders, as they traditionally have had the responsibility for national security and sovereignty issues. No longer are military aggressions alone regarded as national threats. Today, attention is focused more broadly and includes global questions like migration, organized crime, economic competitiveness, and access to water. Both in North America and in Europe security issues are increasingly seen in connection with immigration and organized crime. In that sense, border tasks or functions are constructed by political decision makers. There are no "natural border functions," as there are no "natural borders."

While the strictly legal function of borders is clearly defined, the actual relevance national borders have for their citizens today depends on the political function a national government attributes to them. Historically, national governments have had a tendency to cluster signs of their sovereignty around borders (Haubrichs and Schneider 1993, 11). In other words, borders are used to visualize the line between national territories. Individuals experience the state through symbolism, which is created in order to evoke identification (Bloom 1990, 61). Borders are gatekeepers of a specific national identity, with national flags and banners on display at ports of entry. The more a government uses the border as a symbol and instrument to protect national sovereignty, the more citizens experience a border as regulatory (Clement 1996, 41). The more it is used as a symbol of political integration between the bordering states, the less intrusive a border feels for its citizens and the more likely cross-border contacts are to develop.

The appearance of borders differs according to their given functions. Often the first glance at a border gives away the state's intentions regarding foreign policy and the state of binational relations. Those intentions translate into border images that surpass the functionalism of problem-orientation. Aggressive or hostile relations are as obvious to detect (in the extreme, such as along the former German-East German border, with spring-gun installations on the East German side) as friendly relations are visible (the aims of European integration are, for example, expressed through non-staffed ports of entry). The physical reality of the different intentions affects any cross-border activity—either human or trade-related traffic—and obviously influences the conditions for local and regional cooperation. However, due to the communications revolution, with its non-material exchange, the flows of ideas or capital transactions are generally not impeded by a physical border.

Border issues and the involved actors change due to the quality of binational relations; the better the relationship or the more attuned foreign ideologies are, the more likely it is that non-security issues enter into the binational discussion. Instead of being decided by federal actors alone, debates regarding border issues are being increasingly opened up to a broad variety of political and non-political actors. Also, if economic competitiveness is considered as a means for securing national sovereignty, it does not solemnly fall into federal competency. Instead, it requires multiple partnerships inside the states and across their boundaries. Transboundary interaction has to take political and administrative hierarchies into account, hierarchies defined by the international border.

Many national border policies affect both a country's own citizens and the bordering neighbors. That is especially true for policy fields with a transnational nature, such as environmental issues: "Perceptions of territorial sovereignty are changing, because in environmental matters, states no longer appear to have the right to sanction activities within their frontiers" (Anderson 1996, 36). The question arises as to what extent national policy makers alone are legitimized to make decisions with transnational implications. Accordingly, many policy issues regarding the border present a democracy dilemma within and across nation-states. Thus, international borders both separate and link nations. They are "zones of separation—what belongs to some and what comes under the jurisdiction of others" and at the same time "zones of contact—the meeting place of nations" (Maillat 1988, 199). This duality characterizes the nature of the border and cross-border cooperation.

General Motivations and Barriers to Local and Regional Transboundary Cooperation

Motivations for local and regional transboundary cooperation include a variety of factors, such as economic and infrastructural interdependencies (Hansen 1986, 31), cross-border problems, or long-time cultural and social links that have the potential to create truly transnational life styles for borderlanders (Martínez 1996, 194). The need for cooperation increases dramatically if the border region is confronted with primarily heterogeneous situations, as is true for both the present case studies. Barriers to cooperation include asymmetries between neighboring countries and a lack of cultural understanding or trust between communities. Also, national policies can serve as obstacles for cooperation, provoking an increasing local and regional interaction in federal policy fields.

Economic

Subnational governments and entities have become increasingly sensitive to pressures and international interdependencies (Duchacek 1986, 11), and engage in transboundary cooperative activities such as developing joint economic programs to enhance the economic well-being of their communities and secure international competitiveness. The sister organizations Arizona-Mexico Commission (AMC) and Comisión Sonora-Arizona have for some 40 years cooperated, with an increasing focus on economic development.[2] On a very local level, economic interdependencies are primarily linked to cross-border trade patterns. Some American border cities estimate that about one-third of their retail dollars come from Mexican shoppers (Cochise College Center for Economic Research 1999). Roughly the same interdependence exists in the German-Polish border region. Furthermore, infrastructural projects, ports of entry as well as bridges and roads, also require joint planning on a subnational level. Global phenomena such as the global economy regional trade blocs, for example the North American Free Trade Agreement (NAFTA) or the European

Union (EU), have further increased the importance of cooperation on a broader scale. NAFTA can be considered the dominant positive and negative impulse for the region. While NAFTA has provided a helpful framework securing long-established cross-border businesses, and while regulatory policies have aimed to integrate the maquiladora industries and improve infrastructural equipment,[3] NAFTA also entails associated environmental costs and traffic congestion. It has also significantly influenced patterns of daily cross-border economic interaction, forcing communities to promote structural changes.

Environmental

Along the U.S.-Mexican border another push for cooperation stems from severe environmental problems whose dramatic escalation is due, in part, to the increased economic exchange over the past decades (U.S. General Accounting Office 1996, 1.) A severe lack of infrastructure endangers human health on both sides of the border. Cross-border pollution is regarded as a severe threat for the population and the environment alike. It is widely understood on federal and local levels that these problems cannot be solved within one country: "In today's world, since pollution does not honor national boundaries, overcoming these challenges requires the cooperation of other countries" (Browner 1999, 1). Moreover, pollution along the U.S.-Mexican border can harm economic development, "threatening not only the health and welfare of the region's inhabitants but also the ability of corporations to do business profitably" (Barry 1994, 111). Prime areas for cooperation include water access, joint wastewater facilities, and hazardous waste.

Trust

The level of trust and understanding within a border region has a tremendous impact on the success of any cross-border interaction. In that regard, the recent history of a given border region is especially important. Primarily friendly and cooperative experiences create a completely different situation from one associated with confrontation.

For instance, Mexican culture strongly influences the U.S.-Mexico border region.[4] Social and economic contacts have developed, following multiple family and social transborder ties. Although Oscar Martínez describes the U.S.-Mexican border region as integrated and mentions a distinct "border culture" (Martínez 1996, 193), building trust is still a central element. Margie Emmermann, Executive Assistant for Mexico, Office of the Governor of Arizona, characterized the condition for cooperation with counterparts in Sonora, Mexico: "We had to be friends first before we could become business partners."[5]

In both regions studied, the present border demarcations have been the result of aggressive military conflicts. As part of the public cultural memory, these violent histories influence relationships to the present day. In particular, they make people sensitive to the way in which they are treated. Feeling that one's culture or the human rights of compatriots are not being respected can impair cooperation. For instance, community leaders on the U.S. side strongly disagree with the way the border is policed. While they acknowledge the importance of security issues such as migration and drug trafficking, they consider the federal responses to it inadequate and potentially harmful on several levels. Incidents of harassment and profiling are associated with the massive influx of Border Patrol agents into the border communities. They regard the image created as a sentiment saying, "We love Mexican food, we love Mexican music, we love Mexican culture. We just don't like their people."[6] This image is seen as hurtful for the important process of trust building. Along the border, social and family cross-border ties are so strong that a majority of the interviewed community leaders respond on a very personal level. Psychological lines of identification and identity obviously do not exclusively run according to the national border.

Asymmetries in levels of prosperity and social welfare within the political and administrative structures also may engender a lack of understanding, impeding joint approaches (Scott and Collins 1997, 110). This has special relevance between the United States and Mexico or between Germany and Poland, where federal systems border more centralized ones. In both border regions local representatives call the different natures of government and authority the main obstacle to cooperation.[7] Sometimes these asymmetries prevent development of a shared cultural understanding.

This lack of shared culture is particularly evident along the German-Polish border. Only since the end of the Second World War has the river Oder served as a border between Germany and Poland. Effective local cooperation was hardly possible before German unification and the downfall of communism. In addition, the vast majority on both sides of the border have been affected by violent expulsions and forced migration (Schultz 1996, 80; Brencz 1996, 49). Accordingly, the first basic social contacts here in the beginning of the 1990s had to overcome a strong sense of estrangement and distrust. These problems have been more pronounced because of still-existing language barriers, which lead to severe misinterpretations of behavior. Today, after nearly ten years of rapidly developing contacts, even members of the political elites still misinterpret different mentalities and social behaviors as public offenses,"insults" which limit the will to cooperate.[8]

Differing Government and Border Perspectives

Finally, local cooperation can be impeded by federal policy makers in the national capitals who are accused of a lack of understanding of the border culture and the nature of migration. As the mayor of Douglas, Arizona, said in an interview, "They [the Border Patrol] could stand side by side from here to San Ysidro in California, and they're not going to stop them [undocumented aliens] from coming over" (Hartman 2000). The militarization of the border also affects economic cooperation. In this regard, a business leader from Nogales, Arizona, interpreted the erection of a fence as "a message sent from Washington to the Mexican people to basically stay in Mexico and not to come over to our side,"[9] despite the fact that most American border communities depend on Mexican consumers.[10] In some U.S. communities such as Douglas, Arizona (which in early 2000 had the highest numbers of undocumented border crossings), residents are frustrated by the "failed national immigration policy, and the only solution that they [the federal government] have is throwing more law enforcement at the problem" (Hartman 2000). In response, some residents have taken it upon themselves to detain unauthorized migrants. Not only are these actions considered alien by many in the communities, but also they impede local cooperation with the cross-border community.[11]

Similarly, border communities were frustrated by the way in which the new U.S. laser visa was introduced to replace the old border-crossing cards, and their high monetary cost for individual Mexicans.[12] Another example relates to the attempted imposition of Section 110 entry-exit control requirements that were part of the United States' 1996 Illegal Immigration Reform and Immigrant Responsibility Act. The arguments against it concerned environmental, traffic congestion, and psychological issues, emphasizing that the law failed to recognize the realities of the border because the requirement would bring to a halt the existing and long-standing cross-border movement and trade.[13] The Border Governors Conference lobbied against the proposal, alongside nationwide business coalitions and the Mexican and Canadian governments. Ultimately the requirement was modified. Similarly, Mexico City had attempted to impose a fee on imported cars and, separately, to limit the amount of merchandise a Mexican national can bring back into Mexico to $50 duty-free per day. According to a business leader in Nogales, Arizona, this policy caused a 20 percent drop in sales rates; both proposals were changed after facing severe opposition. Such policies are painful for border communities fighting multiple negative impacts, some of which they associate with NAFTA.

As a response to the problems and out of a growing dissatisfaction with national policies, local and state actors have become increasingly active on federal issues. In addition to the lobbying against Section 110, another example is the push for a new foreign labor program as a means to address both undocumented immigration from Mexico and labor shortages in the United States. The initiative has come from the mayor of Douglas, Arizona. Jane Dee Hull, Governor of Arizona, is at this writing lobbying the concept at the federal level (Hull 1999). Based on the situation in Arizona, the concept offers incentives for a new national approach to economic migration. A Strategy Paper has been published which simultaneously criticizes federal immigration policies, demands new labor programs, and offers solutions based on state and local demands. While it acknowledges federal responsibility, the paper stresses that "border states have valuable knowledge and experience that can help lawmakers design policies that will manage effectively the supply and demand factors that drive illegal immigration today" (Bayless 2001). Similarly, groups such as the U.S.-Mexico Border

Community Coalition have advocated a federal reimbursement to states and counties carrying the financial burden for costs related to undocumented migrants. Such efforts are recognized on the federal level and have motivated several Senate bills that, as this is written, are primarily supported by border states' senators.

In a European example, local criticism is directed against a lack of federal infrastructure funding, which hinders a more rapid economic interaction and causes environmental damage as well as traffic congestion in the hearts of many communities. Also, decisions made at the European level have repeatedly been considered inadequate to meet the unique challenges present along the EU's external borders.

Differences between NAFTA and the EU

Underlying concepts of integration, reflecting long-term political ideas, help determine the role played by borders. The differences in the border functions and images studied are due to differing legal and administrative frameworks as well as different philosophies in North America and Europe, which have influenced the goals and agendas of the EU and NAFTA. The main difference between NAFTA and the EU with regard to borders relates to the integration potential. NAFTA is a trilateral treaty with a clearly defined agenda. Its main goal is to push market integration by eliminating trade barriers, and federal agencies are responsible for enforcing the contract. The overall level of integration compared to the European agenda is considerably lower, limiting the required institutional adjustments. Also, it requires far fewer intergovernmental funds than are used in the European Union (Kaiser 1998, 235). In contrast, the end of European integration, which initially began to develop as a common market in the 1950s, has evolved into much more, with a common currency, free movement of nationals, and supranational institutions. The "endgame" is much more open-ended, with the associated and necessary flexibility that entails.[14]

The NAFTA negotiations showed that at that time, an inclusive political integration was not a likely scenario for the North American near future. After signing NAFTA, President Clinton and President Salinas publicly limited the treaty's goals to economic issues, as a means to pursue an economy without borders and a free trade zone without borders (Europa-Archiv 1994, D62–64). However, economic integration in North America has progressed, raising not only economic, but also social and political challenges (Lorey 1993, 89), some of which have been addressed in environmental, labor, and border-development side agreements. Accordingly, NAFTA is seen as "symbolic of the increased effort both countries are making to find cooperative solutions to bilateral problems" by linking trade and social issues as a new and controversial aspect of international negotiations (Bosworth, Collins, and Lustig 1997, 9). Nevertheless, the economic opening pursued by NAFTA has not yet been complemented by an equal political opening between the member states. Instead "the U.S. government agreed with the argument put forth by President Salinas that to open up the economy and the political system at the same time would only undermine both types of reforms" (Purcell 1997, 141). A widespread fear seemed to exist that further economic, let alone political, integration might compromise a sense of national identity, both in the United States and in Mexico (Bosworth, Collins, and Lustig 1997, 2). While NAFTA has helped economic integration, it has clearly not eroded political boundaries (Keating and Loughlin 1997, 9). Quite the contrary, the process of economic integration has been accompanied by a simultaneous militarization of the border as an instrument to secure and control—and in that sense strengthen—national identity.

The European Union, on the other hand, has been simultaneously pursuing quite different goals from the very beginning. The integration process in Europe has produced supranational elements, as the member states have agreed to pass certain national sovereignties on to the European level. The extent to which the European Union has moved beyond the nation-state and has demolished the traditional concept of sovereignty is still open to debate (Christiansen 1994, 11). In addition to the intention to secure economic competitiveness and to ensure social cohesion, European integration also has been linked to values such as peace, prosperity, pluralism, democracy, and freedom. In that sense, the border image created is one of cooperation and unity. The European Union strongly supports transnational integration. The aim is to create a "Europe without borders"—at least borderless for its member states. Border regions are a favorite topic for European rhetoric; cross-border interaction is a means to achieve the desired continental integration on a subnational level. Accordingly, borders are used as symbols for integrated political interaction. Formal funds have been created to support cross-border cooperation. Furthermore, the EU actively motivates the formalization of cross-border networks and has initiated transnational institution building.

Overall, traditional decision-making processes have changed within the European Union and altered the balance between the different political levels. Governance is perceived through multi-level decision making with a strong emphasis on subsidiarity and decentralization.[15] An integration process is taking place that combines the question of membership with the question of which areas require European governance. Presently, different stages and processes of integration are visible in the various policy areas, including border functions. Here, the area of foreign policy clearly lags behind (Westlake 1998, 3). The treaties of Maastricht and Amsterdam have enforced a differentiation process within the integration. Since the Amsterdam Treaty, enhanced cooperation between member states can be implemented within the institutional framework of the EU and its institutions and procedures utilized. The treaty provides enabling methods for closer cooperation between member states and provides an abstention clause permitting member states to stay out of foreign policy measures decided by others (Deubner 2000). The Schengen Agreement, which eliminates border controls between member states, is one policy area that grants enhanced cooperation while also allowing abstention. The agreement was originally signed by only five member states; however as this is being written, thirteen states have signed on to it and the Agreement has been transferred into the treaty system. The United Kingdom and the Republic of Ireland, however, have opted out; Denmark has never ratified the agreement. All three countries can continue regular border controls with other EU member states. In that sense, even within the European Union, various border images—and accordingly, various border functions—exist beside each other.

Observations on U.S.-Mexican Border Policies and Cooperative Efforts

The ever-present question regarding the function of the U.S.-Mexican border is one of priorities: Should the facilitation of trade and the movement of goods and people take first place, or should control and safety issues have top preference (Kolbe 1999)? With the reality of a borderless economy under way in North America and with many people fearing change, the focus on security measures and the symbolism of the border may be a strategy to publicly parade the defense of national sovereignty and identity. At first sight, the image of the U.S.-Mexico border is one of strong policing, visible in the significant presence of armed border agents, constant patrols with cars or helicopters, high-technology computing, and communications technology. The erection of fences along the border is an indication of separation, "to symbolize the presence of the division of space and identities" (Soguk 1997, 299). This "wall between the two societies" (Barry 1994, 4) stands in crass contrast, however, to the reality of the multiple crossings and contacts. The U.S.-Mexican border, then, has different functions and images for different issues.

The concentration on divisive issues such as narcotics dominates binational relations and debates between the United States and Mexico, leading to a neglect of other, non-security issues which affect the border region and harm local attempts at cross-border cooperation. As Juan Rebolledo Gout, Mexico's Deputy Foreign Minister, said prior to President Clinton's 1999 visit, "Despite all our efforts we never succeed in bringing attention to our huge and complex binational agenda, because we always end up focusing on narcotics" (Dillon 1999). A senior federal official, during the first meeting of the President's Interagency Task Force in Tucson, agreed that in Washington almost all thoughts associated with the U.S.-Mexican border concern drugs.[16] The public image of the border region is also primarily associated with drug smuggling and illegal border crossings, which leads to financing directed to law enforcement.

Although the security issues have changed from defense against military aggression to protection against problems such as drugs, migration, international terrorism, and smuggling, governments still use traditional strategies to defend national sovereignty from unwanted influences and threats, with key politicians regarding the border as a vital instrument to "impose law and order" (U.S. Department of State 1998b). In 1998, the Director of the Office of National Drug Control Policy proposed using a "seamless curtain of electricity—information and technology" (McCaffrey, 1998) to fight the drug challenge portrayed by other senior administrators as a "threat of unprecedented proportions and gravity" to the survival of the nation.[17]

In contrast, environmental and infrastructural questions concerning the border have, for the most part, been decided through a more integrated, cooperative, and multi-level approach. One example is the International Boundary Water Commission (IBWC), which has managed shared transboundary water resources along the border since 1944 and whose experiences influenced the new NAFTA side-agreements. This is remarkable in a region where water is so precious that the public jokes, "I fight you over whiskey, but I kill you for water." Other attempts to develop cooperative environmental solutions for the border region with diverse regional and local participation include the La Paz Agreement in 1983 and the Border XXI Program in 1996. The latter explicitly emphasized public involvement, capacity building, decentralized environmental management, and interagency cooperation (U.S. Environmental Protection Agency 1996, 1). The support of both a multilevel-actors approach and decentralized decision-making processes have—at least officially—been announced as binational political goals.

Post-NAFTA, the two federal governments have been developing new strategies for joint border policies, using "lessons learned" such as needing more transparency, not having an overly limited approach, and ensuring inclusion of regional actors to create new organizations (Sprouse and Brown 1995, 2). These include the bilateral U.S.-Mexican agreement under NAFTA to establish a Border Environment Cooperation Commission (BECC) and the North American Development Bank (NADBank).

NADBank, a classical binational organization with a managing board of members exclusively from the federal governments and agencies, will provide financing for environmental projects certified by BECC to have a goal of sustainable development. BECC was supposed to

offer assistance for the design and financing of environmental infrastructure projects on both sides of the border, with the goal of engaging and supporting local initiatives from the border region (U.S. General Accounting Office 1994, 11). With a multilevel board of ten
directors from the border states, localities in the border region and
participation of members of the public from both countries (U.S. General Accounting Office 1994, 31), BECC's project certification criteria
require strong public participation, steering committees, local organizations, and input from the general public (Taylor 1995). The criteria
do not require binational project development or operation.

Although border residents viewed NAFTA and its related initiatives as a major commitment by the federal governments, its potential
success has been harmed by delays in setting up BECC and NADBank
(U.S. General Accounting Office 1994, 2), because of raised expectations regarding funding and unfulfilled expectations regarding the future of cross-border cooperation. For instance, a Washington decision
in the fall of 1999 to halve accompanying financial provisions[18] sent a
very disillusioning signal to the border at a time when NADBank estimated that continued support by Mexico and the U.S. "for about $1 bil-
lion in grants funds over the next ten years" would be the crucial factor
in meeting environmental infrastructure needs (NADBank 1999, 11).
Moreover, NADBank was criticized as not being designed with community outreach in mind, and the interaction seemed more project-
than policy-oriented (Hale 1996). NADBank/BECC lack a fixed plan for
a long-term binational agenda, and neither has the potential to truly
support a further strengthening of cross-border contacts. Nonetheless, BECC has received a rather positive evaluation regarding its ability to promote sustainability and public participation, including its
ability to promote binational decision-making forms (Varady et al.
1996), and local attempts to extend BECC's agenda beyond water,
wastewater, and solid waste were successful in 2000. As this is written, BECC and NADBank have yet to identify which new environmental infrastructure sectors will be pursued in the future.[19]

Another federal U.S. border initiative is the President's Interagency
Task Force on the Economic Development of the Southwest Border,
stemming from the Empowerment Zone and Enterprise Community
Initiative. It aims toward a better cooperation between the U.S. federal
agencies dealing with border issues and wants to further engage lo-

cally led efforts from the border communities. Although lacking Mexican participants, the task force held hearings throughout 1999 and released a report in winter 2000. More importantly, a binational initiative began in 1997 when Presidents Clinton and Zedillo initiated the New Border Vision, agreeing to devise a long-lasting strategy to transform the border into a "model of bilateral cooperation" (U.S. Department of State 1998b). Although the approach was to be "based on people" rather than law enforcement, Mexican Foreign Secretary Rosario Green Macías stressed that it would need to take into account questions of national sovereignty and respect territorial integrity and the legal frameworks of each country,[20] making it unlikely to lead to the creation of transnational organizations with decision-making powers.

Another U.S. initiative, though short-lived, was the Border Volunteer Corps (BVC), an arm of AmeriCorps created in 1994 to address health, environment, human services, and public safety issues along the Arizona-Sonora border. Richard Carter, former director of the BVC, said that expansion into Mexico had been an explicit goal from the beginning, realized through the project Mi Casa Nueva in Nogales, Sonora. The Casa was a binational effort to grant shelter to homeless children living underground in tunnels. Carter strongly emphasized that the prime reason for its 1995 elimination was that the Corporation for National Service was "terrified of the publicity that would be generated if word got out that federal funds are being used to help Mexicans" (*naminews* 1996).

Despite these new federal efforts, approaches such as the New Border Vision or the New Task Force have not had a lasting effect on the problems along the border. A 1999 GAO Report to Congress on the U.S.-Mexico border concludes: "While such binational mechanisms have been able to make some improvements in certain areas, they have not been able to close the gap between what is needed and what exists" (U.S. General Accounting Office 1999, 3). It is also important to note that so far no single, binational plan exists to deal with the border problems, and no initiative aims to truly empower the border region to address its own problems in a local, sustainable matter with a binational agenda. Instead, even incentives such as BECC's technical assistance are constructed in a way that the border communities have to compete with each other.

The German-Polish Border—Diverse Influences and the European Impact

Presently, the German-Polish border also seems to be caught between fundamentally different images and functions. In the first image, the border is used as a symbol of good binational relations. European, federal, and regional actors try to promote the border for integrative purposes and to ensure good neighborly relations (Stolpe 1997). The federal binational treaties of 1990 and 1991 between Germany and Poland declared their intention to cooperate peacefully and are regarded as essential elements for a peaceful European development (Kettwig 1994, 54). At the same time, there is a second image, experienced both within and outside the region, that of the border as a line dividing "order from chaos" (Tycner 1996, 19). This public image is associated with car theft, drug trafficking, smuggled cigarettes, illegal migration, and prostitution.

With the Schengen Agreement, the European Union has pursued a joint approach on security issues between signatory states and affecting the controlling standards outside what are called the Schengen states. In 1997, Manfred Kanther, Germany's then Secretary of the Interior (responsible for border patrol) called the German-Polish border the "most secured one in Europe" (Pau and Schubert 1999). His successor has continued to increase the number of federal agents and has widened the area granting special rights to border patrol agents. The increased policing function also influences the psychological situation in a border region suffering from a history of distrust. A particularly devastating example is an information campaign warning taxi drivers against accepting riders suspected of having crossed the border illegally (Pau and Schubert 1999). Overall, migration-related issues have had less impact on the border region due to the severe restrictions on receiving asylum in Germany that went into effect in 1993. Since then, the third-state regulation denies asylum rights to persons entering Germany from so-called safe third states, of which Poland is considered one. Accordingly, all asylum-seekers crossing the German-Polish border are immediately sent back to Poland without individual case review. Many human rights organizations, however, condemn this practice, calling Poland's asylum rights too limited to guarantee appropriate asylum proceedings (Henselmann 1999).

At the same time, German and Polish federal border agents have begun to introduce cooperative security approaches in preparation for Poland's entry into the EU. This includes sharing the technical controlling equipment and, since 1999, joint border patrols in both territories.[21] Major funds are spent for language training to better equip agents on both sides of the border for joint activities. On the negative side, in preparation for the EU expansion Poland has already begun to shift its control capacities to its eastern border (Schröder 1999, 9). Along a border already lacking fundamental crossing infrastructure—commercial traffic congestion lasting several days is not unusual—shifting these controls further restricts facilitation and exchange. Thus, the border between Germany and Poland serves at the same time as an isolating and as an integrating instrument. These contradictory functions and developments appear in a border region struggling with the simultaneous pursuit of economic, social, cultural, and political integration.

The border region lacks a history of local and regional transboundary contacts (Schultz and Nothnagle 1996, 11). The main political and financial motivations for any kind of cooperation and integration come from Brussels. In comparison to the experience among EU member states, where transboundary cooperation slowly evolved over the decades, local and regional cross-border contacts along the German-Polish border were initiated by distinct political decisions, with transboundary contacts introduced as a top-down approach rather than the result of slow bottom-up developments. Since 1990, German-Polish cooperation has been strongly encouraged by the German government, government agencies and intergovernmental advisory bodies on different political levels, and European officials (Scott and Collins 1997, 97).

Nevertheless, due to significant external support, some impressive examples of cross-border cooperation have already been achieved. First and foremost is the funding of the Europa-University Viadrina in Frankfurt/Oder, with a binational curriculum and student body. Its sister institute, the Collegium Polonicum, is located in Slubice, Poland. Another example is the binational wastewater treatment plant for the cities of Guben/Gubin. Both projects received multi-level funding and counted on strong political support from beyond the region. Dependency on European influences along the German-Polish border is evident in the chosen structure of cross-border contacts among the "Euroregions." These models of cooperation developed within the European Union some 40 years ago.

In general, within the different political levels and institutions governing the EU there is a strong emphasis on the engagement of local and regional actors as a means to support European identity and the principle of subsidarity. That is also true for cross-border contacts. Transboundary cooperation as an integrated umbrella allowing regional differentiation plays a special role along the EU's external borders as a means of preparing the candidates for membership (Wulf-Mathies 1998). The EU tries to provide technical assistance for the ongoing transformation process. Transboundary contacts are supported to help the candidates for membership (acquis communautaire) to meet the required conditions. By handling the special funds for transboundary cooperation (PHARE-CBC), Poland can become acquainted with European financial instruments. For the German region, a special budget of the regular funds for interregional, transnational, and transboundary cooperation (INTERREG) is dedicated to Poland.

Four such Euroregions have been founded since 1993. They are based on voluntary interactions among communities and local entities, allowing local actors to develop a common goal and vision. The two primary functions of the Euroregion model are to act as distinct representatives of the binational region and to support interaction and integration within the region. To achieve the former, they participate as full-fledged members in federal binational organizations such as the German-Polish Intergovernmental Commission, act as liaisons for the various political levels, and lobby the region's interest at the federal and binational levels. They are also responsible for certifying projects applying for cross-border funding. To achieve the latter, they work both horizontally across the border and vertically among the different political actors responsible, including supporting decentralization efforts in Germany and Poland. In unison with the EU, their overall objectives are the promotion of European integration and friendly neighborliness. In response to transregional problems, they are concerned with economic cooperation, environmental and infrastructural issues, the reduction of unemployment, and cultural understanding. In response to the historic hardships experienced along this border, special emphasis is given to establishing a shared regional identity (Gruchman and Walk 1996, 135).

Euroregions are not meant to create new levels of administration. Instead, they are supposed to provide contacts and act as flexible turntables responding to new problems and requests. They have special relevance as forums to share information and to encourage communication. As a multiplier within a network of contacts they bring regional and local positions into the spotlight and potentially connect the various political and non-political actors involved in cross-border interaction. As voluntary local cooperations, Euroregions are not eligible to formalize binding international contracts; only international treaties can pass these sovereign rights from the federal level on to transnational organizations. Such a treaty is at this writing in preparation along the German-Polish border.

The success of Euroregions as a model for cross-border cooperation along the EU's external borders is hotly debated—from both academic and political points of view. Very often it is regarded as a mere process of institution building without any real impact for integration.[22] However, any evaluation has to pay special attention to the many barriers European transboundary cooperation must overcome. Due to the breakdown of the socialist systems, actors throughout the German-Polish region have since the early 1990s been preoccupied by radical political and economic transformations; a lack of trust and cultural understanding also have major impacts on the level of cross-border cooperation, and economic desperation in the German region has created an atmosphere in which in the mid-1990s German trade representatives declared local Polish products a threat to the East German economy. Moreover, Brussels itself hinders rapid integration: Due to different program designs, terminations, and decision-making responsibilities, the INTERREG and PHARE programs are not completely compatible. For the border region it has so far been nearly impossible to plan and implement larger-scale transboundary projects with joint funding from PHARE and INTERREG. As a result, the funds have primarily worked as incentives for each national part of the region. INTERREG funds have benefited regional planning in the German part of the border region. PHARE funds have been used primarily for road construction and other traffic needs in the Polish part of the border region. While the funds helped to meet essential infrastructural needs in each nation-state, they have, as of this writing, not integrated the border region's cross-border infrastructure as anticipated (Schwab 1997, 12).

Conclusion

The functions of the borders in North America and Europe have changed. Nevertheless, their tasks are still regarded as indispensable for securing national sovereignty and promoting national identity—in accordance with the respective continental integration concepts.[23] The images and tasks associated with the borders differ within the same region due to the subjects and issues associated with them. That creates a situation of unbalanced integration between the case studies, but also within each region. Both are predominately related to the way federal actors embrace border policies. In North America, security-related issues for the most part are exclusively decided by federal agents in each country; binational or multi-level approaches are rare. Environmental issues, however, have for a long time been dealt with in a more integrated matter. Accordingly, programs and organizations supporting joint approaches are the most developed in such areas—although they are inadequate to meet the present challenges. In comparison, due to European integration, process issues along the German-Polish border are being handled in a more interactive manner. While security issues remain a federal and—since most recently—also a EU domain, all other decision-making processes regarding border policies include local and regional input.

Along the border between Arizona and Sonora, a joint border culture and a long history of productive informal cooperation has spurred a multitude of spontaneous bottom-up cross-border contacts. Communities from Germany and Poland, however, are just starting to build up lasting contacts. Cultural misunderstandings, distance, and distrust have to be overcome while at the same time an EU-encouraged top-down institutionalizing takes place. While cross-border cooperation between Arizona and Sonora has been remarkably active on economic and trade-related issues, the European example is one of institution building and formalization. The European Union has created an agenda that supports cross-border cooperation—financially and politically—to the extent that federal governments are passing certain sovereign rights on to binational interregional organizations.

In North America, the situation is one of an increasingly borderless economy accompanied by ever-stricter law enforcement along the border between the United States and Mexico. As pointed out by the U.S. border actors, this development hurts the local and regional potential for economic sustainability and for cross-border cooperation. Most contacts are informal and rely to a great extent on personal contacts. Long-term planning and joint development—both indispensable to meet the infrastructural and environmental problems present —are therefore most complicated. It seems unlikely that the concept of increasing political integration will be part of the North American near future. However, some of the European experiences can be helpful inasmuch as they present new approaches for regional development policies, including strategies, attention, and funding given to border regions and cross-border contacts by the federal governments. The European example in particular holds some interesting lessons for non-security issues.

Traditional structures in North America for local and regional participation have not succeeded in fully communicating the binational interregional interests to higher political levels. So far, the new binational models for more joint approaches with multi-level actors also fall short of the expectation that they could respond more successfully to the multiple environmental and infrastructural challenges present along the U.S.-Mexican border. The reasons are multiple and partly due to the structures in each country. Generally, the border region has neither the financial means nor the political competencies to address the present challenges. The Mexican communities in particular are completely dependent on superior political levels. Moreover, many of the present problems are really border-unrelated developments caused by federal decisions.

Along the Arizona/Sonora border, regions, communities, and border states are actively seeking new chances and cross-border activities to increase their prosperity. These include political, economic, and cultural contacts across the border. Regional policy is specifically aiming toward further economic integration. A process is under way in which truly binational decisions and positions are developed within the border region. Between Arizona and Sonora, the states are progressively trying to coordinate regional and local developments. That process is suffering from the very different political structures present and by the inability of states to reach legally binding agreements. Within the United States and Mexico multiple organizations are trying to lobby for the regional position at the federal level. The question is to what extent federal agents and decision-making processes can respond to those developments.

In this regard, institution building in Europe as a means to disseminate local interregional positions to the various relevant levels of government might be an interesting model to help address this question. It is a unique form of a multinational regional development policy regarding financial needs in such an environment. Although the institutional structures of the Euroregion follow one model, they have enough flexibility to allow for specific local characteristics and are based on voluntary interactions, so that various interests are represented. However, the institution-building process in Europe, geared toward more formalization and a structure that helps to guarantee planning security, poses a major problem for cooperation between regions or communities with significant differences in competencies. The model of the Euroregion, though, as an accepted partner within the binational relations, involved in almost all decisions regarding border policies, gives the border region a chance to lobby and carry their interregional binational positions into various political levels.

Granted, the model is not perfect. The shortcomings of cross-border cooperation along the German-Polish border are due to several reasons. Most significantly, historic development and a strained economic situation have led to fears of competition and have at this writing prevented cross-border cooperation from becoming a top priority for regional and local actors on both sides of the border. Additionally, the European incentives have not proven to adequately respond to the challenges along the EU's external borders. Nonetheless, the experience of institution building can be an interesting example for the U.S.-Mexican case as a means to include border regions more in the overall decision-making processes. Through the special regional funds aimed at the border region, the national and supranational decision makers in the EU also have acknowledged that traditional funding is inadequate to meet the various financial and political challenges present. This is also true along the North American borders, where a political empowerment of border communities seems to be inevitable in order to face the problems at hand.

Along the U.S.-Mexican border, many different organizations on various political levels represent border interests—but no one organization can be identified as the major liaison. The creation of more formal organizations including major local and regional decision makers and nonpolitical actors would have several benefits. With the President's Interagency Task Force, the U.S. federal government has acknowledged a tendency toward uncoordinated, sometimes contradictory activities in regard to the border region. To have one organization as a long-term partner could help to stabilize relations and promote a more coordinated approach. Actors from border states have for a long time criticized a lack of participation when it comes to relevant decisions for the border. "We need to be included from the beginning of the debates, before the issues are discussed," said a senior policy maker from Arizona, who referred to "coming back from Washington to fight off proposals we consider as hurtful." A single binational organization as a liaison could help to solve that dilemma. A more institutionalized process would also allow the beginning of a distinct binational policy-development process, rather than the project-oriented activities limited by the current structure and approach.

Notes

1. The paper is based on primary research, secondary literature searches, and on extended interviews with experts from the border regions. The interviews along the German-Polish border were conducted in spring/summer 1999. The interviews at the Arizona-Sonora border were carried out in winter 1999–2000. The paper focuses primarily on the positions of the United States and Germany.
2. Even though several local entities are part of the Commission, the specific problems border communities experience are not in the spotlight. While the Commission has high political relevance, as it is linked to the governors' offices, it has no authority to negotiate legally binding agreements.

On a local level, several attempts have been made to increase regular binational consultations, particularly by the Southeastern Arizona Governments Organization (SEAGO) in Bisbee, Arizona, which has made such contact building a priority.

3. For an overview of the attention the maquila-industry draws in a binational entity such as the Arizona-Mexico Commission, see Arizona-Mexico Commission (1999).

4. The border scholar Art Silvers estimates that 90 percent of the inhabitants in Arizona's border region are Hispanic.

5. Interview with Margie Emmerman, Executive Assistant for Mexico, Office of the Governor of Arizona, December 16, 1999.

6. Statement by a community leader in Nogales, Arizona.

7. Interviews with senior environmental policy makers from the state of Arizona and with members of the Euroregion Pro Europa Viadrina in Frankfurt/Oder, Germany.

8. Interviews with a senior staff member at the Collegium Polonicum in Slubice, Poland, June 1999.

9. Statement by a trade representative in Nogales, Arizona.

10. The City of Douglas, Arizona, estimates that roughly one-third of all its retail tax dollars are spent by Mexican consumers (Cochise College Center for Economic Research 1999, 19).

11. Interview with senior regional representative in Bisbee, Arizona.

12. Interview with community leaders at the AMC-Plenary Session in Puerto Peñasco, Sonora, November 1999.

13. Interview at the Governor's Office in Phoenix, Arizona.

14. Frequently debated concepts include "Europe à la carte," "géométrie variable," "Kerneuropa" (European Core), or "Europa der verschiedenen Geschwindigkeiten" (Multi-Speed Europe).

15. However, the German subnational levels complain that the push for subsidarity is mainly rhetoric and accuse Brussels of supporting a process of further centralization.

16. A U.S.-Mexico High-Level Working Group on Migration, founded in 2001 by the new presidents Bush and Fox, might be an indication that the federal approach is slowly shifting. The Working Group, with exclusively federal participants, attempts to create a joint framework for migration, border safety, and worker rights. As this is written, no binational concept has been published.

17. In 1999, Thomas Constantine, head of the U.S. Drug Enforcement Administration, warned that Mexican drug trafficking organizations posed the worst criminal threat to the United States (Wren 1999).

18. Information provided by BECC staff.

19. In one example, the Arizona Department for Environmental Quality is conducting a binational air study with monitoring sites in Douglas,

Arizona, and Agua Prieta, Sonora. The study has been used to lobby an extension of BECC's mandate.

20. The Progress Report to the Presidents on the Initiative to Implement a New Border Vision (June 1998) has identified several case studies from which to build a New Vision for the border, though many are dependent on federal funding. One initiative is the Joint Urban Development Program of the two Laredos, a "landmark example of cooperative planning" (U.S. Department of State 1998a).

21. Interview with German Border Patrol Agent, summer of 1999.

22. Public discussion during the conference "Partnerships in Middle and Eastern European Borderlands," organized by Stiftung Entwicklung und Frieden (Foundation for Peace and Cooperation), in Frankfurt/ Oder, Germany, September 4–6, 1998.

23. The European experience can also serve as an example that open borders do not necessarily lead to a process of identity fusion. Quite the contrary, the European process currently suffers from a lack of shared identity, in that there is no European public or common interest.

Works Cited

Ajomo, M.A. 1989. "Legal Perspective on Border Issues." In *Borderlands in Africa: A Multidisciplinary and Comparative Focus on Nigeria and West Africa*, ed. Anthony Ijaola Asiwaju. Lagos, Nigeria: University of Lagos Press.

Anderson, Malcolm. 1996. "The Political Science of Frontiers." In *Border Regions in Functional Transition: European and North American Perspectives*, eds. James Scott, Alan Sweedler, Paul Ganster, and Wolf-Dieter Eberwein. *Regio* no. 9. Erkner, Germany: Institute for Regional Development and Structural Planning.

Arizona-Mexico Commission. 1999. *Arizona-Mexico Commission Annual Review for 1999*. Tucson, Ariz.: Arizona-Mexico Commission.

Asiwaju, Anthony Ijaola. 1986. "Problem Solving Along the African Borders — The Nigeria-Benin Case Since 1889." In *Across Boundaries: Transborder Interaction in Comparative Perspective*, ed. Oscar J. Martínez. El Paso, Texas: Texas Western Press.

Barry, Tom. 1994. *Crossing the Line: Immigrants, Economic Integration, and Drug Enforcement on the U.S.-Mexico Border*. The U.S.-Mexico Series, no. 3. Albuquerque, New Mexico: Resource Center Press.

Bayless, Angelyn Pritchard. 2001, "Labor Shortage and Illegal Immigration. Arizona's Three-Pronged Strategy." Tucson, Ariz.: Arizona-Mexico Commission. <www.azmc.org/downloads/arizonas_strategy.doc>.

Bloom, William. 1990. *Personal Identity, National Identity, and International Relations*. Cambridge Studies in International Relations, no. 9. Cambridge, U.K.: University Press.

Bosworth, Barry, Susan M. Collins, and Nora Claudia Lustig, eds. 1997. *Coming Together? Mexico-United States Relations*. Washington, D.C.: Brookings Institution Press.

Brencz, Andrzej. 1996. "Die Herausbildung einer neuen Kulturlandschaft in den Westgebieten—eine neue Sichtweise." In *Grenze der Hoffnung: Geschichte und Perspektiven der Grenzregion an der Oder*, eds. Helga Schultz and Alan Nothnagle. Potsdam, Germany: Verlag für Berlin-Brandenburg.

Browner, Carol M. 1999. Prepared Statement. Carol M. Browner, Administrator of the Environmental Protection Agency, before the Committee on Finance, U.S. Senate, Washington, D.C. January 28. <www.epa.gov/ocirpage/testimony.htm>

Christiansen, Thomas. 1994. "European Integration between Political Science and International Relations Theory: The End of Sovereignty," European University Institute Working Paper RSC, no. 94/4. European University Institute, Florence, Italy.

Clement, Norris. 1996. "The Changing Economics of Borders and Border Regions." In *Border Regions in Functional Transition: European and North American Perspectives*, eds. James Scott et al. *Regio* no. 9. Erkner, Germany: Institute for Regional Development and Structural Planning.

Cochise College Center for Economic Research. 1999. *1999–2000 Douglas Perspectives: An Overview of Douglas' Economy*. Douglas, Arizona: Cochise College.

Deubner, Christian. 2000. "Harnessing Differentiation in the EU—Flexibility After Amsterdam. A Report on Hearings with Parlamentarians and Government Officials in Seven European Capitals." Forward Studies Unit, Working Papers 2000, European Commission. <europa.eu.int/comm/cdp/working-paper/enhanced_flexibility.pdf>.

Dillon, Sam. 1999. "Mexico Opponents See Politics in Clinton Visit," *New York Times*, February 2. <www.nytimes.com/library/world/americas/021499mexico-clinton.html>.

Duchacek, Ivo D. 1986. "International Competence of Subnational Governments: Borderlands and Beyond." In *Across Boundaries: Transborder Interaction in Comparative Perspective*, ed. Oscar J. Martínez. El Paso, Texas: Texas Western Press.

Europa-Archiv. 1994. Extracts from the speeches given by U.S. President Clinton and Mexican President Salinas after signing the NAFTA treaty. *Europa-Archiv* vol. 2/1994.

Fiedler, Wilfried. 1993. "Die Grenze als Rechtsproblem." In *Grenzen und*

Grenzregionen, eds. Walter Haubrichs and Reinhard Schneider. Veröffentlichung der Kommission für Saarländische Landesgeschichte und Volksforschung. Saarbrücken, Germany: Kommissionsverlag Saarbrücker Druckereien.

Ganster, Paul. 1996. "On the Road to Interdependence? The United States-Mexico Border Region." In *Border Regions in Functional Transition. European and North American Perspectives*, eds. James Scott et al. *Regio* no. 9. Erkner, Germany: Institute for Regional Development and Structural Planning.

Gruchman, Bohdan, and Franz Walk. 1996. "Transboundary Cooperation in the Polish-German Border Region." In *Border Regions in Functional Transition: European and North American Perspectives*, eds. James Scott et al. *Regio* no. 9. Erkner, Germany: Institute for Regional Development and Structural Planning.

Hale, Ron. 1996. "Border Projects Due to Receive NADBank Funds." *naminews*. Issue 17. The North American Institute. <www.northamerican institute.org/naminews/issue17/news.html>.

Hansen, Niles. 1986. "Border Region Development and Cooperation: Western Europe and the US-Mexico Borderlands in Comparative Perspective." In *Across Boundaries: Transborder Interaction in Comparative Perspective*, ed. Oscar J. Martínez. El Paso: Texas Western Press.

Hartman, Pamela. 2000. "Hull: Douglas to Add 180 Border Agents," *Tucson Citizen*, April 27.

Haubrichs, Walter, and Reinhard Schneider, eds. 1993. *Grenzen und Grenzregionen*. Veröffentlichungen der Kommission für Saarländische Landesgeschichte und Volksforschung. Saarbrücken, Germany: Kommissionsverlag Saarbrücken Druckerei.

Heberlein, Horst Christoph. 1989. *Kommunale Außenpolitik als Rechtsproblem*. Cologne, Germany: Verlag W. Kohlhammer.

Held, David. 1995. *Democracy and the Global Order: From the Modern State to Cosmopolitan Governance*. Cambridge, U.K.: Polity Press.

Henselmann, Martin. 1999. "Haben Politisch Verfolgte in der BRD eine Chance auf Asyl?" Arbeitskreis kritischer Juristinnen und Juristen an der Humboldt-Universität zu Berlin, akj. <www.rewi.hu-berlin.de/AKJ/zeitung/99-2/asyl.html>.

House, J.W. 1981. "Frontier Studies: An Applied Approach." In *Political Studies from Spatial Perspectives: Anglo-American Essays on Political Geography*, eds. Alan D. Burnett and Peter J. Taylor. Chichester, U.K.: John Wiley & Sons.

Hull, Jane Dee. 1999. Address before 40th Plenary Session of the Arizona-Mexico Commission, Puerto Peñasco, Sonora, November 14.

Kaiser, Robert. 1998. *Regionale Integration in Europa und Nordamerika*. Baden-Baden, Germany: Nomos Verlag.

Keating, Michael, and John Loughlin, eds. 1997. *The Political Economy of Regionalism*. London, U.K.: Frank Cass.

Kettwig, Knut. 1994. *Rechtsgrundlagen dezentraler grenzüberschreitender Zusammenarbeit im deutsch-polnischen und deutsch-tschechischen Grenzraum*. Frankfurt/Main, Germany: Peter Lang.

Kolbe, Jim. 1999. Address at the first meeting of the President's Interagency Task Force on the Economic Development of the Southwest Border, Tucson, Arizona, November 15.

Lorey, David E., ed. 1993. *The United States-Mexican Border Statistics since 1900: 1990 Update*. Los Angeles, California: UCLA Latin American Center Publications.

Maillat, Denis. 1988. "Transfrontier Regionalism: The Jura Arc from Basle to Geneva." In *Perforated Sovereignties and International Relations: Transsovereign Contacts of Subnational Governments*, ed. I.D. Duchacek. New York: Greenwood Press.

Martínez, Oscar J. 1996. "Border People and Their Cultural Roles: The Case of the US-Mexican Borderlands." In *Border Regions in Functional Transition: European and North American Perspectives*, ed. James Scott, Alan Sweedler, Paul Ganster, and Wolf-Dieter Eberwein. *Regio* no. 9. Erkner, Germany: Institute for Regional Development and Structural Planning.

———, ed. 1986. *Across Boundaries: Transborder Interaction in Comparative Perspective*. El Paso, Texas: Texas Western Press.

McCaffrey, Barry R. 1998. "Organizing Drug Control Efforts along the Southwest Border." U.S. Office of National Drug Control Policy. San Diego, California, August 4. <www.whitehousedrugpolicy.gov>.

NADBank. 1999. *U.S.-Mexico Ten Year Outlook: Environmental Infrastructure Funding Projections*. San Antonio, Texas: NADBank.

naminews. 1996. "Border Volunteer Corps Killed." vol. 16. The North American Institute. <www.northamericaninstitute.org/naminews/issue16/news.html>.

Pau, Petra, and Katina Schubert. 1999. "Bundesgrenzschutz—eine omnipräsente und omnipotente Bundespolizei?" *Bürgerrecht & Polizei* vol. 62. <www.infolinks.de/medien/cilip/ausgabe/62/bgs.htm>.

Prescott, J.R.V. 1987. *Political Frontiers and Boundaries*. London: Allen and Unwin.

Purcell, Susan. 1997. "The Changing Nature of U.S.-Mexican Relations." *Journal of Interamerican Studies & World Affairs* vol. 39, no. 1 (Spring): 137–152.

Schröder, Dietrich. 1999. "Größte Sorge: Personalmangel." *Märkische Oderzeitung*. October 28, p. 9.

Schultz, Helga. 1996. "Die Oderregion in wirtschafts- und sozialhistorischer Perspektive." In *Grenze der Hoffnung. Geschichte und Perspektiven der Grenzregion an der Oder*, eds. Helga Schultz and Alan Nothnagle. Potsdam, Germany: Verlag für Berlin-Brandenburg.

Schultz, Helga, and Alan Nothnagle, eds. 1996. *Grenze der Hoffnung: Geschichte und Perspektiven der Grenzregion an der Oder.* Potsdam, Germany: Verlag für Berlin-Brandenburg.

Schwab, Oliver. 1997. "Euroregionen an der deutsch-polnischen Grenze—gefangen im Politik- und Verwaltungsnetz?" *Raumplanung und Raumordnung* vol. 1, no. 55. Jahrgang.

Scott, James Wesley, and Kimberly Collins. 1997. "Inducing Transboundary Regionalism in Asymmetric Situations: The Case of the German-Polish Border." *Journal of Borderlands Studies* vol. 12, nos. 1 and 2 (Spring and Fall): 97–121.

Seidl-Hohenveldern, Ignaz. 1994. *Völkerrecht.* Cologne, Germany: Carl Heymann Verlag.

Soguk, Nevzat. 1997. "Transnational/Transborder Bodies: Resistance, Accommodation, and Exile in Refugee and Migration Movements on the U.S.-Mexican Border." In *Challenging Boundaries: Global Flows, Territorial Identities*, eds. Michael J. Shapiro and Hayward R. Alker. *Borderlines.* vol. 2. Minneapolis: University of Minnesota Press.

Sprouse, Terry, and Clifford Brown. 1995. "The Emergence of BECC: New Approaches in Addressing Environmental Issues in the U.S.-Mexico Region." Paper presented at the 8th Annual Symposium of the Arizona Hydrological Society, Tucson, Arizona, September 14–15.

Stolpe, Manfred. 1997. "Die Zusammenarbeit in der Oder-Grenzregion enger knüpfen." Speech given by Brandenburg's Ministerpräsident (head of the State of Brandenburg) in Leipzig, Germany. June 20. <www.brandenburg.de/land/stk/reden/1997/p2306.htm>.

Taylor, Lynda. 1995. "Sustainable Development and the Border Environment Cooperation Commission (BECC)." Excerpts from an address to the U.S. Department of Commerce BECC/NADBank Outreach Meeting in Brownsville, Texas. September 29.

Tycner, Janusz. 1996. "Wirtschaft auf polnisch." *Die Zeit.* November 8, p. 19.

U.S. Department of State. 1998a. "Progress Report to the Presidents on the Initiative to Implement a New Border Vision." June 10. Washington, D.C., <www.state.gov/www/regions/wha/980610_border_vision.html>

——. 1998b. Secretary of State Madeleine K. Albright and Mexican Secretary of Foreign Relations Rosario Green Macías, Remarks at Press Conference at the Conclusion of the 15th Meeting of the U.S.-Mexico Binational Commission, Washington, D.C., June 11. As released by the Office of the Spokesman, U.S. Department of State. <http://secretary.state.gov/www/ statements/1998/980611.html>.

U.S. Environmental Protection Agency. 1996. "U.S.-Mexico Border XXI Program. Executive Summary." EPA 160-S-96-001, October. Washington, D.C.

U.S. General Accounting Office. 1999. "U.S.-Mexico Border: Issues and Challenges Confronting the United States and Mexico." Report to Congressional Requesters, GAO/NSAID-99-190, July. Washington, D.C.

———. 1996. "International Environment: Environmental Infrastructural Needs in the U.S.-Mexican Border Region Remain Unmet." Report to the Ranking Minority Member, Committee on Commerce, House of Representatives, GAO/RCED-96-179, July. Washington, D.C.

———. 1994. "North American Free Trade Agreement: Structure and Status of Implementing Organizations." Briefing Report to Congressional Requesters, GAO/GGD-95-10BR, October. Washington, D.C.

Varady, Robert G., et al. 1996. "The U.S.-Mexican Border Environment Cooperation Commission: Collected Perspectives on the First Two Years." *Journal of Borderland Studies* vol. 11, no. 2 (Fall). <http://udallcenter.arizona.edu/publications/publications.htm>.

Westlake, Martin. 1998. "The Book and the Man." In *The European Union Beyond Amsterdam: New Concepts of European Integration*, ed. Martin Westlake. London, U.K.: Routledge.

Wren, Christopher S. 1999. "D.E.A. Chief Warns Senate on Traffickers in Mexico." *New York Times*, February 25. <http://www.nytimes.com/library/world/americas/022599mexico-drugs.html>

Wulf-Mathies, Monika. 1998. "Beziehungen zum Ausschuß der Regionen, Kohäsionspolitik." Address by the EU Commissioner for Regional Policy, Brussels, Belgium. September 25. <www.europa.eu.int/comm/dg16/speeches/sp29_de.htm>.

Additional Resources

Andreas, Peter. 1998. "Escalation of U.S. Immigration Control in the Post-NAFTA Era." *Political Science Quarterly* 113 (Winter) <www.psqonline.org/andreas3.html>.

Arizona, California, New Mexico, and Texas Advisory Committees. 1997. *Federal Immigration Law Enforcement in the Southwest. Civil Rights Impacts on Border Communities.* Report to the United States Commission on Civil Rights (March).

Asiwaju, Anthony Ijaola. 1990. "National Boundaries Commissions as Problem-Solving Institutions: Preliminary Research Notes on Nigeria, Niger, and Mali." In *International Boundaries and Boundary Conflict Resolution*, ed. Carl Grundy-Warr. Durham, U.K.: Boundary Research Press.

———, ed. 1989. *Borderlands in Africa: A Multidisciplinary and Comparative Focus on Nigeria and West Africa.* University of Lagos, Nigeria.

Belausteguigoitia, Juan Carlos, and Guadarrama, Luis F. 1997. "United States-Mexico Relations: Environmental Issues." In *Coming Together? Mexico-United States Relations*, eds. Barry Bosworth et al. Washington, D.C.: Brookings Institution Press.

Beutler, Bengt, et al. 1993. *Die Europäische Union: Rechtsordnung und Politik*. Baden-Baden, Germany: Nomos Verlagsgesellschaft.

Blatter, Joachim. 1998. "Entgrenzung der Staatenwelt? Politische Institutionenbildung in grenzüberschreitenden Regionen in Europa und Nordamerika." Unpublished doctoral dissertation. Halle, Germany: Martin-Luther-Universität Halle-Wittenberg.

Brown, Seyom. 1992. *International Relations in a Changing Global System: Towards a Theory of the World Polity*. Boulder, Colo.: Westview Press.

Browne, Harry. 1996. "Waiting for NADBank." *Borderlines* 30, vol. 4, no. 11 (December). <www.psqonline.org>.

Clement, Norris, Paul Ganster, and Alan Sweedler. 1999. "Development, Environment, and Security in Asymmetrical Border Regions: European and North American Perspectives." In *Curtains of Iron and Gold: Reconstructing Borders and Scales of Interaction*, eds. Heikki Eskelinen, Ilkka Liikanen, and Jukka Oksa. Aldershot, Vermont: Ashgate.

Czempiel, Ernst-Otto. 1993. *Weltpolitik im Umbruch*. Munich, Germany: Beck.

Duchacek, Ivo D., ed. 1988. *Perforated Sovereignties and International Relations: Transsovereign Contacts of Subnational Governments*. New York: Greenwood Press.

Dunn, Timothy J. 1996. *The Militarization of the U.S.-Mexican Border, 1978–1992: Low-Intensity Conflict Doctrine Comes Home*. Austin, Texas: Center for Mexican American Studies.

Enders, Alice. 1996. "The European Agreements and NAFTA: A Comparison of Their Ends and Means." *Internationale Politik und Gesellschaft* no. 3/96.

Fischer, Joschka. 2000. "Vom Staatenbund zur Föderation: Gedanken über die Finalität der europäischen Integration." Speech by German Foreign Minister. May 12. Humboldt-University, Berlin, Germany.

Fry, Earl H. 1988. "Transsovereign Relations of the American States." In *Perforated Sovereignties and International Relations: Transsovereign Contacts of Subnational Governments*, ed. I.D. Duchacek. New York: Greenwood Press,.

Gradus, Yehuda, and Harvey Lithwick, eds. 1996. *Frontiers in Regional Development*. Boston: Rowman & Littlefield.

Groß, Bernd, and Peter Schmitt-Egner. 1994. *Europas kooperierende Regionen: Rahmenbedingungen und Praxis transnationaler Zusammenarbeit deutscher Grenzregionen in Europa*. Baden-Baden, Germany: Nomos-Verlag.

Hansen, Niles. 1994. "Barrier Effects in the U.S.-Mexico Border Area." In *New Borders and Old Barriers in Spatial Development*, ed. Peter Nijkamp. Aldershot, Vermont: Ashgate Publishing Limited.

Heinelt, Hubert, and Margit Mayer, eds. 1992. *Politik in europäischen Städten: Fallstudien zur Bedeutung lokaler Politik*. Berlin: Birkhäuser.

Keating, Michael. 1988. *State and Regional Nationalism: Territorial Politics and the European State*. New York, N.Y.: Harvester Wheatsheaf.

Knight, David B. 1991. "Introduction." In *The Geography of Borderlandscapes*, eds. Dennis Rumley and Julian V. Minghi. London, U.K.: Routledge.

Minghi, Julian V. 1991. "From Conflict to Harmony in Borderlandscapes." In *The Geography of Borderlandscapes*, eds. Dennis Rumley and Julian V. Minghi. London: Routledge.

NADBank. 2001. <www.nadbank.org/default.htm>.

Peach, James T. 1987. "Some Comments on the Current Status of U.S.-Mexican Cross-Border Relations." In *Cross-Border Relations: European and North American Perspectives*, ed. Sevine Ercmann. Zürich, Switzerland: Schulthess Polygraphischer Verlag.

Pechstein, Matthias, and Christian Koenig. 1998. *Die Europäische Union: Die Verträge von Maastricht und Amsterdam*. Tübingen, Germany: Mohr Siebeck.

Scott, James Wesley. 1996. "Dutch-German Euroregions: A Model for Transboundary Cooperation?" In *Border Regions in Functional Transition: European and North American Perspectives*, eds. James Scott, Alan Sweedler, Paul Ganster, and Wolf-Dieter Eberwein. *Regio* no. 9. Erkner, Germany: Institute for Regional Development and Structural Planning.

Seltzer, Nate. 1998. "Immigration Law Enforcement and Human Rights Abuse." *Borderlines* 50 vol. 6, no. 9 (November). Alberquerque, New Mexico: Interhemispheric Resource Center. <www.us-mex.org/borderlines>.

Singer, Alex. 1993. *Nationalstaat und Souveränität*. Frankfurt/Main, Germany: Peter Lang.

Solis, Arturo. 1998. "Human Rights on Mexico's Northern Border." *Borderlines* 51, vol. 6, no. 10. December. Alberquerque, New Mexico: Interhemispheric Resource Center. <www.us-mex.org/borderlines>.

Spalding, Mark J. 1999. "NADBank and the Public." *Borderlines* 53, vol. 7, no. 2 (February). <www.us-mex.org/borderlines>.

Spener, David, and Kathleen Staudt, eds. 1998. *The U.S.-Mexico Border: Transcending Divisions, Contesting Identities*. Boulder, Colo.: Lynne Rienner Publishers.

Stoddard, Ellwyn R. 1986. "Problem Solving along the U.S.-Mexico Border: A United States View." In *Across Boundaries: Transborder Interaction in Comparative Perspective*, ed. Oscar J. Martínez. El Paso, Texas: Texas Western Press.

U.S. Department of State. 2001. Joint Statement of the U.S.-Mexico High
Level Working Group on Migration. Press Statement by Spokesman
Richard Boucher, Washington, D.C., April 4. <www.state.gov/r/pa/prs/
ps/2001/index.cfm?docid+2013>.

Wessels, Wolfgang. 1998. "Flexibility, Differentiation and Closer Cooperation: The Amsterdam Provisions in the Light of the Tindemans Report." In *The European Union Beyond Amsterdam: New Concepts of European Integration*, ed. Martin Westlake. London, U.K.: Routledge.

Wirth, John D. 1996. "Advancing the North American Community." *American
Review of Canadian Studies* (Summer). <www.northamericaninstitute.org
/na_community/advancing.html>.

5

Made-to-Measure Strategy: Self-Governance Initiatives in the Dreilaendereck

Malgorzata Irek

LOOKING AT THE POLISH-GERMAN border, one might easily come to the conclusion that the sole reason for its existence is to give local people an opportunity for quick and easy profit. The border offers potential access to economic and social goods on both sides, and the differences in economic potential provide lucrative business opportunities. Inevitably, one wonders what are the agents shaping the prosperity of the border. How far is it influenced by "socioeconomic" background and historical heritage? To what extent is it an effect of a wise policy of central governments, or the work of the invisible hand of the market? To what extent was it achieved by local communities? To what extent,

This research has greatly profited from the help of interview partners from the four towns and the following people, who shared with me their information, documents, and personal networks, and I thank them all: Hanna B. Majewska, vice president of Via Regia in Goerlitz and chancellor of the Department of YMCA in Zgorzelec; Ireneusz Aniszkiewicz, deputy mayor of Zgorzelec; Ulf Grossmann, deputy mayor of Goerlitz; Erhard Gaertner, project manager in the Innovations Relay Center within the ETB in Goerlitz; Jerzy Ozga, former deputy mayor of Zgorzelec; Jozef Sontowski, vice president of the municipal governing body in Zgorzelec and officer of the local business clubs in Goerlitz and Zgorzelec; Mieczyslaw Wysoczanski, manager of a local firm, Dudex; Jan Olbrycht, president of the Silesian Parliament and former major of Cieszyn; Jacek Jakubiec, officer in the Euroregion Nysa; and Wladyslaw Komarnicki, managing director of Interbud-West in Gorzow and a member of the Polish-German Commercial Chamber.

if at all, is transborder cooperation on the local level necessary for the welfare of the area? Is there any interdependence between governments and local communities, and if so, can it be expressed in a measurable way?

Fieldwork conducted in January–June 1999 in Zgorzelec, Poland/ Goerlitz, Germany and Slubice, Poland/Frankfurt-Oder, Germany, towns split by the Polish-German border and their adherent municipalities, sought to answer those questions by tracing local initiatives and assessing their meaning for the respective communities. The data were acquired through standard fieldwork methods: participant and non-participant observation, unstructured interviews, primary sources such as official brochures and memoranda as well as unpublished reports and documents in local archives, local and regional newspapers, government bulletins, publications on research done by others—especially local scholars—as well as my findings from former fieldwork in this region. To avoid projection of any kind on the fieldwork materials, the interviews were not structured and, where possible, informal.[1] The interview partners were chosen to represent the border community in the most comprehensive way.

The majority of the fieldwork was in Zgorzelec/Goerlitz—situated in a picturesque mountain region of Luzyce/Lausitz on the southern part of the border, in the so-called "Worek Turoszowski," or in German "Dreilaendereck." The region has well-developed heavy industry and owes its name to a bag-like shape allowing for the physical proximity of Germany, Poland, and the Czech Republic.[2] A second pair of split towns of similar size, Slubice/Frankfurt-Oder, about 140 kilometers north of Zgorzelec/Goerlitz, was chosen as a point of comparison.

Background

Germany (about 357,000 square kilometers) has a 566 kilometer-long border with Poland (about 312,000 square kilometers) in the east and a border with the Czech Republic in the southeast, which have become the external borders of the European Union (EU). To appreciate the obstacles that need to be overcome before bridging the German-Polish border, one has to know its history of conflict, dating back to the early

Middle Ages. From the late eighteenth to the early twentieth centuries, Germany was one of the three powers that had divided Polish territory between themselves (Pobog-Malinowski 1991, 369–378). Poles were treated very nearly as slaves; to justify territorial domination, they were presented in Germany as an inferior race incapable of autonomy. In response, Poles developed a deep resentment of the German oppressors, enhanced after the Second World War by the fear that Germany would again invade. Poles are still deeply concerned that Germany's economic strength may be brought to bear on their assets if Poland enters the EU.

Poland was liberated from Germany in 1919, only to be invaded again 20 years later. As a result of the Second World War, Poland lost six million people out of 36 million, the country was looted, and its technical base, cultural goods, and intelligentsia were destroyed. Independence was lost, as was a huge amount of eastern territory—about 70,000 square kilometers—to Soviet Russia. In its place, Poland obtained about 30,000 square kilometers to provide a home for the "volunteer" resettlers from the East who had been expelled by the Soviet army and suffered under typical wartime crimes (*Deutsche und Polen* 1991). Because of this, the German government officially recognized the German-Polish border only in 1989 as an act of good will to ensure German unification. The German-Polish treaty of peace was only ratified 45 years after the end of the war, in November 1990.[3]

Meanwhile, Poland had signed a treaty of peace, mutual help, and friendship with the friendly GDR (East Germany), known as the Treaty of Zgorzelec. Despite the lingering wartime animosities and the conflict resulting from the fact that the border actually cut right across the middle of German territory, it was named the "Border of Friendship." Both states made efforts to demonstrate brotherly cooperation on the border, which usually only further aggravated the situation.[4]

Despite highly centralized systems of governance during the socialist period and the virtual impossibility of formal action at the local level, a tradition of informal contact and actions developed, providing the basis for present-day cooperation. These contacts were maintained during periods of open borders, which, unlike any border of a capitalist country, could be crossed by showing a normal ID, without a passport and usually even without an invitation.[5] In fact, it was through the employment of the Polish workforce commuting between the two sides of the border, long before the fall of socialism, that local authorities came to maintain regular contacts and that local people came to demonstrate initiatives in bridging the border. Their physical proximity forced neighboring communities to develop their own ways of cooperation, not necessarily adhering to the laws of their respective states, to which local authorities wisely chose to turn a blind eye.

The change in the political system brought decentralization of government, which allowed local communities more freedom to "take matters into their own hands." The international treaty of friendship concluded between Poland and Germany in 1991, in which Germany finally recognized its eastern border, provided a legal framework for cooperation between bordering regions on the local, communal level.[6] This trend was further strengthened by EU regulations and financial incentives, such as the PHARE and INTERREG programs, which fund two- or three-way cooperative projects. To tackle problems arising from differences in economic potential, several plans and concepts for cross-border cooperation have been devised (Kurcz 1992), including an effort to implement a maquiladora program (Janzen and Osekowski 1998, 187–202).

The new treaty, as well as the transition itself, has created a better environment for the old cross-border organizations like the multinational Parliament of European Border Towns and the AGEG, as well as the local ones. In the Zgorzelec/Goerlitz region they are: the trilateral "Begegnungscentrum Dreilaendereck," "The Congress of Silesian Cities," and the "Society of Lausitzian Towns," incorporating four German and two Polish towns. It also has made possible the rise of new structures such as Euroregions,[7] all aiming at creation of a common identity.[8] However, in practice all major decisions in Poland are still made at the central level,[9] which can be explained both by the fact that policy on the border must not clash with state interests and by a simple lack of relevant legal provisions, although the majority now originate through local pressure.[10]

The fall of the old system and the rise in German unemployment eliminated the demand for a legal Polish workforce, which traditionally had played a significant role in both local economies, since they were well paid and also acted as trading entrepreneurs in the two countries, both suffering from a poor distribution system and shortages of basic goods (Irek 1998, 12–13). Their place was taken by illegal workers, estimated at 500,000 by German authorities (Cyrus forth-coming).[11] Under the new circumstances, the German and Polish governments agreed to a rigid limit of employees granted permission to work by government bodies in the Polish capital, although the agreement does not take into account the specific needs of the border population.[12] In 1999 there were 17,000 legal Polish workers in Germany, working mostly on contracts in the building industry, as well as 200,000 seasonal workers in agriculture, with three-month work permits (Cyrus forthcoming). There are no restrictions on German employment in Poland, and the number of Germans working illegally is estimated at more than 60,000 (Komarnicki 1999).

Zgorzelec, Poland/Goerlitz, Germany

Profile

Zgorzelec and Goerlitz are two parts of a single town, which was divided in 1945 by the new German-Polish border going along the Nysa River. Zgorzelec, the Polish part, which was formerly just a suburb of Goerlitz, has 37,000 registered inhabitants (not counting its peripatetic traders, tourists, smugglers, prostitutes, and criminals from Poland and the former Soviet Union). It is a booming, rich town in very good economic condition, with a strongly developed small-enterprise sector and a huge gray zone dating back to postwar times.

Due to its truly peripheral geographical location, as well as its status as a border zone under the supervision of the Polish army, Zgorzelec used to be regarded as a place of exile for various social outcasts. Its population has always been multiethnic, with a mix of migrants from the eastern territories of Poland lost to Russia under the Yalta Treaty and from the poor regions of central Poland, as well as former convicts and ethnic minorities such as Ukrainians, Jews, and Greek communists who fled the Greek civil war. Aside from such novelties as green pepper, gyros, and other exotic foods, the Greeks also brought and developed opium production, which is why the town is a well-known center of the drug business. In the early 1990s the town became a Mecca for poor Romanians travelling west to wealthier countries, and recently Ukrainian, Belarusian, and Russian businessmen and illegal workers have appeared. There are also some contacts with the so-called "blacks"—illegal Asian migrants, who cross the Nysa River on their journey to the West. In this context, contact with Germans after the opening of the border was not a cultural shock. Indeed, it was quite realistic for both towns to develop a common Silesian identity.

The major factor facilitating the area's integration is the open border. Under the 1991 treaty, all Polish citizens who possess passports can cross the border as tourists. There is also a special border zone agreement, which allows the inhabitants of the region to cross the border on their normal ID,[13] as long as they stay within the zone. The reopening of the border in 1991 and the corresponding international treaty paved the way for the economic and cultural integration of both parts of the town. Zgorzelec and Goerlitz proclaimed that they are one European town, and even put up a monument to their own glory. This huge stone, which, as local people remember, previously hailed the glory of the Soviet Army, now has an inscription proclaiming the unity of Zgorzelec and Goerlitz.

Zgorzelec is flourishing, and at the time of this research had one of the lowest rates of unemployment in Poland. There is great purchasing power in the town, due to shadow activities resulting from the very existence of the border, which in turn gives occupation to numerous shopkeepers and the service sector. Generally speaking, the services are at least twice as cheap as on the other side of the border, and therefore attract German clients. This is especially true of the barbers, beauticians, and dentists, but also of night clubs and restaurants, not to mention brothels. There are also 70 new companies, of which 34 are joint ventures with German capital. The rich citizens of poor, economically disadvantaged Poland buy up ruined houses in rich Germany, which eliminates the need for the local authorities in Goerlitz to pay for their renovation.

While Zgorzelec has profited and is profiting from "the great migration westwards," Goerlitz, which now has only about 64,000 inhabitants, is decaying for the same reason. In the nine years since German unification, more than ten thousand of the best-qualified people have left the town, seeking a better life in the richer West. Heavy industry has collapsed and the unemployment rate is one of the highest in Germany—officially, 20 to 25 percent. In the meanwhile the situation has been further aggravated by the migration of the unemployed; German families of Polish extraction (known as Poles with German documents), living further into Germany, have come closer to their fatherland, their main economic motivation being the possibility of cheap shopping in Poland.

Even with these difficulties, the local authorities of Goerlitz demonstrate the utmost flexibility and common sense, trying to exploit all possible advantages of the border situation. Unlike the central government, they do not see the illegal employment of Poles as a threat to the German workforce because, as explained by an official publication of the Goerlitz Town Hall, "employing cheaper labor gives the possibility to save costs, which is vital for the new, inexperienced East German small businessman, who otherwise could not compete with the rich Western capitalist. . . . On the whole the illegal employment of Poles does not take jobs from the German workforce, but is instrumental in creating new jobs. Therefore any stringent action by border officials against illegal employment should not necessarily be approved of" (Timm 1996, 9).

Cross-Border Traffic

As mentioned above, the open border creates opportunities for residents of the region to take advantage of both countries without the necessity of permanent migration. They cross for a variety of reasons, including to shop, to work, and to visit families. The most common is "shopping tourism," whereby inhabitants of each country visit the other in search of unobtainable or cheaper goods, which are then usually taken home without paying customs duties. As long as the amounts are not obviously commercial this does not count as smuggling; usually the matter is at the discretion of the customs officer.[14]

Mixed German-Polish families also cross the border on a daily basis, as do children attending the international nursery and genuine tourists, artists, and members of different international friendship societies. Workers employed in Goerlitz and its vicinity also commute on a daily or weekly basis, although local authorities on both sides have no statistics on this. The legal Polish workers are primarily seasonal, contract workers who can prove that they are not taking a job from a German or EU citizen, as well as those who have a business or a joint venture company in Germany. There are also Polish craftsmen doing service on the German side by appointment. Most illegal Polish workers are employed in small businesses (men) and housekeeping (women). Similarly, "Dienstleistung- und Reparaturtourismus" (loosely translated, "service tourism") concerns mostly Germans, who seek cheap services in Poland but then do not declare them as an added value when recrossing the border, especially in the area of car servicing.

Since the Polish-German border is at this writing also the external border of the EU, problems like smuggling of people and drugs, illegal import-export, and prostitution occur there as well (though the problem will likely move east once Poland and the Czech and Slovak Republics join the EU). Citizens of different non-EU states do cross the German border illegally, chiefly to seek some sort of asylum, but they have little impact on the border towns since they try to move quickly far from the border. Ironically, illegal migration and people-trafficking contributes to the welfare of both cities, providing their citizens yet another chance for the quick accumulation of money. For both towns, a greater problem is the vagrant beggars, who commute between the two towns and live in train and bus stations.

Local Initiatives

As one of the local officials said, "Everything that happens on the border has started as the idea of some wonderful local fool." The difficulty is in creating the best environment for these ideas so that they may be implemented. The local community has long been trying to address this problem, so the recent increase in decision-making freedom has been well received, despite painful consequences such as the complete chaos in public health services. So far, local initiatives have been undertaken by local governments, business societies and individual businesses, and nongovernmental groups.

Many local initiatives take place in the context of Euroregions. Euroregion Nysa, which encompasses the Zgorzelec/Goerlitz area, was founded in 1991 on the initiative of local communal structures, with the blessing of the respective governments and the three presidents.[15] Its most valuable initiative to date has been the creation of common intervention forces in case of natural disasters or ecological catastrophes, which often happen in this heavily industrialized area. Before any decisions are made on the central level, the local communities use each other's resources across the border. Economic cooperation in the Euroregion, though, is described by all parties as insufficient and difficult, a problem since Euro funds are accessible only to two or more partners working on one project.

Town Halls

The town halls of both towns have long traditions of cooperation, forced on them by postwar economic difficulties, such as the fact that after the town was split in 1945, the water pumps were on the German side and the gas factory on the Polish side. In 1991, once they could make their own agreements and in response to the demands of the local population on both sides, the Rada Miejska Zgorzelca (Magistrate) and the Parliament of Goerlitz agreed to sign a "Contract for Partnership and Cooperation Between Goerlitz and Zgorzelec," amended in 1996. Two years later, in April 1998, the two towns declared their unity as one *Europastadt* (European Town).

Both sides agreed to "develop close contacts and work together in partnership and support the partnership by all means possible. The towns shall exchange ideas, knowledge, and experience,"[16] as well as support all initiatives leading to the improvement of the quality of life of their inhabitants. Four working groups include: industry, town planning, infrastructure, and economic co-operation; health and social care and the environment; culture, tourism, sport, education, and youth exchange; and order and security.[17] To stress the sense of partnership and equality, there is always a balance between Polish and German members in the Working Groups and treaties are signed by two German and two Polish representatives.

Another form of local government initiative at town hall level is the "Office for Culture and Information" founded in 1997, run by a German married to a Pole, and paid for by the Goerlitz Town Hall.[18] The Office publishes a quarterly information sheet, distributed to 18,000 households in Zgorzelec and its vicinity through the Polish post, listing all cultural events ("Informator: Biuro Kulturalno-Informacyjne

Zgorzelec-Goerlitz"). As an international organization located in Poland, it can claim funds from all sources sponsoring German-Polish friendship, such as the Friedrich Ebert Stiftung, local and state government funds, and especially PHARE and INTRERREG money. It also responds to a very urgent local demand for culture; Zgorzelec is a town with a growing number of nouveaux riches, who seek to show themselves at the theater, opera, music house, or picture gallery, none of which exists in Zgorzelec. On the other hand, decaying Goerlitz, with its picturesque old town, numerous museums, picture galleries, theater, ballet, opera house, theme park (with old-time train), planetarium, and zoo, is seeking to find an audience for its economically unjustified cultural enterprises.

This attempt by Goerlitz to be a *Kulturstadt*—"culture-rich town"—and draw tourists is also in the best interests of Zgorzelec, and both try to mark their presence in Europe by organizing as many international events as possible, such as the Feast of Silesian Music, the Gardening Exhibition, or an exhibition of children's paintings on the connecting bridge (Letza 1998). Another valuable initiative facilitating life on the border is the Internet link between the two town halls and the hot line between the two border guard units, which helped Zgorzelec notify its German counterparts when Polish skinheads chose to come to Zgorzelec to demonstrate their anti-German sentiment in reply to the infamous German provocation in Slubice/Frankfurt-Oder.[19]

Recently Goerlitz regional television was connected to cable television in Zgorzelec, and a local German newspaper, the *Wochenkurier*, is published in two languages and distributed via the Polish post. Advertisements in German, written by Zgorzelec inhabitants, state: "Polish woman accepts any work in Germany" (meaning any illegal work), or "Cheap windows made to measure,"[20] suggesting a Polish craftsman selling his products abroad at a competitive price, without paying border tax or value-added tax. All this occurs with the silent approval of the local authorities. The newspaper initially was published on the Polish side and distributed by Polish post against existing regulations, which subsequently were amended. Like many other border activities, the initiative came first and the formalities were satisfied later.

This cooperation between local authorities is independent of high-level political changes in both countries. The authorities in Goerlitz say, "Our aim is to make the border work to our advantage, not disadvantage." Indeed, the border secures every fourth job in the trade of the town. *Einkaufstourismus* (shopping tourism) is so important for Goerlitz that it has fought for two years to create a common bus line bringing Polish shoppers to its shopping centers.[21] The buses come both from Poland and Germany, and one can pay for the ticket either in marks or zloty. There are also special free "joy rides" organized for shoppers from such distant towns as Jelenia Gora, and offers are advertised in the *Wochenkurier*, as well as in commercial advertisements delivered to Polish houses. The major chain stores accept payment in Polish money, and advertisements are in two languages. German shoppers, tourists, and bons vivants also play an important role in the economy of Zgorzelec, as demonstrated by the open market created solely for German shoppers, with favored goods, prices written in German, and payment in German marks—which, although strictly illegal, is no longer prosecuted, or even noticed. Another initiative facilitating transborder integration is "Intertaxi," a system making it possible for taxi drivers (with special permission) to cross the border without queuing.

Business Associations

In sharp contrast to the very active town halls, business associations on both sides do not feel they are doing much, realizing that they are competing in the same market. The Poles have the advantage of much lower production costs, while the Germans profit from cheap credit and the trademark "Made in Germany."

Animosities on both sides are great enough to prevent initiatives such as a training course for Polish craftsmen, which was to be organized by the Society of Craftsmen in Goerlitz and Weisswasser and paid for with EU money, but the Polish Business Club and the Commercial Chamber of Zgorzelec preferred changes in those customs laws that prevent them from legally entering the German market.[22]

Despite the lack of direct business with each other, business associations are good for public relations and breaking down mutual prejudices. "We meet a lot but we don't do much," they say. "The Poles are not willing to cooperate because they are afraid of German excellence," say the Germans, while the Poles think of themselves as better craftsmen and refuse to accept any training. In the spirit of Euroregion, however, the local commercial chamber in the Jelenia Gora (Zgorzelec's district) changed its name to Euroregional Commercial Chamber and organized a trilateral conference discussing a new system of financing common enterprises and visions.

In 1993 the German Chamber of Commerce in Goerlitz, sponsored by EU funds, founded a consulting office for the Euroregion Nysa to foster transborder cooperation, support for local initiatives (especially small and medium "technically oriented" enterprises), and transfer of technologies between Polish, German, and Czech businesses. Called the ETB, it turns the peripheral geographic positions of the firms in the border area and their physical proximity to each other (meaning inexpensive transport) into an advantage marred only by long waits at customs. The official partners of the Goerlitz office are the Euroregion offices in Jelenia Gora and Liberec, and so far the firm has a thousand clients on the German side and as many Czechs and Poles on the other. These clients receive free advice about patents, information on possible partners (via a CD in four languages listing 450 small firms in the three countries), and information on available technologies and training programs. Moreover, it organizes an annual international conference about existing trading networks and public relations possibilities attended by the representatives of industry, trade and commerce, local and central governments, business associations, and commercial chambers. As an ETB officer stated, "These projects make it possible for small and medium producers of this ex-communist border area to mark their existence on the international market. Without our support they would stand no chance there" (Erhard Gaertner, project manager, IC, personal communication).[23]

Individual Businesses

For the individual businesses in the vicinity of Zgorzelec, successful transborder cooperation has deep roots preceding the Transformation, based on self-reliance and individual networking. Their welfare was strictly dependent on the border, and the visibility of their economic ties with Germany depended on how friendly conditions were. Like an iceberg, one could see only so much of the top, with the rest underneath in the "irregular economy."

As mentioned, 34 Polish companies are registered with German capital, mostly joint-venture companies using German capital, though there are also Polish companies with German citizens investing via a proxy Polish citizen. A common practice is to use cheap Polish labor on the Polish side using materials, usually textiles, brought from Germany to Poland. A ready-made product is then brought back to Germany with the label "Made in Germany." Often the Polish partner is some privatized, formerly state-owned plant looking for investors.

Although the textile industry has decayed in Goerlitz since the fall of communism, it has further expanded in the Zgorzelec area, prospering with privatization and the involvement of new German capital. Some firms continue the cooperation based on a good relationship that originated under socialism. A very popular activity of German companies is also the importation of cheap Polish building materials, which do not meet stringent German environmental regulations. Another common practice is for a German firm or individual to buy a ready-made house from a Polish firm for installation in Germany, making possible the employment of cheap, well-qualified Polish workers.

Polish citizens may also take part in a limited company on the German side, as exemplified by the entrepreneurial Polish builder who spotted a market niche in Goerlitz for restoration of historic houses and decided to do business in Germany without migrating there. With three Polish and four German citizens, he founded a limited company in Goerlitz with a 51 to 49 percent capital ratio and employed 40 highly qualified Polish restoration specialists and builders (taking advantage of the law in that there were no Germans available who could perform the job). Three years later he founded a new firm with one German citizen and 95 to 5 percent ratio of Polish to German capital, thanks to the flexibility and common sense of local authorities, who granted him a German visa as a person very much desired in Goerlitz. In the interim, however, legal grounds on which to hire Poles had been eliminated, since hundreds of women who had become unemployed after the collapse of the textile and optics factories had been retrained for the jobs in demand, including restoration specialists. Knowing that these inexperienced, retrained females often quit the harsh conditions of the building industry for health reasons and, in fact, could not replace the experienced, strong, and more effective Polish males, he reached a compromise whereby he employed one German worker for every Polish one.

There are also private consulting firms in Zgorzelec/Goerlitz, selling "know-how," mostly to small companies in other regions of Poland, Germany, and the Czech Republic, because the local companies in the border zone already possess the "know-how" and can simply go across the bridge and find their partners themselves or through the ETB, without having to pay a substantial fee of about 2,000 DM a year—which is about a third of an average yearly Polish income. The names of these firms are very similar, for example ECB or EDB, where "E" stands for "European" and "B" for "Bureau." They are fierce rivals of the ETB and the Goerlitz Chamber of Commerce, whom they accuse of "wasting the taxpayers' money" on expensive, useless projects and undermining the market for private consulting.

A fine example of a private-sector initiative is a consulting firm in Zgorzelec, a subsidiary of a German firm originated by a nearby citizen, who created an industrial database for the region due to the Transformation and joblessness, and discovered that Poland was a tabula rasa for the German entrepreneur. In the Polish branch, the staff are German-speaking Poles and the manager is a rare Polish-speaking German who commutes from Germany. Financially independent, the firm targets small and medium-size entrepreneurs (up to 20 employees) in both countries who are looking for new technologies, capital investments, possibilities to sell or buy products and raw materials, and to enter the EU market. For a fee it offers an Internet service in three languages and finds partners for cooperation without assessing their credibility. It is registered in the EU and uses its web site, but is not sponsored by any institution.

Nongovernmental Organizations

Although the numerous friendship organizations do not directly affect the economy of the border zone, they play a very important role in the area's integration, bringing people together and breaking down prejudices and animosities. They can also be described as hothouses of ideas for the betterment of the quality of life on the border. The most eminent are Via Regia and two Euro-Operas, whose names suggest linkage with the tradition of universal Europe.

Via Regia, named for the medieval trading route connecting Santiago de la Compostela in southern Europe with Kiev in the Ukraine and running through Goerlitz, was founded in 1990 by German Evangelical circles. Its goal is the "shaping of international spirit and raising of a truly multicultural society,"[24] and it holds weekly meetings in a Zgorzelec pub, where people from both countries enjoy themselves under the excuse of learning German and Polish. The first president of the organization is also the editor of a high-quality trilingual magazine, *Viadukt*, devoted to the problems of the border zone, and its vice president is a Polish teacher who devotes all her time and money to transcultural collaborations such as the exchange of Polish and German youth. In addition, Via Regia circles proposed creating a school for NATO cadets in the region to take advantage of the empty Polish army buildings and empty German flats and to address the growing crime rate.

The Euro-Operas also demonstrate initiative by local enthusiasts, with the first, founded by a German music hall director, suggesting a huge opera and music hall hanging as a bridge over the Nysa River, symbolic of ties across the border and home to numerous international events. (The "culture office" alone supported 26 German-Polish events just in 1998, not to mention activities of other permanent organizations like the Polish-German children's orchestra, or yearly meetings of musical families from the two countries. See Czajkowski 1998; Letza 1998.) A second Euro-Opera society was founded in Dresden (the district town for Goerlitz). Its chief achievements so far are a huge symbol of united Europe painted on the top of an historic Polish mill (the subject of dirty jokes by the local population due to its very organic shape) and a monopoly on the use of Jakub Boehme's house, given to them by Zgorzelec Town Hall and renovated with German funds.

Transborder contacts also are encouraged by the Catholic Church, which already had numerous transborder organizations such as the YMCA by the time of Transformation. Today, though, it is much easier to organize activities specifically connected with the border area, such as youth meetings or common trips along the border. The Evangelical Church in Goerlitz organizes numerous ecumenicist events such as concerts in churches or human brotherhood marches with lighted torches symbolically carried across the bridge. There is also an international "culture meetings center" (*Begegnungscentrum*) in a nearby cloister, and a similar center is planned on the Polish side. All are subject to fundraising, and financial loyalties seem to be national rather than religious despite the Church's universal character.

Overall Image

The general impression is that of an overwhelming spirit of local pride, initiative, self-help, and well-being, an official image presented to outsiders. Zgorzelec/Goerlitz present a coherent common policy, symmetry of power relations, and openness to the public. In both towns high-ranking officials are given responsibility for cooperation. Access to all the information for this study was facilitated by the general policy of the authorities of both towns, who were eager to give all possible help and information.

Slubice, Poland/Frankfurt-Oder, Germany

To get a better sense of whether the Zgorzelec/Goerlitz experience is typical for the German-Polish border, fieldwork was conducted in another pair of towns with similar backgrounds—Slubice/Frankfurt-Oder. In sharp contrast, the authorities in Slubice were rather unhelpful. They seemed focused on applying for EU funds and were not keen on giving any information about local initiatives for transborder cooperation.

The towns have a combined populations of approximately 100,000 inhabitants, as well as a common tradition of huge gray zones, problems with drugs, prostitution, and well-developed organized crime. Other similarities to Zgorzelec/Goerlitz include the experience of a transition to a market economy and employment of the local Polish workforce before the Transformation. Slubice's only big factory has collapsed, along with the state-owned farms, which were an important agent creating jobs in this agricultural area. Further, restructuring of the biggest production plant in Frankfurt-Oder eliminated 3,000 jobs, leaving the town with a 15 percent unemployment rate.

Members of commercial bodies complain about a lack of action to improve the commercial cooperation between the two towns and to help restore the lost jobs. They claim that their efforts to get into the German market and cooperate as partners are not supported, with the only smooth Polish export to Germany being the smuggling of cigarettes and trafficking "the blacks."

The general feeling in Slubice is that of being an insignificant player with no industry of its own, dominated by its powerful neighbor and having to accept the Frankfurt-Oder terms to obtain its goal, a significant difference from the sense of partnership existing in Zgorzelec/Goerlitz. A crowning example of the asymmetrical power distribution is the infamous Slubice/Frankfurt-Oder provocation, described earlier. Other examples include anti-Polish manifestations in Frankfurt-Oder, held at the Bridge of Friendship (border crossing with Poland), as well as numerous cases of attacks on Polish students in Frankfurt-Oder, on which the authorities refused to comment.

Nevertheless, as in the other cities, Slubice residents seem to be busy exploiting the border situation, profiting from the "irregular economic activities." Official data reveal that 5,490 of the total 17,000 inhabitants in Slubice have been registered as owners of an enterprise, which would mean that every third person in this town, including babies, invalids, and the aged, has been a business owner![25] This statistic does not include private medical services, insurance agents, more than 1,000 traders on the "German market," and the owners of casinos and other forms of entertainment (there are six big brothels in Slubice alone). This may explain why typical dwellings of the "unemployed" are double-glazed apartments with tiled bathroom and kitchen, each with good cars and its own satellite area for digital TV.

The local authorities concentrate on betterment of the economic situation of the town through foreign investment (private or institutional). An example of cooperation was development of the Polish counterpart of Viadrina (Germany), a subsidiary of the Poznan (Poland) university "Collegium Polonicum" with a campus for students from both towns (greatly envied by other border towns, especially Zgorzelec), which was founded with EU funds. Moreover, the publications founded by EU transborder cooperation programs have been used to pull in foreign investors, chiefly German, and to promote local small business on a larger scale. The cooperation of Frankfurt-Oder, infamous for its racist sentiments, with Polish Slubice is an example of how international funding can influence the situation on the border. Frankfurt-Oder is compelled to cooperate with Slubice, since it is no match for the nearby Berlin in terms of receiving prestige and funding. Thus, the welfare of both towns greatly depends on their common efforts to access international funds. The hope for changing the claustrophobic climate of Frankfurt-Oder is connected with the international milieu of students in the new European University, which was created in the spirit of Euroregion (both are named Viadrina) and which for the town itself is a matter of prestige.

In a telling difference, however, Slubice, unlike Zgorzelec, has no single body responsible for total cooperation and no high-ranking official specifically in charge of it. A single unit in the Town Hall is responsible for "promotion of culture and sport," and responsibility for commercial cooperation is dissipated among different departments, often in the hands of lower-rank officials, reflecting the reality of the low levels of cooperation. The office for "promotion of culture and sport," strategically placed next door to the office of Euroregion Pro Europa Viadrina (open only one day a week), was able to hand out official bulletins sponsored by EU funds. These bulletins paint a rosy picture of transborder cooperation and grandiose plans for the future such as building new Polish highways (cutting right across the last remaining rain forest), environmental improvements, encouragement of Polish export to Germany, and a common architectural concept for both parts of the town (Stankiewicz 1998). However, behind the elegant facade presented to outsiders, there is no real action. In fact, the authorities of both pairs of towns lack a platform on which they could exchange their experience and ideas. Their contacts with each other stem from a single fruitful meeting of representatives of towns split by the border, held in Gorica on the Slovenian-Italian border, where the idea of creating a Forum of Border Towns originated. The first meeting was to be held in 1998 in Cieszyn on the Polish-Czech border, but it did not materialize because of a lack of funding.[26] It appears from these two cases that it may be difficult to generalize about whether the ties and cooperation between Zgorzelec and Goerlitz are in fact typical of the German-Polish border.

Conclusions

The fieldwork materials, obtained by tracing local initiatives and assessing their meaning for the respective communities, have shown that local initiatives of transborder cooperation are in place and can significantly contribute to the general welfare of the area and successfully tackle its problems. The success of those initiatives depends mainly on the urgency of its problems, the degree of economic necessity, the common sense of local authorities, and the good will of inhabitants. The initiatives can be facilitated or made more difficult by the international political climate and the degree of understanding between the respective governments responsible for creating a legal framework for bilateral contacts between the local populations.

Further, this comparison of these two sets of localities situated on the same border has shown that in each place there is a need for a different strategy within the same legal framework and the same socio-historical background. This confirms the requirement of extreme flexibility at the border area which can be best guaranteed by granting possibly the largest freedom of decision making to the local authorities. In both pairs of towns, the communities had customized strategies of exploiting the border. Zgorzelec, with its strong industrial infrastructure, can be self-reliant and can afford partnership on equal terms with its German counterpart, Goerlitz; the small, insignificant Slubice, with no industry of its own, on the other hand, has to accept the Frankfurt-Oder terms to obtain its goal, which is getting foreign investment, be it private or institutional. The case of Frankfurt-Oder/Slubice proves that local initiatives also can be to some extent steered by governments and international organizations via funding, but a key factor shaping life on the border is a sheer wish for profit. However, the border situation can bring profit only if both sides agree and are allowed to cooperate.

It is the pragmatic approach of the local populations that allows them to overcome a centuries-old historical conflict, as well as practical obstacles, and to join hands in making the most of the border. Thus, examples of desirable practices include joint planning, Internet links, common bus lines, border universities, shared cultural institutions, establishment of communication channels (both "hot lines" that permit local governing bodies on both sides to communicate with each other and with representatives of decision makers on the central level of either states), and regular meetings of local governing bodies. It could also be useful to establish some international organization aimed at annual or biannual meetings of representatives of local governing bodies of cities split by the border in which information on the up-to-date best practices could be exchanged.

It also appears from the research that the respective central governments can do little to solve the problems of the local populations, simply because they are too far away to understand them and to react quickly enough. On the other hand, they can greatly aggravate any difficulties by insisting on strict adherence to regulations that often are sadly out of date, by imposing red tape on the simplest activities, and by neglecting the local communities' needs and ambitions—all under the pretext of "reasons of state"—a concept used as freely as that of a "symbol" in literature.

The ultimate implication of this research for the policy makers is that local communities of the border area should have the space, authority, and means of self-governance. It must be, however, within a framework that would not defy the "reasons of state" but which would provide complete flexibility, an absolute necessity for this area, which cannot be guaranteed by the central government. By the time such a framework is created, the main factor when dealing with the border should be simple common sense, rather than "going by the book."

Notes

1. The actors were asked to talk freely about life on the border and contacts with the other side. Other research was consulted only after the completion of preliminary analysis of the fieldwork materials. At that stage a list of specific questions—mainly concerning the missing parts of a puzzle— was prepared and directed to those actors who could possibly answer them.
2. Since Zgorzelec/Goerlitz could not be isolated from the network of other towns in the region, places were included such as Zittau, Germany/ Bogatynia, Poland/Visniova, Czech Republic; and Zawidow, Poland/ Habartice/Frydland/Liberec, the last three in the Czech Republic.

3. For an adequate description of postwar German-Polish relations see *Deutsche und Polen* 1991, 55–59.

4. During the serious 1980s economic crisis in Poland, German workers were told to work extra hours without pay or on a free day like Saturday or Sunday, for the sake of "Polenhilfe" (help for Poland). On the other hand, whole Polish border districts were regularly deprived of electricity (and heating), even when winter temperatures dropped to –25°C, because of "friendly help" for the GDR, which involved feeding Polish electric power into the German grid. As a result of such misguided central/international policies, any shortage of goods or services that was experienced on either side of the border was blamed on the neighboring country. (Irek n.d.)

5. The border had already been open to Polish workers since the 1950s, but to the Polish tourists only since the 1970s. It was closed early in the 1980s to prevent the Solidarnosc "bug" from penetrating the healthy East German state, although millions of Poles still crossed in transit to West Germany. Every Saturday GDR citizens "invaded" neighboring Polish towns like Zgorzelec and Slubice to buy up all possible foods, as well as desirable goods like jeans and leather clothes, contributing to immense Polish growth of private-sector production and services. Poles visited Germany to buy goods they lacked, such as shoes, children's clothes, and certain foods, but this did not contribute much to the region's welfare because there was practically no private sector in the GDR. On the other hand, the thousands of Polish workers commuting daily to German factories increased that country's GDP (Irek 1998).

6. For the text of the treaty see *Viadukt* 1991b, 14–15.

7. Euroregions are voluntary cooperations between municipalities and local entities in different nation-states, which coordinate cross-border activities in terms of economic development to encourage cross-border employment, investment, and economic activities. One of their consequences is to make old centers peripheral and former peripheries central. Another aspect of Europe's regionalization is the creation of eight megaregions for and by the EU, all explicitly transcending national borders and, at this writing, linked to particular policy areas ("areas of transregional cooperation" [European Union 1995]). As with EU regional policy generally, the rationale is to equalize economic and social development between different parts of Europe (Parkin 1999).

8. Unlike the Mexican-American border, until recently the binational population in this border area barely existed. The inhabitants of the Polish side are chiefly resettlers from the eastern parts of Poland granted to the Soviet Union by the Yalta Treaty. The population that claims German origins and cultural heritage lives deeper in the country, chiefly in Upper Silesia.

9. During my research, there was a change of administrative structure in Poland, which by January 1999 had replaced the existing 49 *Vojevodshafts* with 16 larger units as part of a decentralization process. Despite initial chaos, locals have been very optimistic about the change, hoping that their projects will no longer disappear in the governmental structures and that their lives will not be decided by some uncaring person in the capital.

10. The latter is the greatest problem for the new Polish democracy which, unlike the former GDR, did not inherit a coherent legal system appropriate to a market economy, nor the support of 20,000 highly trained West German bureaucrats and the advantages of EU membership. (See *Viadukt* 1991a.)

11. On the German side three illegal Poles are estimated for each legal one, though many Poles have dual citizenship, making them appear as Germans in the German statistics and as Poles in the Polish ones. These numbers seem negligible compared to the total populations, although they may be more relevant relative to the border population.

12. A crowning example of local flexibility, common sense, and good will occurred a few years ago when the Goerlitz hospital suddenly found itself without staff, since many East Germans, especially those well qualified such as nurses, had migrated westward in search of better payment after German unification. To solve the problem, Zgorzelec Hospital quickly arranged for its "superfluous" employees—70 nurses—to work in Germany.

13. Every Polish citizen obtains an ID at the age of 18. People traveling abroad must apply for a special travel passport issued by the Polish state. Additionally, a Polish citizen wishing to visit any of the non-EU countries usually has to apply for a visa issued by the authorities of the chosen country. During socialism, to obtain a West German visa one had to queue several days and nights in the German Embassy in Warsaw. Thus, crossing the border with only an ID is a great simplification.

14. According to a very rough estimate, German tourists spent about three billion deutsche marks yearly at the Polish border markets alone (Cyrus 2000).

15. The local municipalities in the participating states chose ten representatives each to form a Euroregion inauguration committee. Lacking the power to make decisions themselves on the international level, they also invited a representative of the state. They decided to create a separate Euroregion office in each of the three countries rather than one superficial international head office. The Polish head office is 60 kilometers from Zgorzelec in its district town of Jelenia Gora, the Czech head office is about 50 kilometers from Zgorzelec in the district town Liberec, and the German one is about 20 kilometers from Zgorzelec in a small town,

Zittau, on the Polish-Czech-German Border. (Jacek Jakubiec, officer in the Euroregion Nysa: personal communication.)

16. "Vertrag ueber die partnerschaftliche Zusammenarbeit zwischen den Stadten Goerlitz (BRD) und Zgorzelec (PL)."

17. The first group's objectives include developing a common concept for the urban development of the towns, common Internet representation, renovation of the Old Town, creation of more border crossings, and support of economic cooperation by private firms on both sides of the border. The second group focuses on health-service exchanges, implementation of the "Clean Nysa" program, cooperation in dangerous situations such as floods or fires, fighting the drug problem, and common training courses and conferences. The objectives of the third group include exchange of cultural achievements, development of education programs, common concepts of tourism and a "regional culture," organization of international sporting events, and organization of training. Finally, the fourth working group focused on working together in maintaining order in public places and in fighting crime.

18. The *Kultur- und Informationsburo* was formed to be a "binding agent between Zgorzelec and Goerlitz and simultaneously, a starting point for common projects."

19. German officials in Frankfurt organized a "trap" for illegal Polish workers. Leaflets advertising jobs in Germany were spread on the Polish side, with no detailed information other than the date and address of the meeting with the future employee (it happened to be at a shopping center). On the advertised day the job seekers, together with innocent shoppers, were ambushed by police with dogs and brutally arrested. The incident occurred in the early days of the Transformation, but vivid memories remain locally.

20. The *Wochenkurier* is a free paper which appears weekly in 40,311 copies plus 11,000 copies in Polish which are distributed directly to the households in Zgorzelec.

21. The idea of facilitating the movement of shoppers by creating a bus line began with a German citizen and was passed to the Goerlitz magistrate, followed by the mayor's office and the Coordinations Commission, which sent it to the respective governments for permission. Agreements were made with both sets of border guards for buses to pass the border without queuing (passenger cars can queue for up to 12 hours on each side). An agreement was signed with a German transport firm and with a Polish one. Now this is the only self-supporting, profitable bus line in Goerlitz.

22. Indeed, progress is moving backward, as attempts by Polish craftsmen to enter the German market have led to a requirement that all documents have to undergo nostrification (an exam taken in German in front

of the German Commission). Previously, diplomas and certificates of the Polish Chamber of Commerce were honored on the German side.

23. Cooperation with Poland generally is viewed as more fruitful than with the Czech Republic because of more competitive prices and quality, greater flexibility, and a greater willingness to cooperate.

24. From an unpublished manuscript by Hanna Majewska, the founder and president of the Polish branch of Via Regia: "Via Regia: kontakty Zgorzelec-Goerlitz."

25. The list of registered entrepreneurs, "Wykaz ilosci przedsiebiorcow od 1989.011.01 do 1999.11.03," is in the Department of Commerce in Slubice Town Hall.

26. Personal communication with Jan Olbrycht. Cieszyn/Tesin is an example of a situation comparable to the U.S.-Mexican border, in that a large population of Poles lives on the Czech side.

Works Cited

Cyrus, Norbert. Forthcoming. "Komplementäre Formen grenzüberschreitender Migration: Einwanderung und Mobilität am Beispiel Polen." In *Migration und Stadt*, ed. Klaus M. Schmals. Opladen: Leske und Budrich.

Czajkowski, Ralf. 1998. "Aktivitaeten des Kultur-und Informationsbuero im Jahre 1998." December 14. In the Archive of Miejski Dom Kultury in Zgorzelec.

Deutsche und Polen, Informationen zur Politischen Bildung. 1991. vol. 142/143 6897F. Bonn: Bundeszentrale fuer politische Bildung.

European Union. 1995. *Europe 2000+.* Brussels: European Union.

Irek, Malgorzata. 1998. *Der Schmugglerzug.* Berlin: Das Arabische Buch.

———. n.d. "Common Sense." Unpublished.

Janzen, J., and C. Osekowski. 1998. "Niemieckie koncepcje wspolpracy na pograniczu z Polska (1990–1992)." *Studia Zachodnie* vol. 3.

Komarnicki, Wladyslaw. 1999. "Report on German Protectionism." In private archives of Interbud-West in Gorzow, Poland.

Kurcz, Zbigniew. 1992. "Pomysly na pogranicze polsko-niemieckie." *Odra*, no. 11.

Letza, Wieslawa. 1998. "Zalocznik do sprawozdania MDK, dotyczacy wymiany kulturalnej Zgorzelec-Goerlitz: Wykaz inicjatyw popartych przez Kulturbuero." December 16. In the archives of MDK w Zgorzelcu.

Parkin, Robert. 1999. "The Development of Regional Identities in an Integrating Europe: A Challenge to the Nation State?" In *Transnational Communities*, ESRC Programme Working Papers.

Pobog-Malinowski, Wladyslaw. 1991. *Najnowsza Historia Polityczna Polski.* vol. 1. Gdansk: Oficyna Wydawnicza Graf.

Stankiewicz, Maja. 1998. *Slubice.* Bydgoszcz: Tekst.

Timm, Joern K. 1996. "Die Zusammenarbeit zwischen Goerlitz und Zgorzelec." In *Saechsische Staatskanzlei*—IV. Goerlitz: Town Hall publication.

Viadukt, Ein Journal fuer die schlesische und sachsische Oberlausitz und ihre Umgebung. 1991a. No. 5/6: 5.

———. 1991b. "Vertrag zwischen der Bundesrepublik Deutschland und Republik Polen." *Dokumentation.* No. 7/8 (July-August): 14–15.

Additional Resources

Goerlitzer Wochenkurier. 1999. March 3.

Information Bulletin. 1998/1999. "Informator: Biuro Kulturalno-Informacyjne Zgorzelec-Goerlitz." 12/01/01/ 1988/99; 03/04

Komarnicki, Wladyslaw. 1999. "Report on German Protectionism." In private archives of Interbud-West in Gorzow, Poland.

Kostrzyn-Slubice. 1998. *Special Economic Zone.* Bydgoszcz: Tekst.

"Vertrag ueber die partnerschaftliche Zusammenarbeit zwischen den Stadten Goerlitz (BRD) und Zgorzelec (PL)." 1993. December 2. In the Archives of Town Hall Zgorzelec.

PART THREE

Russia

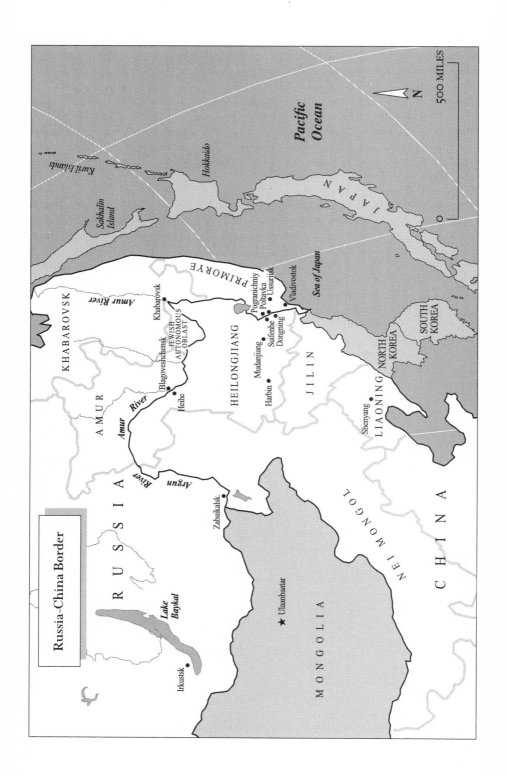

Russia-China Border

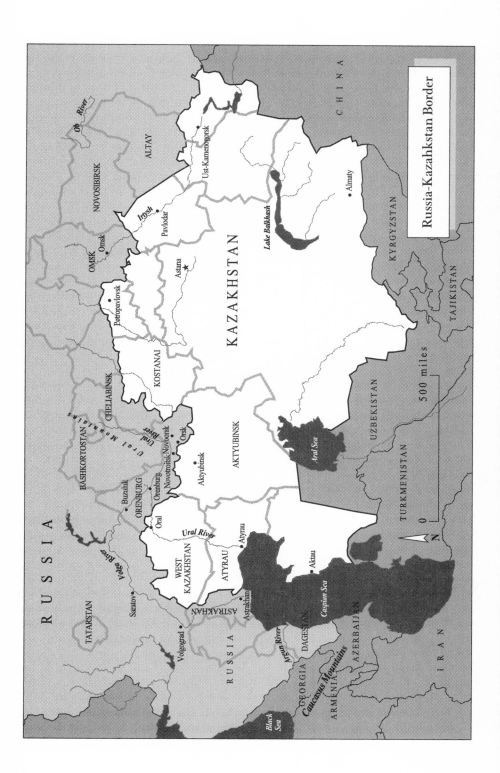

Russia-Kazahkstan Border

6

At the Crossroads: Russian-Chinese Border Interactions

Viktor Larin and Anna Rubtsova

IN THE EARLY 1990s, after the collapse of the USSR, Russia faced growing migration from outside its borders that required creating new state and regional structures to manage it and to develop a new migration policy. The USSR's disintegration and the regionalization process that weakened ties between the federal center and regions made regulation and coordination of migration issues more difficult but also gave the Russian regions a good deal of independence in certain spheres, such as establishment of direct ties with the governments of neighboring territories on the issues of cross-border trade and tourism. While the process has contributed much to the development of regions, it also has caused some difficulties and contradictions in relations with the federal center, such as when documents adopted by regional authorities contradict federal law or when some federal laws are ineffective because they contradict the interests of the region.

Although it has been very difficult for the authorities of both levels to find "the golden mean," federal and regional interests must be balanced to help maintain stability in the country. That is why the destiny of Russia's Far East region, strategically important because it borders the Asian-Pacific region, as well as the issue of Chinese migration, cause controversial discussions among federal and regional mass media, scholars, and politicians. This chapter aims to understand and address not speculations, but the realities, of Chinese migration to

Russia's Far East, including how many Chinese live in Russia (legally and illegally), what their interests are, how they fit Russia's federal and regional interests, the nature of Russian-Chinese interactions, the influence of Chinese migration on Russia, and future prospects and processes for control at both the federal and regional levels.

Methodology

This chapter is based on two studies: the results of a Carnegie Moscow Center project on Chinese migration to Russia funded by the Ford Foundation and the MacArthur Foundation, and a survey and field visits engaged in for this project. The former includes several field studies in 1996–97, 1998, and 1999 in the Russian Far East and the Moscow region, and two trips to the Russian Far East in 1998 and 1999.[1] The latter includes an analysis of the replies of survey participants—72 employees (39 Russian and 33 Chinese) of different organizations and 26 experts (14 Russian and 12 Chinese)—regarding the state of Russian-Chinese relations, common perceptions, and prospects of these relations. It is also based on the field observations from three field trips and meetings in both Russia and China.[2] The survey's geographic area, as well as a list of the survey participants and the experts (those whose job it is to analyze and evaluate Russian-Chinese relations) are presented in Tables 6.1, 6.2, and 6.3.

Analysis of the survey replies were informative regarding the professional level and personal qualities of people working on Russian-Chinese interactions. For instance, organizational interests often led individuals to narrow mental outlooks, passive responses, and a limited scope of thought, due to their lack of a regional or national understanding of the problems of Russian-Chinese interactions. In contrast, the experts' higher levels of education and analytical ability, and their deeper involvement in the Russian-Chinese interaction process, provided them with a wider outlook and let them evaluate the border situation more critically, including making suggestions on how to raise effectiveness and extend the sphere of collaboration.

TABLE 6.1
Survey Participants in Russia

	Officials	Federal organizations	Science education	Business	Tourism	Transport	Others	Total
Vladivostok	3	–	2	2	1	–	–	8
Blagoveshchensk	5	3	1	1	2	2	2	16
Khabarovsk	4	–	2	–	1	–	–	7
Ussuriisk	–	–	1	1	–	–	–	2
Pogranichny	–	–	1	–	–	2	1	4
Dal'nerechensk	1	–	–	–	1	–	–	2
Total	13	3	7	4	5	4	3	39

TABLE 6.2
Survey Participants in China

	Officials	Federal organizations	Science education	Business	Tourism	Transport	Others	Total
Harbin	1	–	1	11	4	–	–	17
Dongning	–	–	–	2	2	–	–	4
Heihe	–	–	–	1	1	1	–	3
Suifenhe	2	–	–	6	1	–	–	9
Total	3	–	1	20	8	1	–	33

TABLE 6.3
Russian and Chinese Experts Participating in Survey

	Officials	Federal organizations	Science education	Business	Tourism	Others	Total
Russia	7	1	2	2	–	2	14
Including:							
Vladivostok	1	1	1	–	–	1	4
Blagoveshchensk	3	–	1	–	–	–	4
Khabarovsk	2	–	–	–	–	–	2
Ussuriisk	–	–	–	1	–	–	1
Pogranichny	1	–	–	1	–	1	3
China	1	–	3	5	3	–	12

Background

Previously closed and tightly controlled by Moscow, Russia's Far East now has a relatively open 4,259-kilometer border with China.[3] It also faces fundamental imbalances in the distribution of population and resources; Russia is resource-rich and population-poor, while China is population-rich and resource-poor. Both national and regional Russian press and officials express their alarm over the problem of a "yellow threat." They fear that with mass resettlement from China, Chinese can outnumber Russians in the Far East region, endanger Russian security by separating the Far East from Russia, aggravate competition on the Russian labor market, create social tensions, drain natural and hard currency resources, and worsen the crime rate and sanitary and epidemic situation in Russia. While some of these fears may indeed have a sound basis in reality, it is essential to understand why this situation has arisen and to evaluate the concerns. The realities include asymmetries in population size and rates of employment and weakened ties between the Far East and the rest of Russia, circumstances which portend the inevitability of Chinese migration to Russia.

Demographics Along the Border

Estimates show that the population density of territories near the border of the Russian Far East region is ten to fifteen times less than in the neighboring Chinese provinces. According to the statistical data, the population of the Russian Far East numbered just over 7.3 million people in 1998 and was decreasing, while the population of the northeastern part of China numbered 106 million people and was increasing. (Of these, 7 to 8 million, the equivalent of Russia's Far East population, are unemployed.) The population decrease in the Far East is exacerbated by an outflow to European Russia and to the Ukraine, as well as by natural population loss. From 1993 to 1998 the population of the border regions decreased by 456,000 people, nearly a quarter of Russia's two million population loss. Russia lacks the demographic and economic resources to carry out significant population resettlement programs to its Far East regions.

Reliable information, though, is lacking regarding the size, composition, and behavior of the Chinese population in Russia. Size estimates vary from 500,000 up to 2.5 million or even five million.[4] Nevertheless, the 1996–97 and 1998–99 Carnegie Moscow Center surveys, using data from the Federal Migration Service, the Federal Border Service, local experts, and local passport/visa services, showed that the number of Chinese in the Far East region is overestimated by the mass media and by those political leaders who prefer to gamble a "Chinese card" in order to get more money transfers from the federal center. Some Far East experts estimate that the number of Chinese in the Far East in 1992–93 did not exceed 50,000 to 80,000 including some 10,000 to 15,000 legal contract workers and 10,000 to 12,000 students (Minakir 1996, 94). There are also shuttle traders who arrive in Russia in order to sell their goods and then return to China, but the number of registered permanent residents is very small.[5] (Vitkovskaya 1997, 10). It is doubtful that the number of illegal aliens exceeds the number of legal migrants. According to the Interior Ministry officials in Primorsky krai (Primorye's local administrative unit), the share of those tourists who left this krai of Russia on time (tourists are the major source of overstayers) was 64 percent in 1994, 68 percent in 1995, and 97 percent in 1997, while in 1997–98 it exceeded 99 percent. That works out to about 6,000 to 7,000 individuals in 1994–95, about 600 in 1996, about 350 in 1997. These figures prove that this migration is not as uncontrolled as many people try to present it, and that the number of Chinese illegals on the Russian territory is not as large as is claimed by some officials.

Reasons for Chinese Interest in Russia

As mentioned, internal demographic pressures had caused high unemployment in China (Jilin province alone had 100,000 "awaiting jobs"), leading Chinese authorities to desire expanded economic interactions with Siberia and the Russian Far East to further socioeconomic development. They focused on exporting produce to Russia, services oriented toward Russian tourists and businessmen, and an increase in the number of Chinese merchants in Siberia and the Far East, with the border towns becoming outlets to the Russian market as well as bases oriented toward the export of industrial and agricultural manufacture. Cooperation with the South of China and development of relationships with the North (the countries and areas of Northeast Asia) became the official Chinese government policy as early as 1986, with special policies for each province regarding its economic capability, geographical location, and natural resources.[6] New rules regarding how to govern the border areas were introduced by China in 1988, with two zones of economic collaboration that had proven to be the most viable and Russia-oriented—Heihe and Suifenhe—taking the leading role. In fact, the State Board of China promulgated a special decree (#21) that created border economic collaboration zones for these almost unknown settlements.[7] Chinese authorities and businessmen recognize the role and responsibility of the governments of both countries in the development of border relationships, as exemplified by the mayor of Suifenhe, who believes that the city owes its prosperity primarily to the government of China. In contrast, neither the Russian government nor the government of Primorye takes into proper consideration the development of Suifenhe's Russian counterpart, Pogranichniy, which has not changed much over the last ten years.

Characteristics of Chinese Migration to Russia

Chinese migration to the Russian Far East is predominantly commercial, with Chinese migrants primarily engaged in wholesale and retail trade, followed by study or training, and work on a contract basis. The majority of Chinese migrants who came for study or training, however, do not study, or give up their study to start trading or other business shortly after their arrival, particularly since the 1992 signing of the Russia-China agreement on visa-free border crossing for tourist groups (it included rather affordable tour prices and relatively easy procedures for gathering documents).[8] These agreements favored an inflow of Chinese tourists, mostly shuttle traders taking cheap goods and agricultural products to the Far East. The peak year for Chinese crossing the Russian border was in 1998, when there were about half a million crossings. Their presence is viewed positively by the local population, given the economic recession and high unemployment in the Far East, irregular salary payments, and small pensions.

The shuttle traders' usefulness, and an example of the flexible approach of local authorities and their ties to the local Chinese community leaders, is the twenty-four-hour Chinese market in the town of Ussuriisk. It is the largest in the region, well organized, and considered successful. It has a capacity of 1,500 places, with some 800 Chinese trading there in the daytime and 200 at night. Chinese merchants live in two-leveled vans in which the first level is a trading place while the second one is a living apartment. A hotel complex on the market territory offers reduced prices for frequent visitors, with warehouses, a restaurant, a casino, karaoke, and laundry. The city budget receives yearly about seven million rubles (approximately $300,000) of taxes from this market. The Russian director has some ethnic Korean deputies as mediators between the Chinese and Russians.[9] All merchants are obliged to pass through the sanitary control, and there is a system of penalties for leaving garbage on the market's territory. The criminal rate is very low because the merchants want good relations with the local authorities and thus search for and punish violators themselves. Also, the market protects Chinese merchants against violations of the law by providing law enforcement bodies and security for local inhabitants. The market administration is planning to cooperate with the Chinese police in searching for those who committed crimes on the Russian territory and fled to China. But unfortunately, this example of a successful and mutual cooperation is not common in the Far East.

The Economic Situation in the Russian Far East

Weakened ties between the Russian Far East (whose financial needs had been half subsidized when it was supplying the military-industrial complex) and the other regions of Russia have led to a deterioration of the region's economic situation. Primorsky krai's industrial production in 1996, for example, was 53 percent of that in 1991, Khabarovsky krai's was 29 percent, and Amur oblast's was 39 percent. Growing prices for energy and transportation costs also made it difficult to deliver consumer goods and food from the European part of Russia. Since 1992, the Far East has suffered a number of crises, such as the 1992 food crisis (partially softened by the possibilities of cross-border trade with China) and energy crises in the winters of 1993, 1994, 1996, and 1997.[10] The deteriorating economy and reduced interactions with the rest of Russia have led the Russian Far East to become increasingly dependent on neighboring Asia-Pacific countries such as China (in 1993 over 90 percent of commodity circulation in Amur oblast, and 65 percent in Khabarovsky krai, were with China; see Figure 6.1).

Crossing the Border

There are thirteen border passes between China and the Russian Far East, some of which are used for cargo and others for people (there are five in Primorye, two in Khabarovsky krai, three in the Jewish autonomous area, three in Amurskaya oblast).[11] The border crossing, poorly organized and slow, with a nonexistent service standard, poses yet another stumbling block to the development of trade and the exchange of people.[12] In 1996–1999 about 200,000 to 280,000 Chinese and about 250,000 to 300,000 Russians traveled through these passes yearly, including a significant number of Russian "commuter merchants" and Chinese traders.

FIGURE 6.1
Primorsky Krai and Amur Oblast Trade with China

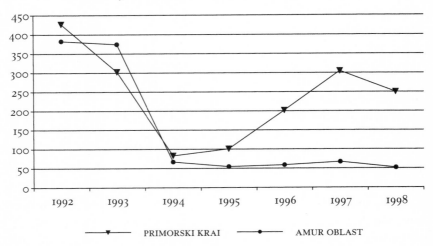

Source: Monthly Bulletin on Trade with Russia & East Europe. July 2000. p. 130, 135.

As of May 2000, only trip buses were allowed to cross the border, with a Suifenhe transportation company managing the trips from the Chinese side and two companies monopolizing the service on the Russian side.[13] At Sosnovaya Pad, a ten-minute ride from the village of Pogranichniy, the Chinese have expanded the pass to eight crossing lanes for people, instead of four, and the railway station expanded from three to six. Chinese authorities say it takes approximately ten seconds to check one person on the Chinese side and two to three minutes on the Russian side. Russian customs officials attribute the difference to the Chinese not checking the personal luggage of "commuter merchants." There is a serious threat of drug smuggling from China and that of valuable wood and fish resources and undeclared currency from Russia, which makes Russian customs check the luggage carefully.

Russian checkpoint soldiers have a good reputation among Russian tourists and "commuter merchants." They are considered sympathetic and honest, but their attitude toward the Chinese is quite strict, due to the number of Chinese trying to enter Russia with incorrect documents and fake passports; bribes are not uncommon. Generally, the actions regarding border crossings in both countries do not favor foreigners, since regulations are not clearly formulated. This leaves the authorities in charge of border crossings to interpret regulations. "Commuter" group leaders say that every one of them is obliged to "thank" customs off the record for favorable attitudes when being checked, often by allowing the customs employee to take something that looks nice to him or her.

Crossing the border on the Chinese side is not complicated for those who do it regularly, since problems are easily resolved with bribes.[14] Interestingly, businessmen seem more respected than scientists. Our researchers were not allowed to visit Suifenhe, which can mean that the Russian-Chinese agreements about a Suifenhe/Pogranichniy free trade zone in reality exist only on paper. The vice-governor of Khabarovsky krai also was not allowed to pass by the Chinese border staff when he tried to find out how the Free Trade Zone works.

Russian and Chinese survey participants remarked that over the last few years the Chinese have improved their customs service, whereas that on the Russian side possibly worsened, except for those who travel by air and go through the international terminals in Vladivostok and Khabarovsk. Despite the long, tiring, inefficient, and sometimes humiliating process, most Russians do not see a great problem, simply accepting that "Customs just torments people," according to one survey participant. Their tolerance may relate to the progress made since the low point of 1993 and 1994, when Russian administrative and federal structures were reorganized and crossing was both chaotic and a danger to people's physical and emotional well-being.

Levels of Cross-Border Interactions

After being closed for nearly 30 years, demilitarization of the Russia-China border, liberalization of trade, and removal of the "iron curtain" provoked a kind of euphoria, causing an initial lack of migration control and numerous violations of the law. Many citizens of China stayed in Russia without registered documents, and many became proprietors of lands and estates, often purchased indirectly through dummies. No appropriate legislation existed to regulate these issues. However, instead of finding ways to legalize Chinese migrants, such as developing different categories of resident permits or creating conditions for civilized leasing of property and land, the Russian migration service drastically changed its policy from one of "open border" migration to one with strict limitations on entry.

Russian-Chinese interactions today have been formalized by a series of international agreements and contracts, which control the process of political and economic interaction between these two countries with otherwise limited contact.[15] Interactions are international, national, regional, or individual, although this chapter focuses on the nature of regional and local interactions by government bureaucrats, businesses, individuals, and nongovernmental organizations.

International

This level refers mainly to the sphere of "high politics" rather than economics, since international trade stagnated in the second half of the 1990s against a background of active political rapprochement and joint diplomatic actions whose goal was a "strategic partnership."

The international level of Russian-Chinese border interaction connects with others in the sense that it defines, but does not regulate, interactions at lower levels. These border contacts, though, have been handicapped by the lack of a legislative basis for their existence and development, particularly prior to November 1997. At that time, an "Agreement on principles of collaboration between the Russian Federation and Chinese provinces, autonomous regions, and cities" was signed in Beijing, establishing legal and formal bases for the regional level relations. Also in February 1998, the Russian and Chinese governments reached agreement, valid in the border areas as of June 1999, about simplifying the way Russians and Chinese citizens could trade. It provides a simplified border crossing for Russian Federation citizens (by means of valid passes meeting criteria set by Russian and Chinese law) to trade centers in Heihe and Suifenhe and for Chinese citizens (by means of valid overseas passports without visas) to trade centers in the towns of Zabaikalsk, Blagoveshchensk, and the village of Pogranichniy.

National

In 1993, the Russian presidential decree "On the Measures on Implementation of Immigration Control" introduced immigration controls at the border checkpoints. In 1994, the decrees "On Immigration Control" and "On Measures on Preventing Uncontrolled External Migration" also were adopted, providing for the formation of immigration posts in towns of Primorye, Vladivostok (both seaport and airport), Nakhodka, and in the railway station of Grodekovo. Following the visit by then Russian Prime Minister Chernomyrdin to the Far East, however, the Russian government unilaterally canceled its policy of a de facto "open border" and imposed a visa regime of entry for Chinese in January 1994. Visas cost from $50 to $150, and quotas for Chinese workers were fixed, although a January 1994 consular agreement with China allowed those with diplomatic and official passports entry to China and Russia without visas. Those who had regular passports, however, could not freely travel to China and Russia (unless they were in tourist groups using the visa-free crossing). New customs and excise duties also were imposed, which had a negative impact on border economic relations and favored the rise in shuttle trade. Thus, federal policy moved toward strict controls, limiting immigration and the rights of Chinese on Russian territory (Vitkovskaya 1997, 19).

Regional

At the same time, however, the regions were getting more independence regarding migration policy. For instance, tourism committees in the Far East joined with border services and passport and visa departments to develop and sign agreements with neighboring Chinese provinces on border tourism in order to regulate the process of border crossing. According to the agreement signed by Primorsky krai with the China province Heilongjiang, special letters of invitation were issued for registered groups of Chinese tourists. This facilitated and regulated the number of Chinese tourists and tourist agencies, but the system was canceled in 1997 when the border checkpoint between Primorsky krai and Heilongjiang was placed under the jurisdiction of the Far East Border District.[16] Study tours again grew popular in 2000 but face obstacles such as long waits at the border and bad roads.

Formally, the exchange between regional bureaucrats is rather active. Informally, though, this bureaucratic level seems to make little difference in terms of organizing and conducting business activity or individual exchanges. One of the experts noted that "rare and usually formal official contacts do not have any significant influence upon the development of regional contacts." Authorities' representatives' meetings rotate between Russia and China irregularly, with the host country paying expenses. The outward result of this situation is hundreds of visits and banquets, as well as agreements and contracts, which are not very meaningful and are left, for the most part, on paper. Intercity contacts (Blagoveshchensk/Heihe, Ussuriisk/Mudanjiang, Suifenhe/Pogranichniy, and others) also have a formal and ceremonial flavor, not correlated with the development of trade and personal contacts.

A major part of such agreements, which flourished in the 1990s, were documents that determined the main areas and orientations of the interaction and provided some means for realization of the desired collaboration.[17] Most agreements did not yield practical results, lacking either mechanisms for accomplishment of the agreements, delegation of responsibility for their fulfillment, or continuity in staff changes in local administrations and legislative organs. That periodic bureaucratic attempts on the Chinese side to regulate border interactions and reduce corruption also failed to bring about significant change was attributed by many to Russian indifference.

Nonetheless, regional authorities often have a decisive word in determining visa regimes and residence permits (the so-called "propiska") at the regional level. Border regions have the right to define quotas for attracting contract labor workers as part of the regionalization of migration policy.[18] Local authorities try to attract Chinese contract workers because they are cheaper than Russian ones, very undemanding and hardworking, and are ready to live in any conditions. Local authorities also have a great influence on the fate of shuttle traders who come to Russia with tourist visas and who constitute most of the Chinese migrants to Russia.[19] Penalties collected from merchants overstaying their visas supplement local budgets, while filling the pockets of some officials and local policemen. This leads authorities to be particularly apprehensive about losing real power over the territory as tougher control measures increase the number of illegal migrants by pushing them toward illegal business, which reduces the state's control over the situation.

Individual

Many Russian-Chinese interactions occur as individuals engage in "business" or educational tourism on both the Russian and Chinese sides, although there are also criminal and cultural ties. Individual business relationships are limited by several circumstances. First, it is complicated to legalize the necessary documents for the consulates in Shenyang (Liaoning Province) and Khabarovsk, in addition to which the consulates are inconvenient for those who live in Primorye and Amurskaya region in Russia and in Heilongjiang Province in China. Second, it is difficult to cross the border, and a one-time visa is quite expensive ($50), even for businessmen, leading many to disguise themselves as tourists, which is cheaper and quicker, though a tourist group must include at least five people and allows limited movement and stay. Third, a deep gap remains between the two peoples in psychological and cultural aspects. However, these problems have not affected criminal activity, as cross-border interactions often are protected by authorities and federal organs. Criminals are involved in mass smuggling of contraband such as wood, fish, non-ferrous metals, wild forest plants, rare fish products, and drugs. This smuggling is the only real, Chinese-related threat to Russian security, but ironically it is spawned not by China, but by the Russians themselves.

In 1997, 449,000 people (of whom 146,600 were tourists) traveled from China to Russia; in 1998 that number was 464,200 (of whom 198,600 were tourists). The major flow of tourists comes to Russia across the border in either the Amurskaya region (see Table 6.4) or Primorye (see Figure 6.2). Both Russians and Chinese often use a tourist guise for "commuting" trade because the border crossing for tourists is

TABLE 6.4

Russians and Chinese Crossing the Border in Amur Oblast, 1993–1998
(in thousands)

	1993	1994	1995	1996	1997	1998
Number of Russians visiting China	185.0	95.0	119.0	118.0	160.0	132.0
Including:						
Tourists	106.6	70.8	107.3	97.8	135.5	109.3
On business	57.2	13.3	2.9	3.9	8.4	7.6
Transport workers	21.2	10.9	8.8	16.3	16.1	15.1
Number of Chinese visiting Amur oblast	177.0	48.6	70.5	96.6	105.5	115.2
Including:						
Tourists	73.0	32.2	41.9	46.3	51.9	59.7
On business	80.7	10.9	18.1	33.5	39.8	43.6
Transport workers	23.3	5.5	10.5	16.8	13.8	11.9

Source: Blagoveshchensk State Committee on Statistics for Amur Oblast. 1999. *Major Indicators of Foreign Economic Ties of Amur Oblast and China.* pp. 2–3.

easier, using lists only, without entry visas. Russian "commuters," estimated at 30,000, form a special category of the border population. They are small traders who sell their goods at markets, and buy other goods independently in China. Over the period of ten years during which this form of trade has existed in the Russian Far East, a layer of professional "commuters" has developed for this nerve-wracking, difficult, and risky work, whose participants have become either suppliers or deliverers. They are mainly middle-aged women with a college-level (or lower) education, strength, and endurance (they have to carry bags weighing 30 to 40 kilograms), aggressiveness (which borders on impudence), and resourcefulness (needed to assure a customs official that 20 pairs of shoes are all meant for her family, and that seven hats are one for each day of the week, and so on). Many of those who go to China regularly have close personal relationships with Chinese in Suifenhe and Heihe beyond business, based on trust, help, and personal affection. Many "commuters" realize that "the Chinese have the same kind of attitude toward you as you have toward them."

FIGURE 6.2

Primorsky Krai Trade with China and the Dynamic
of Chinese Movement to Primorye

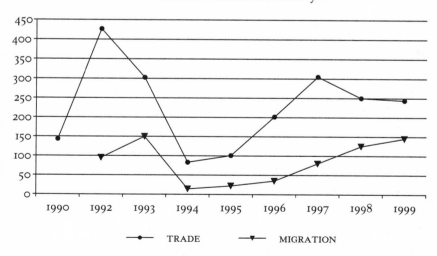

Source: *Monthly Bulletin on Trade with Russia & East Europe.* July 2000. p. 130; *Perspectives of the Far East Region: The China Factor.* 1999, 9. Moscow: Carnegie Moscow Center.

Business

Businessmen and organizations engage in the most popular form of exchanges—those based on bilateral agreements (business, tourism, science, and education) and regulated by market spontaneity, mutual demands, and financial opportunities. In general, mutual contacts play a key role in economic prosperity and are a means of survival for the majority of trade and tour companies, as well as for transportation companies of the border areas. With unreliable postal service and systems not well-equipped for electronic mail, businessmen keep in touch via fax and telephone, although this is expensive. The interdependence seems to grow proportionately with the closeness to the border and intensity of interactions. A Russian expert remarked that the connections "are not regulated well, not controlled well by federal authorities or those in Primorye, and are oriented mainly toward achieving commercial goals."

Nevertheless, a majority of Chinese trade organizations depend on contacts with Russia, and they eagerly search for new sources and partners to increase their profits. In the 1990s, a fairly steady number of Chinese Russia-oriented companies were formed, most of which have already acquired trusted partners, building strong relationships based on reliability and a good reputation. Some contacts of Chinese firms (those that participated in the survey) go as far as the Urals, western Siberia, and the European part of Russia. According to one trade-company employee, the slogan "survive by any means" was adopted by many Chinese Russia-oriented firms in the 1999 worsening of the Russian economy.

Cultural

In contrast to many other border communities worldwide, few blood relations exist between these border town inhabitants. Only a few hundred Chinese in the Far Eastern region have applied for Russian citizenship, and few Russians live permanently in northeast China. Personal contacts between Russians and Chinese are subservient to business interests and serve mainly as a basis for making business contacts. Thus, cultural exchange actually plays an insignificant role. "I don't remember any cultural or informational events," said a deputy to the Duma of Khabarovsky krai, while an expert from Pogranichniy village stated that "cultural, social, manufacturing, and that kind of relations are rare," and Chinese survey participants simply stated that there is nothing like that happening. Any cultural exchange that does occur is formal, embracing a narrow scope of people and insufficiently promoted, which does not help much in overcoming cultural gaps between the two peoples. In fact, many people who participate in these cross-border interactions realize that, to the contrary, significant cultural differences influence daily communications and economic collaboration.

Local Perspectives on Migration from Border Towns
Blagoveshchensk, Russia/Heihe, China and Pogranichniy, Russia/Suifenhe, China

Generally, both Russian and Chinese survey participants were rather cautious in their opinions and replies, especially regarding power structures. Also, both Russians and Chinese were more sincere, critical, and pessimistic in personal conversations than they were in writing.

The Russian Perspective

The presence of Chinese on Russian territory was viewed in different ways by various groups in Russian society. Federal and regional law-enforcement bodies that have control over the presence of foreigners believed the introduction of a visa-free cross-border regime was a mistake, a policy for which Russia was not ready. They said cross-border smuggling increased and that the sanitary situation worsened.[20] They also were dissatisfied that the majority of merchants enter Russia as tourists, and suggested dramatic changes such as forbidding tourists to engage in trade, a visa regime for all categories of foreign citizens, and a reduction of stay for tourists from the current 30–45 days to ten days, ideas not necessarily consistent with the views of the local communities because they did not take into account the local benefits of commerce.

Local administrations, even conservative ones, who were more interested in trade relations and profit for the region, demonstrated a more flexible approach, supporting freedom of movement for populations of border regions. They recognize that merchants cross as tourists because it is cheaper and that introducing a visa regime for all categories could decrease cross-border trade. Instead they suggested improvements such as "valid for one occasion only" permits giving the right to trade, as well as appropriate legislation that regulates the movement of Chinese on Russian territory and protects them from police arbitrariness. Local Russian administrations seem envious that Chinese leadership is implementing a policy of developing its border regions, and they wish Russian federal officials would follow this example when working out regional programs.[21]

Russians differed in their evaluation of the collaboration, with some describing relations as "good," "normal," and "friendly," while others, especially in Vladivostok, called them "shamefully passive" and "chaotic." In Blagoveshchensk residents implied that the neighboring Chinese town of Heihe was a "vampire," benefiting from its proximity to them. Most Russians in the border territories see no practical advantage to being China's neighbors, other than "more convenient trade" and a short transportation route and lower costs when going to China; the Chinese threat is abstract to them, and most see no negative aspects to living in the border area. Most of the Russian experts were unusually skeptical in evaluating the present state of the Russian-Chinese border, with only two characterizing the state of affairs as "positive" and "satisfying" and the rest evaluating it as "extremely low" and "unsatisfying," with negative aspects relating to crime, poaching, currency exportation, and labor market competition. They admit, though, that Chinese migration does not play a significant role in the life of the Russian border towns and villages, and that the possibilities of migration are not being exploited.

The Chinese Perspective

The Chinese have a different evaluation, believing that internal migration from the countryside to the towns, resulting in fast demographic growth and concomitant social problems, is one of the negative aspects of close proximity to Russia, although a third saw no drawbacks to being neighbors with Russia. Also in contrast to the Russians, the Chinese see a direct connection between such closeness and the well-being of their towns, stimulating city development (Suifenhe) and trade relations (Heihe). However, Chinese migrants interviewed indicated they face the following difficulties in their entrepreneurial activities in Russia: the need to bribe the police (67 percent of those polled); bribery among officials (30 percent); crimes against Chinese merchants committed by Russians (35 percent); low purchasing power of the population (35 percent); imperfect rules of company registration (30 percent); demands for bribes by custom officials (25 percent) and tax officials (9 percent); and the impossibility of getting a long-term visa that gives the right to trade, or a residence permit (18 percent).[22] Further, the majority of them consider the attitude of the local authorities toward Chinese migrants as "not very positive" (around 35 percent), and some as even hostile (around 8 percent) while around 10 percent consider it to be friendly, around 25 percent say it is neutral, and 22 percent had no opinion.[23]

Despite these difficulties, and despite concerns regarding Russian criminal groups' potential involvement and profits, many of the Far East experts and entrepreneurs spoke of creating a free trading zone. The profits Chinese companies received from border trading with the USSR/Russia in the late 1980s to the early 1990s helped the remote border towns and villages to thrive.[24] The economies of Suifenhe and Heihe are totally Russia-oriented, with a higher-than-average annual income per person. Interaction with China plays a no less important role for the Russian villages of Blagoveshchensk and Pogranichniy. (Vladivostok, Khabarovsk, and Harbin are not as close to the border and thus less oriented toward each other.) In these towns, the inter-town exchange is very intensive. The mayor's assistant in Suifenhe says that in their town of 100,000 people there are a thousand Russian people daily, mostly merchants, and over 30 hotels for foreigners. In 1999, about 100,000 tourists from the Far East visited, mainly small traders spending a few days to buy a new supply of goods since only 50 kilograms of cargo and up to ten of a kind of goods are duty-free. The center of town, on a spot smaller than 1 square kilometer, has hundreds of shops, wholesale bases, restaurants, and sewing workshops which are specifically oriented toward Russian tourists.

Nevertheless, those who live in the border area towns and are regularly in contact with each other know little about formal relations between the towns. Overall, China seems to have benefited from these interactions, whereas Russian border territories mainly suffered disappointments. The authorities and the residents of the southern Far East have not achieved favorable economic results with China and think future prospects are dimmed by a history of negative outcomes. Some Chinese experts believe that the border towns' relations will inevitably change, as the present "commuter trade" or "people's trade" is doomed. Transformation to "more civilized" trade forms (through large firms and companies) is inevitable, they say, and it will be economically and politically advantageous for both countries, though socially potentially troublesome.

Recommendations

Experts were unanimous concerning the importance of Chinese migration to the Russian Far East, with one representative of the migration bureau describing Chinese migration as "a favorable circumstance for the Russian Far East." Almost all opposed tightening conditions for Chinese crossing the border, believing this would only harm the interests of Russia. The experts supported stricter controls over the people migrating and stricter measures toward those who break the law (including imprisonment), but opposed re-establishment of the "bamboo curtain."

Chinese businessmen put most of their hopes into greater official aid when considering expanded border interactions between the two countries. Regarding improving border interactions, the Chinese experts made the same suggestions as those who are actually involved in the process: improve legislation and increase the role of the authorities. However, they feel uncomfortable when crossing the border, and speak about the Chinese businessman's fear of the crime situation in Russia and about mentality differences between the two peoples, all obstacles to closer interaction.

Surprisingly, with no exceptions the Russians directly or indirectly suggested, on the matter of improving interaction, that the authorities should be involved in building a more favorable economic and legal framework. Their energetic suggestions speak for themselves: "improve accommodations at the border passes," "set up favorable terms for investment in the border territories," "simplify border crossing and customs rules," "reduce visa costs," and similar ideas.

Factors That Influence Cross-Border Relations

Having examined the dynamics of the border regions and the types of cross-border interactions that occur, it is time to turn to factors that influence these relations, both negatively and positively. Many experts and local officials think the existing border-crossing regime works against the region's interests. Sometimes it seems that the only commonality is the meetings that take place on either side. Moreover, border interactions seem limited to sector-to-sector exchange: authorities relate to other authorities, merchants relate to merchants, tour companies relate to tour companies, and so forth. Cross-interactions are rare, with relationships generally based on economic and political interests, rather than ideology. (Russians rarely turn to Chinese authorities, although some organizational representatives admitted to keeping in touch with Russian authorities, particularly the foreign economic relations committees of local administrations.)[25] In the research, many of those interviewed raised similar themes, discussing obstacles to successful cross-border cooperation, ranging from specifics such as the cost of visas to perceptions regarding cultural differences.[26] Below we consider four factors: the role of federal governments, the role of other actors, Russian attitudes, and cultural perceptions.

The Role of Federal Governments

Local officials and migrants frequently stated that cross-border trade and migration is harmed by the absence of an appropriate and reasonable legislative basis that could regulate it and make it more profitable for both sides, including creation of a system of different permits for the migrants.[27] One mutual wish, for both Chinese and Russians, was for real assistance and support by the authorities. "In fact, all the hindrances are the result of activity of the authorities," stated one Russian survey participant. A Chinese businessman agreed that "the biggest problem is the lack of assistance provided by the authorities in the border trade." Thirteen Chinese and 11 Russian survey participants mentioned the necessity of assistance from the authorities. More generally, they commented on the lack of financing and attention from the federal center to the problems of border regions of the Far East, particularly the lack of regional development programs. With regard to infrastructure, the existing ports of entry at the border have seriously deteriorated and need to be equipped with modern computer systems and other equipment in order to increase their capacity. Although the number of ports of entry has been halved from the 360 that existed under the USSR, the migration load has increased. There is also duplication by the Border and Migration Services of each other's work and corruption among customs and law-enforcement officials. These agencies need to stop wasting money, to organize their work more efficiently, and to separate their functions.

The Role of Other Actors

In a Russian joke an official asks his colleague, "What does one need to be a rich man for the rest of his life?" The answer is: just one meter of the state border. Though it contradicts Russian laws, the existence of ports of entry owned by private companies also increases the difficulty of cross-border movement. This is consistent with the theme discussed earlier that criminal gangs and individuals, not the state, are benefiting from border trade. While borders and ports of entry normally are run by the federal agencies, some on the Russia-China border are owned by private operators who impose their own taxes and spend no money on infrastructure maintenance. These companies were state-owned eight to nine years ago but were quietly privatized at the beginning of market reforms, automatically becoming owners of some ports of entry. Now the federal agencies lack the money to buy them back from private hands. Moreover, these private companies are still listed in the agreements signed in the early 1990s, demonstrating that legislation is hundreds of kilometers behind reality.[28]

The joke regarding becoming rich from the border is also applicable to another set of actors who complicate cross-border connections—criminals. Chinese participants (in personal conversations more than in writing) focused on the so-called Russian militia (the local police) and its corruption and open extortion. Every Chinese interviewed on this topic described cases in which he himself had given bribes to Russian militiamen. The chief assistant for foreign economic relations of the government in Heilongjiang province was convinced of epidemic corruption in the Russian militia. In China, by contrast, crime is related to the flow of the unemployed from the countryside villages. Theft or robbery are not uncommon in Suifenhe and Heihe, with Russian tourists often the victims. Chinese authorities generally respond to the complaints, but cannot find the criminals. They are, however, restraining aggressive actions of Chinese merchants, which they had not done in the past.

Russian Attitudes Regarding the Chinese

A third impediment to cross-border collaboration, particularly for Russian local authorities, is that they do not understand the importance of China for Russia's economy and foreign policy. They are overlooking all the benefits of Chinese proximity; they are simply afraid of China. This has resulted in negative incidents such as anti-Chinese mass media hysterics backed by the authorities, "witch hunts" for illegal Chinese, and failed collaborative projects such as the construction of a bridge over the Amur river. Moreover, authorities have used the "Chinese question" to improve their image making as effective patriots and "statesmen." For example, the election slogan by a mayoral candidate in Vladivostok, N. Beletsky, was "Vladivostok is simply besieged by Chinese. We do not need such partners." One of the reasons they do not understand and take advantage of the potential benefits of China's proximity is that the financial situation of the administration and federal authorities does not depend on border interactions. At the same time, some officials have a self-interest in keeping in contact with China, leading to decision making based on personal preference rather than economic merit.

Cultural Perceptions

Related to this is a fourth set of obstacles to the development of economic and personal relations between the two populations—a cultural gap. Specifically noted was the traditionally closed character of Chinese communities, the two languages, and differences in cultures and ways of life in Russia and China. Some Chinese survey participants noted that "Russian mentality and their way of doing business differs from that of the Chinese greatly." Chinese scientists, in private conversations, say that cultural misunderstanding is one of the main obstacles to extending interaction between Russians and Chinese. Similarly, Russians state that there are specific "oriental character traits," a belief which breeds conflicts. These perceptions may well be the cause of mutual blame, with the Chinese saying that "the Russian side often breaks agreements or does not keep their contracts," whereas Russians state that "the Chinese partners are not reliable" and "they do not keep agreements." Often it is a simple misunderstanding of psychology or of the negotiating style of the other side. The result is that Russians think there are "many promises but no business" from the Chinese side, whereas Chinese say that "the Russian side does not value its reputation" and that "since 1994 the reputation of the Russian side has been getting worse and worse."

Consistent with this historically limited integration are views regarding mixed marriages to promote integration. More than 52 percent of Chinese said they would not like to marry a Russian citizen, and around 68 percent of Russians answered the same about Chinese, while only nine percent of Chinese and about three percent of Russians would like to marry each other (Gelbras 1999, 9–37). Similarly, although almost all the Chinese who trade at the markets of the Russian border towns speak some Russian, as do restaurant owners, hotel personnel, and small shop owners in the Russia-oriented part of Suifenhe, few Russians speak Chinese, even among those who work with China on a regular basis. A good example is a nine-year employee of a Russian tour bureau who takes people to China but has learned only four Chinese words (and even then distorts them beyond recognition). The Russian exceptions are those who graduated from universities or specialized schools, despite the fact that Russian officials and transportation, scientific, and educational employees note that lack of language command is a hindrance to normal exchange. In contrast, most Chinese acquired basic knowledge of Russian from short courses, although some of them studied it at schools or even at universities. They use mainly "street-slang," the language in which Russian "commuter traders" speak to them.

Nevertheless, there are a number of positive factors that give hope for improvement of the current situation. The first is the human factor. The attitude of local authorities toward cooperation with the Chinese, as a rule, is very positive and cooperative. The majority of local leaders seem to be reasonable and clever people, and they strongly support establishing mutual contacts with their Chinese neighbors. They now all have quite successful experiences of personal relations with Chinese local community leaders and with the leaders of neighboring Chinese provinces, and they visit each other on a regular basis. Furthermore, many cities and towns have started cultural and educational exchanges, signing agreements on the local level. A society of Russia-China friendship with branches in many Far East border cities has been organized, exemplifying the important types of steps that need to be taken toward cultural integration. Another positive sign is consideration of joint environmental monitoring projects. This sphere is still rather sensitive, there are numerous violations, and efforts must be intensified; still, some steps toward more civilized means of using joint resources have been taken.

Conclusions

Overall, the Russian-Chinese border is ill-regulated and ineffectively developed because of a divergence in the interests and goals of the two sides, horizontally (Russia and China) as well as vertically (between the Russian center and the territories of the Russian Far East). The northeastern provinces of China act according to state strategy and policy concerning Russia, whereas the Russian side is permanently uncertain regarding its China policy, lacking a unified approach or an understanding of China's value for Russian national interests and national security. Hence, the existing disorder of regional policy, the subordination of state interests to local interests, and the placing of technical questions ahead of strategic and potential-benefit questions.

Consequently, the present attitude toward China in the Russian Far East is not only ambiguous, but also to some extent hypocritical. Officially people call for Russian-Chinese friendship and use slogans about the inevitability of collaboration, but in reality, fears, hopes, and disappointment rule the hearts of a majority of the politicians and the ordinary citizens, as evidenced by the tone and policy of the local media. Publications devoted to Chinese expansion and economic (and military) aggression far outnumber articles devoted to China's history, culture, and present situation. Nevertheless, both Russians and Chinese living along the common border understand that there is no alternative to looking for the means of improving collaboration and overcoming future obstacles.

Indeed, the majority of Russians living in the border territories evaluated prospects for future Russian-Chinese relations as positive, although they were concerned about Chinese migration, growing economic dependence on China, and unresolved territorial problems. However, the real dangers are connected not to China's policies but to the actions of Russia itself, to the calculated and serious policies of Russia in the Far East, and to its ability to develop and protect its Far Eastern territories. All the Russian experts and most of the survey participants evaluated relations with China as highly important and favorable for Russia. But they considered it a necessity to "clearly identify the scope of Russian strategic interests on a long-term basis," "create a better-defined strategy on interaction with China," and to establish special programs for border collaboration and the development of border areas, "similar to the Chinese." "If Russia leads with reasonable policy, there is no danger to it from China," claims an expert from Blagoveshchensk. "There are favorable prospects if Russia leads with skillful state policy. But if the policy is unskillful, Russia will lose the Far East," states his colleague from Vladivostok.

One of the most important policy areas to develop, and one with collaborative potential, is migration policy. However, the lack of information on the actual situation in the border regions is a serious problem. This results, in part, from the unwillingness of the federal center to pay enough attention to the problems of the Far East region, from regional authorities who use the threat of a Chinese expansion as an ace in the political games with the federal center (and sometimes provide unreliable information), and from the closed character of Chinese communities in Russia. It demands an effective, research-based policy of interaction and collaboration with China, especially in the border regions, and a migration policy that takes into account the specific character of the Russian regions. Within the framework of the general migration program, regional programs must be developed, and regional authorities should have more power to regulate migration issues in the border territories.

At the same time, however, it also is important to recognize that restrictive measures are ineffectual and promote corruption. It would be wiser to create a legal basis for the presence of Chinese migrants in Russia by looking for acceptable forms for legalizing Chinese migrants and their activities in Russia. The Chinese diaspora leaders in Russia also need to be vested with responsibility, to develop cooperation between themselves and local authorities, and to establish and continue a mutually beneficial partnership with the People's Republic of China.[29]

Either way, the Russian authorities and the Russian people need to accept the projection that Chinese migration is inevitable and that by 2050 the Chinese may become the second-largest group of people in Russia after Russians. Thus, it is vital to work out long-term integration programs on both national and local levels, which is impossible to do without cooperation between federal and local authorities. Failure to do this may lead to yet another ethnic conflict, of which Russia has had enough.

Notes

1. The paper uses materials provided by Galina Vitkovskaya, Director of the Program on Migration and Citizenship of the Carnegie Moscow Center, Zhanna Zayonchkovskaya, Institute of Economic Forecasting of the Russian Academy of Science, and Vilya Gelbras, Institute of Asian and African Countries. It also draws on the results of several field studies and two field trips to the Russian Far East carried out by the Program on Migration and Citizenship of the Carnegie Moscow Center.

2. The field trips were in Vladivostok-Pogranichniy-Sosnovaya Pad (the automobile border crossing)-Suifenhe-Harbin, in April and June 2000. Transportation was by Vladivostok tour buses, regular route coaches (Suifenhe-Pogranichniy, Ussuriisk-Pogranichniy, Suifenhe-Harbin) and

railway. Chinese authorities did not let the researchers into Suifenhe one of the three times because of faulty documents.

3. The border is 705 kilometers land, 3,484 kilometers river, and 70 kilometers lake. The eastern side is 4,204 kilometers while the western is 55 kilometers. Three portions of the border (Bolshoi Ussuriysky and Tarabarov Islands on the Amur River and Bolshoi Island on the river Argun) remain in dispute.

4. Chinese sources believe no more than 300,000 Chinese are living in all CIS countries, which represents around one percent of the Chinese diaspora worldwide.

5. The head of the Primorye passport and visa service stated there were only 37 permanent Chinese residents registered in the krai in 1999.

6. Heilongjiang Province was to be a model and a sort of corridor for Chinese expansion to the North via extraction of certain kinds of products and raw materials from Russia (such as wood, fish, chemical fertilizers, and ferrous and non-ferrous metals). Most of the products and materials would go to the central and southern areas of China. In exchange, cheap Chinese goods in high demand would be delivered to Russia.

7. Today, however, it is the entrepreneurs, rather than the authorities, who must look for partners for collaboration, a situation that explains their comments regarding the need for better governmental support of border collaboration.

8. According to this agreement, tourist groups of not less than five persons headed by the representative of a certain tourist company (initially the tourist companies were owned by the state) had the right to cross the border without visas. A visa, on the other hand, remained relatively expensive, with one entry costing $50 (or $70, depending on the term of visa issued) and a triple-entry visa costing $150.

9. Chinese trust Koreans more than Russians because the Korean diaspora lived in the Russian Far East for many years. Though they have much in common with the Chinese, they know the Russian language and local situation.

10. These crises led to special Presidential Decrees: 1996 "Decree on the Responsibility of Officials ... in Primorsky Krai" and 1997 "Decree on Additional Rights and Obligations ... in Primorsky Krai."

11. The most popular are the Blagoveshchensky pass (which is a water pass), Grodekovsky railway pass (near the villages of Pogranichniy and Primorye), and the passes at Poltavka and Sosnovaya Pad (also in Primorye), with the crossing in Poltavka having the worst reputation.

12. For example, those who go by bus leave Vladivostok at 5:30 to 6:00 in the morning in order to be at Sosnovaya Pad or the Poltavka pass at 10 a.m., where it could take one to two more hours to cross. In April 2000, the researchers spent seven hours in a bus on the Russian side, along with

Russian "commuter merchants" and Chinese tourists, with no shade or restrooms. In June, the delay on the Russian side took less an hour, but on the way back it took three hours.

13. It costs 180 rubles ($6.40) for a 10-kilometer section of the route from Pogranichniy to Suifenhe by Russian bus and 130 yuan ($15) return by a Chinese one. In comparison, it costs only 100 rubles ($3.60) to go the 200 kilometers from Vladivostok to Pogranichniy.

14. For example, it costs a passenger ten yuan at Sosnovaya Pad pass to avoid taking one's things out of the bus, and resolving document problems costs 100 yuan, according to a Russian tour firm director. The Chinese side also requires Russians to have a medical note from a doctor concerning AIDS (which tourists and "commuter merchants" buy at tour firms for 15 to 30 rubles) or to pay money. Similarly, Russian quarantine authorities require Russian tour group leaders to have papers verifying that they have had an educational course on "prophylactic measures against cholera" or they are fined 500 rubles each (a ten-minute course costs 120 rubles).

15. From 1992 to 2000 more than a hundred intergovernmental documents were signed.

16. As a result, some tourist agencies that had been fined or had their licenses canceled by the krai's administration for violations of law continue issuing invitations for Chinese tourists in order to increase their profit, complicating the work of the border service at the checkpoints.

17. For example, Heilongjiang Province signed such treaties with Primorye, as well as with Khabarovsky and Krasnoyarsky krais, and with Amurskaya, Chitinskaya, Irkutskaya and Kemerovskaya oblasts. In 1992 and 1995, Primorsky krai signed almost identical agreements regarding trade-economy, scientific-technical, and cultural collaborations.

18. This was especially important in rural districts, where local inhabitants do not want this work.

19. Khabarovsky krai has created the most favorable conditions, as tourist visas are valid for a month and may be extended, so that traders can sell their goods without the risk of deportation or financial penalties (most Chinese interviewed had paid penalties to policemen). In Amur oblast, a visa is issued for two weeks, and for three days in Primorsky krai. Since it is not possible to sell goods on such short terms, traders always violate fixed visa terms, as revealed by the large numbers of illegal migrants found during police raids.

20. The media reported that four cases of cholera brought from China were registered on the territory of the Russian Far East for the first time since 1921, in August 1999.

21. Some Chinese border villages have grown for 15 years into prosperous towns oriented to trade with Russia.

22. The information is based on the 1998–99 survey carried out among Chinese in Moscow and in the Far East cities of Khabarovsk, Vladivostok, and Ussuriisk. The results of the survey and the related conference presentations have been published by the Carnegie Moscow Center. (Gelbras 1999).

23. Perhaps some of these challenges could be alleviated by implementing the suggestions of Russian experts and entrepreneurs who work with Chinese to establish a category of "trading agent" for Russian and Chinese companies' representatives with a multiple visa, or creation of joint ventures with the right to employ a labor force and to import goods.

24. Often the state fails to benefit from cross-border trade due to criminal groups and the unorganized merchant "tourists" who are part of the "shadow economy" and do not contribute to the regional budget.

25. Russian exceptions are the scientific and educational organizations whose directors have a wider scope of views and interests, and well-managed commercial institutions, such as "Ussuri-centre." Called "the Chinese market" in the town of Ussuriisk, it breaks the locally set negative image of the nature, opportunities, and effectiveness of border connections with China, as well as that of the potential for Chinese migration in the Russian Far East.

26. According to the survey, Russians believe key obstacles to interaction include imperfect legislation (73 percent), bureaucratic interference (61.5 percent), Russian government inactivity (46 percent), and lack of legal basis (33 percent). Only 15 percent believed there was no advantage in collaboration, while 15 percent also believed that cultural differences are an essential hindrance to the development of relationships. Russian experts were more critical, attributing the lack of cooperation to imperfect legislation (100 percent), bureaucratic hindrances (69 percent), and lack of legal basis and Russian inactivity (61.9 percent). From the Chinese perspective, obstacles to collaboration ranged from general statements about the unfavorable economic situation in Russia to accusations of Russian ineffectiveness and the different mentalities of the two peoples. Specific obstacles to interaction, according to Chinese experts, were imperfect legislation (64 percent), lack of legal basis (42 percent), economic incompatibility of the two countries (42 percent), and crime problems (36 percent).

27. There were also complaints regarding the long time it takes to acquire an official passport, the expense of a visa, and the necessity of going to Shenyang or Khabarovsk to get a visa.

28. There seems to be a similar situation with tourist agencies. The 1992 agreement on visa-free border crossing for tourist groups contained a list of companies that have the right to do this business; they used to be state-owned companies but are now private and trying to gain as much profit as possible.

29. As mentioned earlier, some interviewees proposed the idea of a "trading agent" who could be employed by both Russian and Chinese companies and given a reasonably priced multiple visa or a one-time-only permit to trade in Russian territory.

Works Cited

Gelbras, Vilya. 1999. "Preliminary Results of Investigation of the Chinese Migration Problems in Moscow, Khabarovsk, Vladivostok and Ussuriysk." Moscow.

Minakir, P.A. 1996. "Chinese Immigration in the Russian Far East: Regional, National, and International Dimensions." In *Cooperation and Conflict in the Former Soviet Union: Implications for Migration*, eds. Jeremy R. Azrael and Emil A. Pain. Santa Monica: RAND.

Vitkovskaya, Galina. 1997. "Russia: Cross-Border Migration in the Russian Far East," Carnegie Moscow Center, October. Available on the UNHCR web site at <www.unhcr.ch/refworld/country/writenet/wriruso3.htm>.

7

The Russia-Kazakhstan Border: A Comparison of Three Regional Cases

Grigorii G. Kosach, Alexei S. Kuzmin, and Vladimir I. Mukomel

THE BREAKUP OF THE SOVIET UNION in 1991 had far-reaching effects for the country as a whole and for its constituent parts. It established official state borders where formerly there were only administrative borders such as those between German Länder (for example, North Rhine-Westphalia and Rhine-Palatinate), or between U.S. states (such as Texas and New Mexico). In this study, we describe the current state of transborder relations and activities in three Russian border regions (oblasts)—Omsk, Orenburg, and Astrakhan—and their direct neighbors, Kazakhstan's administrative formations. These regions were chosen because they are key to a certain geographical area: Omsk in western Siberia, Orenburg in the southern Urals, and Astrakhan in the Lower Volga, which correspond to regions in northeast, northwest, and southwest Kazakhstan, respectively. Using case studies, we review the history and economies of these three regions of the Russian Federation, examine the current situation regarding cross-border interactions and opportunities for cooperation, discuss challenges to such cooperation, and draw some conclusions regarding the state of play on these issues and their likely future.

We gratefully acknowledge the work of consultant Jacqueline Edlund Braun, who compiled this paper based on our more detailed research reports.

As a matter of foreign policy, the Russian Empire created Omsk to establish Russian control over Turk- and Mongol-speaking states in Altai and present western Mongolia. Orenburg was to be the main fortress for further Russian expansion in the direction of the Kazakh Steppe and Central Asia. The Russian occupation of Astrakhan, which was the capital of a state risen from the ruins of the Golden Horde, stressed its functional significance as an important center for the movement of people and goods on the Volga River and Caspian Sea to the Caucasus and Near East. The Soviet era did not change the essence of these interests, although relations among these three regions of Russia and their Kazakhstan neighbors since the dissolution of a unified state have changed considerably. The post-Soviet evolution, in spite of the promise of opportunities opened by inter-Russian regionalism, did not bring essential reforms to the economic interests of these regions.

For the most part, the authorities as well as the citizens of all three Russian regions do not aspire to establish close and multilateral relations with their former compatriots in what is now a new country, Kazakhstan. Of course, exceptions do exist, but the factors that drive them are neither stable nor long-term. More specifically, for the Omsk region, the economic and cultural interaction with Kazakhstan would be characterized as "nothing to share, nothing to fight about." There is a notable lack of contact and mutual economic interests that might fuel cooperation or maintain transparency of the borders. The Orenburg regional administration's desire to develop economic ties with Kazakhstan is designed first to rescue the industrial giants who occupy an enclave position in the regional economy and second to develop the regional economic environment as a whole, based on its substantial economic dependence on Kazakhstan, its former agrarian and raw materials periphery.

In its Astrakhan section, the border in many ways resembles a barrier, showing few signs of transforming itself into a contact frontier, with one notable exception. The extensive hydrocarbon resources in Kazakhstan enhance the possibility of cooperation between the two regions because Kazakhstan lacks the capacity, which Astrakhan has, to organize the infrastructure required for an efficient, modern level of hydrocarbon production, as well as the highly skilled labor force needed to develop those resources. Cooperation in this area also has a spillover effect in demands for Astrakhan's transit capabilities to transport oil and for orders placed with its shipbuilding industry for drilling rigs, supply vessels, and tankers that will be needed to develop the vast reserves on the northern Caspian shelf.

With the exception of Orenburg's industrial giants and Astrakhan's hydrocarbon development potential, Russia-Kazakhstan economic interaction in all three parts of the interstate border is becoming increasingly rare. The economic potential of the Russian regions is much higher in comparison with their Kazakhstan neighbors, so Russian leaders spend their resources trying to develop relations with other partners—other Russian regions, states of the western zone of the Commonwealth of Independent States (CIS), the Far East, Western Europe, and the United States. Nor is the private sector yet strong enough to be a decisive factor in Russian foreign-trade activities. Moreover, the "system" opponents of the executive authority—regional political movements and local branches of all-Russian opposition parties —are more interested in fortifying the border's barrier status than in relaxing it. The authority bodies of all three regions, as well as the opposition, do not believe a high level of transparency on the Russian-Kazakh border is necessary. On the contrary, they believe that the border's transparency constitutes a security threat both to their own regions and to Russia as a whole, a belief not completely unfounded for reasons that include poorly defined borders, drug trafficking, migration, and interethnic tensions. All of these problems have led to efforts to fortify the border, making it more difficult to transport goods and people.

Methodology

Omsk

To study the role of the Kazakhstan border in the life of the Omsk region and its inhabitants, during the summer of 2000 one of the authors (Alexei Kuzmin) conducted a sociological survey of 258 persons in the city of Omsk, in the southern border districts of the region. Survey participants included regional and local authorities, regional politicians, experts (including university professors, researchers, administrative body counselors), industrial and trade management personnel, medical and educational personnel, and "common people" in Schebarkul (for example, truck and bus drivers, peasants, merchants, and factory workers). The results of this survey, as well as other data (from regional newspapers, official documents, and published and unpublished regional studies), form the basis of the ongoing discussion of border and transborder relations as seen from the Russian side.

Orenburg

The study of transborder cooperation covering Orenburg, Orsk, and some other towns in the eastern part of the region (including Novotroitsk and Mednogorsk) was conducted in June and July 2000 by another of the authors (Grigorii Kosach).[1] Participants in the informal interviews included representatives of border districts, industrial enterprises and commercial firms, officials of the regional administration and town municipalities, deputies of the legislative assembly, representatives of the federal government bodies, the leadership of the Kazakh and the Cossack movements, businesspeople, and representatives of education and law enforcement. The author also used conclusions from previously published papers, information from the Orenburg, Aktyubinsk, and Moscow press, official information from the Orenburg regional administration, and native scholars' studies.

The perspective is a Russian one because of a high level of Kazakh "reticence," which made it impossible to gather their perspective, despite persistent attempts with the officials of the Kazakhstan regional authorities, local journalists, leaders of national movements, the teaching staff of the Aktyubinsk University, and leaders of commercial sociological centers. This was, nevertheless, a useful exercise, as it demonstrated clearly the position of the Aktyubinsk administration and the unified character of the Kazakhstan state system as they relate to the prospects of Russian-Kazakhstan border cooperation. Overtures from Russian individuals and officials would likely meet the same reluctance.

Astrakhan

In the Astrakhan region, the third writer (Vladimir Mukomel) initially distributed two questionnaires to stakeholders in boundary collaboration as well as to experts representing the regional, regional-center, and local-authority bodies, the scientific and industrial associations, and the national and cultural societies. However, potential respondents who ran businesses in Kazakhstan or who were officials with responsibility for communications with Kazakhstan became reluctant to agree to the interviews, despite preliminary conversations in March 2000 in which they demonstrated their willingness to take part in the research.[2] The study's format was then changed to use two focus groups, both of which were conducted by Astrakhan sociologists in July 2000 in the Krupskaya regional scientific library, in free and informal surroundings.

A total of ten respondents took part in each focus group, including representatives of the commercial firms, representatives of building firms and the customs office, representatives of the local administration (the district bordering the Kazakh Republic, made up of ethnic Kazakhs), officials of the regional administration (responsible for national policy), and representatives of service firms. The appraisals of the principal questions in both focus groups were nearly identical, so there was no need to differentiate the results by source-group. The participants were frank in their responses, due to the promise of anonymity in report documents, the informal surroundings, and the selection of the participants who either knew each other or had friends in common with the researchers.

Background

Omsk

The 1,783 kilometer-long Russia-Kazakhstan border in western Siberia separates the Russian Omsk region and the corresponding regions of northeast Kazakhstan. This border originated in the early eighteenth century, when the Russian colonization of Siberia shifted south and the Kazakh khanate grew north and west. Omsk was established in 1716 as a fortress on the so-called Siberian Line and played an important role in the shifting power structures among the Turk- and Mongol-speaking states in Altai and western Mongolia, the Russian colonists, and the traditionally nomadic Kazakh society. At brief points in their history, Kazakhs and Russians joined to ward off attacks, but for the most part, Russians and Kazakhs tended to settle in different areas of the region, and Kazakh markets lay outside the zone of usual Russian habitation. The historically limited contact between the peoples of these two regions likely contributed to the "peaceful" character of the Russian-Kazakh cultural and economic border.

The primary industries in the Omsk region's economy are oil refining and petro-chemistry, including production of tires, and some construction. The economy showed a ten to fifteen percent annual decline since 1992, typical for the post-Soviet era, although that seems to have halted in 2000, as the inflation index dropped from 3,200 percent to 20 percent. The Omsk region today is multiethnic, although Russians constitute a clear majority with 80 percent of the population. Kazakhs, with 3.5 percent of the population, make up the fourth largest ethnic group; fewer than one-third of the 76,000 Kazakhs in the Omsk region live in cities. Moreover, while nine of the 31 districts of the Omsk region border Kazakhstan, their population density is low, with only 275,600 people of the region's two million total inhabiting them. Many border villages, in fact, lost their entire populations during the 1980s and 1990s, becoming uninhabited.

Orenburg

The Orenburg region has a special status among the regions bordering Kazakhstan due to its historical role, its economic interests, and the fact that its border forms one-third (1,876 kilometers) of the whole frontier. In 1743, Orenburg became a fortress town that formed the link between lines of defensive fortifications (the "Orenburg Line"), although it lost this status in 1862 after the Russian conquest of Central Asia shifted the frontier south. Orenburg was created as an "imperial" city, the third most important in the region after Moscow and St. Petersburg, with government documents noting that it would become "the stronghold and advanced post" of the empire, as well as the leading center of the Russian-Kazakhstan and Russian-Central Asian trade and industrial relations.

The Orenburg region today is the most southern Russian administrative unit in the Ural region, bordering the Republic of Tatarstan, the Samara and Saratov regions, the Republic of Bashkortostan, the Cheliabinsk region, and the Republic of Kazakhstan.[3] It considers itself the Russian "gateway to Asia," via neighboring Kazakhstan (Futurianskii 1996, 3–4). Orenburg has a surface area of 123,900 square kilometers and a total population of 2.2 million inhabitants, almost two-thirds of whom are urban. The Ural River, the main but unnavigable waterway, crosses the Orenburg region and is the geographical borderline between the European and Asian continents. The region also includes two economically important rail lines and two paved roadways, along with airports in Orenburg and Orsk with air service to Russia and Kazakhstan.

The region's largest cities are Orenburg (600,000 inhabitants), Orsk (300,000), and Novotroitsk (108,000) in the east of the region, and Buzuluk (86,000) and the main center of the local oil output, Buguruslan (54,500), in the northwest. Twelve of its 35 rural districts border the Republic of Kazakhstan. Although the Russians are the majority in the population, with 72.3 percent, and the region is unquestionably dominated by the Slav national groups (mostly Orthodox Christian), it is also a multinational region, with Tatars, Bashkirs, Chuvashes, Mordvinians, and Germans. Current migrants include Armenians, Azerbaijanis, Chechens, Ingushes, Tajiks, and Uzbeks. The most numerous of the local national minorities (the Tatars at 7.3 percent and the Kazakhs at 5.1 percent) seem to be marginalized, with minimal Kazakh representation in the local power structures. Nonetheless, the Orenburg Kazakh minority is a considerable demographic quantity in several parts of the region, fluctuating from 13.1 to 52.5 percent in six of the eight eastern districts.

Orenburg's previous extensive regional economic interactions, specifically a common production area that included this Russian region as well as Kazakhstan (for oil, gas, metallurgy, and agriculture) also contributed to its special role. The most important branches of regional industrial production are energy fuels (natural gas and oil), the ferrous and non-ferrous metal industry, and mechanical engineering. The centers of oil-product output and chrome-ore processing were created in the Soviet period, turning the region's eastern districts into a dynamically developing area of economic growth and urbanization, although completely dependent on deliveries of Kazakh raw materials. In addition, the vital activity of the enormous industrial complex of Orsk and Novotroitsk depended on the agricultural enterprises of its Kazakhstan neighbors. In fact, in the Soviet period, Orenburg-Kazakhstan relations were based mostly on the traditional scheme of an industrial center (Orenburg) with an agrarian and raw materials periphery (northwestern Kazakhstan). In turn, the engineering works of Orenburg and Orsk were the main producers for the northwestern regions of Kazakhstan.[4]

Astrakhan

Since the liquidation of the Astrakhan khanate and its establishment as a territory of Russia, the region founded by Peter I in 1717 has served both as a Russian military-political outpost in the south and as a transport junction linking Russia with Central Asia, India, the Crimea, and Transcaucasus. Even before becoming part of Russia, the region was an important commercial center on the famous Silk Road. Its early history and numerous later cultural developments contributed to forming a peculiarly multiethnic and multi-religion population in a tolerant atmosphere. In fact, according to the 1989 census, representatives of more than 150 nationalities made the Astrakhan region their home: 72 percent Russians, 12 percent Kazakhs, 7 percent Tatars, as well as smaller percentages of Kalmyks, Chechens, Azerbaijanis, Belorussians, Nogayians, Armenians, Darghinians, Gypsies (Roma), and many others. Regional authorities try to avoid the explosion of extremism linked with a similarly complicated situation in the Northern Caucasus.

The region, with the city of Astrakhan (population 488,300) at its center, comprises 11 administrative districts[5] and has a total population of over a million, of which two-thirds are urban and one-third rural. Its economic base is the fuel, energy, and agro-industrial complexes, though there are also a number of chemical, machine-building, light industry, and building enterprises. Traditional industries include shipbuilding, ship repair, fishing, and vegetable and melon farming.

Similar to other Russian regions, the Astrakhan region faced a pro-longed economic recession and a decline in living standards following the socio-political and economic institutional transformation of the post-Soviet era. An 18 percent increase in its goods and services produced between 1998 and 1999 resulted from improving the external economic situation in the fuel and energy complex, creating favorable conditions for import-substituting production development, and the region's increased investment attractiveness due to its natural resources, its geopolitical position, and its stable political situation.[6]

Economic growth is also made possible by the region's transportation infrastructure of more than 600 kilometers of railways, 3,000 kilometers of highways, and about 1,500 kilometers of waterways. The region continues to develop as a transportation hub, as it is able to provide year-round transportation with Iran and the Middle East, Pakistan, and India; it has access to the Volga River; and it uses its railway and road network for transporting goods to other Russian regions. The communications system has also been modernized and enlarged. However, one of the most important economic issues is the need to eliminate the "shadow economy," which would increase revenue to the regional budget. By the experts' estimation, this shadow turnover accounts for 40 percent of the economy (*Volga* 1999b); in particular, the markets and places of unofficial trade form 50 percent of the goods turnover in the region, including the real estate market (*Volga*, 1999a).

Transborder Cooperation and Interaction

Omsk

Both overestimation and underestimation of transborder cooperation are common in contemporary scientific discourses and public opinion within both Russian and Kazakh societies due to a variety of perspectives on whether the border is transparent, unnoticed, or impassable. Although no state border existed in the region for nearly two centuries, there has been a cultural and economic border. Thus, one would expect transborder contacts to be common, given the similarity in ethnic composition of the population of the bordering regions, the lack of language problems to hinder communication, surviving economic links from the Soviet era of "One Extremely Large Plant," and existing railroads and highways.

However, a glance at a detailed map of the region shows few connections by rail, highway, or other transportation, as well as a lack of industrial incentives. Specifically, the border is crossed only by two main railways, namely the western branch of the Southern Siberian railway, which runs from Petropavlovsk in Kazakhstan to Omsk, and a minor, single-rail branch leading to Kokshetau. Only two of the five paved roads could be considered major highways (namely, the Petropavlovsk-Omsk and Omsk-Pavlodar), and some become unpaved near the border. This centralization of space and the accompanying degradation of the transport infrastructure in the administrative borders at the Soviet, Republican, regional, and even district levels have been extensively discussed in the literature on geography, but the Omsk case seems to be one of the most extreme (Kolosov et al. 2000). Moreover, most of the industries are oil refineries and petrochemical plants, and even the construction industry is mostly linked northward to the oil-rich Tiumen region and not south to Kazakhstan. Unlike the case of the Orenburg region, whose industry depends on raw materials from Kazakhstan, in the Omsk region there is no industrial incentive to develop further cooperation.

The Omsk governor and the mayor of Omsk stated that friendly relations with Kazakhstan were crucial for the well-being of the region. However, there are no signs that these statements are more than mere politeness, given that none of the more than 200 joint ventures in Omsk—with countries as varied as Iraq, Slovakia, Venezuela, and Vietnam—are with its neighbor Kazakhstan. That helps explain why none of the local authorities and only three of the regional authorities surveyed for this report expressed even scant interest in transborder contacts and cooperation. Only eight of those interviewed had visited Kazakhstan in the last five years (and six of those went for personal reasons). Only two of the participants had made visits in the last two years, and both visits were in response to crimes committed in the region (more than 3,000 head of cattle stolen by Kazakhstan inhabitants in Odesskoie district, and 35 kilometers of stolen electric wires in Novowarsawka district). So for local and regional authorities, the border appears at best a barrier, at worst a peril.

Even among those in the region who would have reasons to go to Kazakhstan to visit family or close acquaintances—namely, the Kazakhs (who have large family networks and often migrate to take up residence with a new spouse's family) and Kazakhstan emigrants to Russia during the 1990s (13 percent of the total in our survey)—there has been little or no contact. Of this latter group, few make visits back to Kazakhstan; 45 percent do not plan to visit it at all because they have hardly anyone left there; and some 35 percent of those who do have close relations in Kazakhstan are "doing their best to save their families from Kazakhstan," as one ethnic German immigrant stated. Visits to Kazakhstan during the Soviet period were only slightly more frequent, averaging five days a year. Even the existence of railroads and highways to Petropavlovsk, Kokshetau, Pavlodar, and Astana did not stimulate interest in transborder cooperation. This lack of contact is perhaps because residents of the Omsk region do not need any of the goods available from northern Kazakhstan or because the complex character of the Omsk economy enables it to meet most of the needs of its population.

Although overall we found little cross-border cooperation in this region, there were a few positive examples. For instance, the educational facilities of northern and central Kazakhstan have been inadequate for the needs of its population since the Soviet period. The problem is exacerbated by Kazakhstan's Astana State University becoming Kazakh-speaking only, putting further pressure on East Kazakhstan University, North Kazakhstan University, and Eurasian Independent University to meet the educational needs of the non-Kazakh population of central and northern Kazakhstan. Twelve Omsk higher-education institutions educated an estimated 3,000 to 8,000 Kazakh students each year from 1993 to 1999, but only a third of the educational costs of these students from Kazakhstan are reimbursed by the Russian federal and regional budgets. Nevertheless, the quality of education in Kazakhstan was deemed by respondents to be "immeasurably bad," so they continue to admit gifted pupils, despite budgetary problems such as an inability to pay teachers their salaries.

With regard to medical care, since the 1994 decline in the Kazakhstan public health system, the Omsk-Kazakhstan border transparency statute has been utilized by 100 to 300 Kazakhstan citizens a day to enter the Omsk region for medical treatment. No medical personnel surveyed for this report felt able to refuse medical treatment in the case of a medical emergency or a severely ill person. Thus, between two and three million rubles are spent each year by public health institutions in the region on medical aid to Kazakhstan citizens, and only one-third of these expenses are reimbursed.

Orenburg

The picture that emerges of border interactions with Kazakhstan in both the Soviet and post-Soviet eras shows that the inner districts of the region were not focused on cooperation with the neighboring state. Cooperation with the adjoining Kazakhstan regions was important only for the central and eastern districts, with their industrial interests. For example, the heads of executive power bodies of twelve Russian districts bordering Kazakhstan showed no interest in developing contacts with their colleagues from the neighboring state during the interviews, with the exception of the heads of administration of two central (Sol-Iletsk and Akbulak) and one eastern (Novoorsk, with the towns of Orsk and Novotroitsk) districts. The three districts have more or less regular contacts (including trips to Kazakhstan) with the representatives of the Aktyubinsk administration, aimed at resolution of problems of land tenure and cultural and business relations. None of the other Orenburg authorities maintains even such limited contacts. Little cooperation between the two countries takes place, even regarding crime. Only the committee responsible for organizing cultural days for the Orenburg Kazakhs maintains stable relations with the departments of the neighboring Kazakhstan *akymats* (local administrative units).

These differing levels of contact, similar to those in Omsk, relate at least in part to the lack of transportation infrastructure, including few connections with Kazakhstan. A second reason is that both Orenburg and Kazakhstan's neighboring districts tend to specialize in arable farming and cattle breeding, which excludes more developed forms of active commodity circulation. Third, as noted in interviews with officials of the Department of International and Foreign Economic Relations, the rigid, unified character of the Kazakhstan state system increases the difficulty of creating a truly integrated regional area. But they stressed that it was outside the Orenburg administration's competence to promote its change, with the principal factor being "the firm and clear position of the two countries' leadership." They also acknowledged that cooperation with the Kazakhstan neighbors would have even greater results, if it were not for "passivity on the part of the Russian side." The rise of a functioning civil society, currently in its embryonic stage, and the economic and political pluralism that follows, is necessary for new forms to come into existence. Yet cooperation does occur at the regional government level, through commercial ventures, in education, and through shuttle and rural trade.

Regional Administration. After the collapse of the Soviet Union, "the common production area," which included the adjoining Russian and Kazakhstan regions, became a nostalgic memory for the Orenburg regional administration. The administration—with ever-growing irritation toward the attempts of Moscow industrial and financial groups to institute control over local monopolies and natural resources[7]— began searching for ways to survive in this new environment, and preserving the industrial enclaves became the answer.[8]

Initially, the Orenburg administration tried to diversify its external economic contacts by emphasizing that the only opportunity to "overcome the growth of negative economical tendencies" (for the Orenburg region and for Kazakhstan) was "restoration of effective economic relations between the republics of the former Soviet Union" (Borisyuk and Sivelkin 1997, 25–26). Seeking contacts with Belarus, some Ukrainian regions, Krasnoyarsk krai, other Russian regions, and foreign companies failed to bring about serious economic or social changes.[9] Orientation toward Kazakhstan, its leading foreign trade partner, turned out to be more advantageous: in 1997, Orenburg's exports to the neighboring state were 71.9 percent, and Kazakhstan delivered 86.2 percent of the total import production necessary for the Orenburg region (Gorshenin 1999, 47).

"We step forward firmly from the position of further expanding good-neighbor relations with the Kazakhstan partners, despite the transformation of the administrative borders with the contiguous [regions] into the frontier with the Kazakhstan Republic" (Yelagin 1999a, 3), noted the former head of the Orenburg regional administration. In doing so, the Orenburg region preserved its "specific character," including the fact that "the border determines the priorities" (Yelagin 1999b). Administrative and financial circles, however, presumed that

Kazakhstan would likely remain the producer of agricultural and industrial raw materials (Tsykler 1997, 36–38), unable to become a real industrial power, at least in the near future. Naturally, it would then need a base for consumption and processing of its products. Such economic relations could also help preserve internal stability.

Other objective conditions that stimulated the integration process were the existing mineral resources in Kazakhstan and the world-class industrial, scientific, and technical capacities of Orenburg, whose workers possessed high levels of professional training and general education. In 1996, "barter operations"—the heritage of the Soviet planning and distribution system—were the leading form of economic interaction between the two regions, amounting to 57 percent of the region's total barter bargains with all the CIS countries (Laskov 1997, 14). The Orenburg administration continued to seek new ways of interaction that would stimulate the development of direct capital investment in each other's territories. Of the registered joint companies in the Orenburg region, by 1996 41 out of a total of 180 had been created with the participation of Kazakh partners; by 1999 this number was 45 out of 209.[10] Although economic relations between the two stabilized in 1997–1999, some problems still occurred in transborder cooperation, such as the future reliability of agreements regarding delivery of unprocessed oil and gas from Kazakhstan to the Orenburg region in 1997. Also, by 1999, some 17 percent of all Orenburg and Orsk enterprises connected with Kazakhstan had gone out of business, and one-third of the enterprises had grown considerably weaker in that same period. The most typical problems of business cooperation with Kazakhstan partners faced by these enterprises were questions of payment, the difficulty of obtaining long-term registration, and the bureaucratic red tape of the Kazakhstan officials.

The Orenburg regional administration believed in a regional approach to production problems and sought to remedy the situation by establishing agreements with the administrative bodies of the neighboring regions of Kazakhstan. On 26 June, 1997, the heads of the administrations of the Orenburg, West Kazakhstan, Aktyubinsk, and Kostanai regions signed a "Treaty on establishing and developing basic directions of partnership," a "Treaty on cooperation in protection of the environment, use of natural resources, and providing ecological security on contiguous territories," and an "Agreement on cooperation in protection of population and territories in a state of emergency of a transferred nature." These agreements addressed a broad range of border cooperation issues, and also served to focus both sides on the problems of trade and economic relations. The "Treaty on establishing and developing basic directions of partnership" reaffirmed the eagerness of the participants "to expand economic cooperation, promote the development of science, advanced technologies, [and] free enterprise."[11] The creation of joint ventures and joint investments in the enterprises of mutual interest, the use of natural resources, and the development of a transportation infrastructure have become the key tasks for interregional cooperation. The motives for Orenburg, though, as reinforced in the author's interviews with officials, related to their desire to further their own regional economic interests, and that of the Russian state more broadly, including development of gas fields and other opportunities.

Further development of border cooperation raised the issue of corresponding demands by the Kazakhstan regions to their government regarding "economic independence of regions," a degree of which the Orenburg region had already gained under an agreement with the Russian federal government. Only in this way, they thought in Orenburg, could the two countries promote the maintenance of "the common market economic area" to unify money circulation, taxation, customs duties, and rates of exchange. Discussion of problems of regional cooperation occurred at two meetings in the summer of 1998, but the region needed federal support to carry out its own initiatives. This included creation of a "Europe-Asiatic center where it would be possible to focus trade and economic relations of the CIS countries" in "a zone of free trade or Exchange Court" (Yelagin 1999a).

Contacts with the representatives of the federal power continued, with then-Russian Minister for Foreign Affairs Primakov arriving in Orenburg after a visit to Kazakhstan and addressing the transformation of the Orenburg section of the Russia-Kazakhstan frontier into an "experimental laboratory for organization of the border regional cooperation" (*Orenburzhje* 1998). Orenburg was to become the site of the next meeting of the interstate Russia-Kazakhstan committee. In Orenburg it was thought that the tradition of the eighteenth-century Border Commission would be revived in this way. Unfortunately, all these undertakings came to very little; even signing treaties is not enough when the official administrative structures are checked by a border that is increasingly becoming a barrier.

Commercial Ventures. The post-Soviet era has brought the emergence of new forms of bilateral cooperation built on commercial interests. Orenburg-Kazakhstan commercial cooperation, as was revealed by the sociological research conducted by the author, has entered the initial stages of its development (only six of 25 organizations surveyed have direct production relations with Kazakhstan). Nevertheless, commercial contact is becoming a reality, creating the opportunity for still other forms of contact between the two countries.

Commercial cooperation has been developing only in the areas of the region that directly adjoin the border with Kazakhstan—the cities of the center and east, Orenburg, Orsk, Novotroitsk, and Mednogorsk. The organizations involved in this cooperation are for the most part closed joint-stock companies (for example, cellular communications). Nevertheless, all these companies were created, as their representatives stressed in their interviews, for the sake of "making a profit and developing the contacts with the Kazakhstan side" and, with one exception, are self-financed.

In every case, initial contacts with the Kazakhstan partners were made by the leaders of the companies. Quite a few of these leaders and their workers were of Kazakhstan origin. In the interviews with their representatives, there was a positive evaluation of migrants from Kazakhstan and their role in the economic development of the region (this differs greatly from the case of the industrial giants, to be considered below). Two of their main motivations for developing contacts with the neighboring state were the availability of relatives in Kazakhstan and the preservation of friendly relations with its citizens so as to facilitate promotion of their products or services in Kazakhstan (for example, in placing their advertisements). It was also important for efficient production that their workers know the Kazakh language. Often they succeed by creating a niche in the Kazakhstan market for a product not yet locally produced, for example cellular communications, mayonnaise, and ice cream.

However, the lack of competition in the Kazakhstan market, which has made them successful, also makes them particularly vulnerable. For example, in the early 1990s, the Orenburg liqueur-vodka distillery had a monopoly on the vodka market in Aktyubinsk, Kazakhstan. But in 1995, another distillery started up in Aktyubinsk, and the Orenburg enterprise was forced out. This leads these organizations to advocate for an active state policy aimed at developing relations with Kazakhstan and working out measures to promote regional integration. Another challenge includes supporting contacts with their foreign partners, making these entrepreneurs into definite supporters of border integration, and preserving a high level of border transparency.

Border Trade. Yet another type of commercial interaction is that of small-business owners who engage in "shuttle" exchanges. These are individuals who purchase cheap consumer goods in other markets, such as in Turkey or Moscow, and then bring them back to the region for resale where there is a lack of such affordable goods. Shuttles arose in all the countries formed within the bounds of the post-Soviet regions and have spread throughout the territory of the southern Urals and western Kazakhstan. One group of shuttles started as the providers of goods (clothes, footwear) from Moscow and Turkey (via the direct Orenburg-Istanbul airline). Another group supplied goods that had been delivered by their Russian colleagues in Orenburg to the cities of the neighboring Kazakhstan regions. In 1996, cheap Turkish goods became available in Orenburg through the new Aktyubinsk-Istanbul air route via Kazakhstan, stimulated by the difference in the exchange rate, which was also the main factor behind the availability of cheaper Kazakhstan agricultural products (vegetables, melons, meat) in the Orenburg region. The Russian financial crisis of August 1998 and the measures taken by the Kazakhstan government that strictly limited export to the contiguous Russian regions have changed the situation radically, in effect putting an end to the "shuttle" business.

Until August 1998, when cross-border trade experienced a recession likely related to Orenburg's introduction of protectionist measures, the most active participants of the border trade were the rural inhabitants of the border areas of the central and eastern districts of the region. Some 15.5 percent of the Orenburg region's residents characterize their trade with the citizens of the neighboring Kazakhstan regions as "constant"; 13.4 percent as "rather frequent"; and 21 percent as "from time to time." Eight percent of the Russian participants of the study and 14 percent of the ethnic Kazakh participants characterized the trade with Kazakhstan residents as "of the utmost importance for the material well-being of their families" (Amelin and Vinogradova

1997, 105–107).[12] Demonstrating the eagerness of the Kazakh diaspora to join the process of regional economic interaction despite the marginalization they currently experience in the Orenburg region, two Orenburg businessmen of Kazakh origin have become deputies of the Legislative Assembly. One is the chairman of a collective farm and the other is an executive manager of the agricultural joint-stock union, both of them representing districts in the region with considerable shares of Kazakh population.[13]

Higher Education. A fourth sector of cooperation includes Orenburg's higher education institutions, which, facing difficult financial situations similar to those of many Russian education establishments, look to new solutions. To a certain extent, the coordinated activity of the higher educational institutions of Orenburg (Orenburg State University, Orenburg State Pedagogical University, Orenburg State Medical Academy, and Orenburg State Agricultural University) has had positive results in this direction. The opening of their consultative centers (in Aktyubinsk, at least) and the participation of their instructors in preparing students from Kazakhstan for entering these institutions have gone a long way toward promoting their institutions at a time when annually fewer than 5 percent of students from the Aktyubinsk region go on to further study in Orenburg. The system of paid education is acceptable for students from Kazakhstan because it has been used there in years past. The development of bilateral relations in the sphere of higher education is envisaged by the agreements concluded by the Orenburg and Kazakhstan regions.

However, it must be noted that this interaction is not a real form of border cooperation. The Kazakhstan students arriving in Orenburg (and, to a certain extent, in Orsk) are generally ethnic Russians. They, along with the few non-Russian Kazakh students, do not consider it possible to return to their mother country after finishing their education in the neighboring Russian region. This cooperation is, in fact, a latent form of migration from Kazakhstan.

Astrakhan

The expansion of Astrakhan's cooperation with Kazakhstan and other countries, along with its outlet to the Caspian Sea, have been key features of the region's ability to adapt to an increasingly globalized world economy and to reforms of Russian sociopolitical and economic institutions. Problems in transborder cooperation have special significance because the Astrakhan region maintains the transport passages and communications among the countries of Central Asia and Europe. According to western specialists, transportation via Astrakhan is half as costly as other alternatives (however, the Iran section of the route is unpredictable from an insurance point of view). Simultaneously, there are definite prospects connected with developing a land transport route via the land frontier with Kazakhstan. However, the land transport network is a weak link in the regional system of transport communications. Regional roads are not adapted to heavy haulers and container traffic; some are in poor condition and do not meet modern road transportation requirements. Delays in modernizing the transport network could very well translate into the international cargo transporters' leaving the region for better conditions elsewhere. To avoid competition, in September 2000 Russia and Kazakhstan signed an agreement on the realization of coordinated transportation policy and development of the Eurasian transport corridors that pass through these countries (Mirkitanov 1997, 6).

Our research found that there are some legislative agreements regarding boundary collaboration in this region, but there are no mechanisms for their implementation. Currently, cross-border interactions occur primarily among economic interests, business associations, labor markets, cultural groups, educational institutions, and environmental interests. Both commercial and non-commercial Astrakhan organizations cooperate almost exclusively with the Atyrau region of Kazakhstan. This is the case for several reasons: the border location of the Atyrau region, traditional relationships formed in the Soviet period, and the fact that the Atyrau region, to a large extent, concentrates finances resulting from the Tengiz field development. In addition, the availability of spare cash from the boundary region's authorities and population has become a strong incentive to collaborate with the Kazakh region.

Economic Contacts. These ties with Kazakhstan are maintained by government bodies, by commercial organizations (including joint-stock companies, limited-liability companies, and private companies) and, to a lesser extent, by public organizations (such as the Kazakh cultural society Zholdustyk). According to the rough data, some 20 large and medium Astrakhan firms (or their branches), and Kazakh firms created by Astrakhan citizens, now operate in Atyrau. According to the experts consulted for this study, Astrakhan enterprise activity in Kazakhstan is concentrated in retail and wholesale food trade, the wholesale consumer goods trade, various types of building (originally connected to the development of the oil and gas production infrastructure), and certain service sectors. The regional authorities are now beginning to focus on promoting commercial and economic relations not only with Atyrau but also the Manghistau region as well (by means of foodstuff deliveries from Astrakhan). They are also working toward opening new stores in the region as part of a supermarket chain headquartered in Astrakhan.

The majority of organizations working with Atyrau are private ventures, independent from the state and self-financed, with the exception of the Astrakhan shipbuilding facilities, which fill large orders for hydrocarbon-producing firms in Kazakhstan due to their existing industrial capacities and a highly skilled labor force.[14] Astrakhan can ensure (to the extent possible) the creation of the marine oil production infrastructure—constructing drilling rigs, floating production supply vessels, tankers, and so forth. These enterprises can depend on the credits, taxes, and loans from the regional budget. All participants in economic activity are engaged in the export of goods, labor, means of production, and so forth. The experts surveyed were of the opinion that there is nothing to import from Kazakhstan—except oil and fish, and with these two import items there is little opportunity for private firms. The import and transit of oil are the arenas of the largest national and international companies ("LUKoil," CPC), but only a few businessmen import fish because of its poor quality, difficulties with customs, and other factors.

Nevertheless, Astrakhan's transborder cooperation with Kazakhstan cannot yet be called stable. The establishment of business activity in Kazakhstan is motivated by the aspiration to increase trade and profits and by the absence of competitiveness in Atyrau. Almost all commercial enterprises in Kazakhstan have been established only since 1997. In the course of conducting the focus groups, it became apparent that this commercial activity was triggered by two factors: the beginning of large-scale hydrocarbon development (the Tengiz field and the Caspian shelf), which resulted in foreign investment inflow and growth in Atyrau market capacity; and the conclusion of a collaboration agreement between the Astrakhan and Atyrau regions.

The potential hydrocarbon reserves of the Caspian shelf adjacent to the Astrakhan region—Azerbaijan, Kazakhstan, and Turkmenistan—are estimated at 28 billion tons. In March 2000, LUKoil, the largest oil company, officially declared that seven oil- and gas-bearing deposits had been discovered on the northern Caspian shelf. The fuel industry makes up 42 percent (as of 1999) of the regional industry. The potential of Astrakhan regional development is based on these considerable oil and gas resources. Eighty percent of the gas resources in the Volga region, which at the present production level will produce for 300 years, come from the Aksaray Steppe. In 1999, 8.7 billion cubic meters of natural gas were produced in the region. Moreover, 200 kilometers of the oil pipeline being built from Tengiz in the northeast of the Caspian coast in Kazakhstan to Novorossisk on the Black Sea passes through the Astrakhan region. The region is expected to accrue around $3 million in oil transit taxes in the first year that the pipeline is in operation (projected to be online July 1, 2001). In 2014 to 2017, this sum will increase to as much as $39 million. The companies constructing the pipeline (including some Astrakhan enterprises) will pay taxes to the local budgets and thus increase revenues available to local authorities (Tjukaev 200a).

Business Associations. For the most part, Astrakhan businesses cooperate with Atyrau regional authority bodies (which act as the clients) or with foreign firms formally registered in Kazakhstan. Contacts with the representatives of solely Kazakh private capital are exceptional, and no respondent in the study had heard of the creation of joint private ventures. As a rule, the founders, directors, or deputy directors of Astrakhan enterprises are responsible for communications with their partners in Kazakhstan. For more or less stable business to take place, it is necessary to carry on "private" meetings with the representatives of Kazakh authorities. In organizing the contracts with Kazakh organizations, Astrakhan businesspersons try to communicate with the leaders at the appropriate level. In doing so, they depend on people who have lived in Atyrau or know someone there. Even then, communications with Kazakh organizations are by no means predictable, as all the participants in the focus group noted.

The collaboration of the Chambers of Commerce and Industry (CCI) in the Caspian region countries is developing within the framework of the International Council on Caspian Business (with the initials ICBC). The constituent meeting of the council was held in Astrakhan in 1996, and included the Chambers of Commerce and Industry of the Russian Federation of the Astrakhan region, Kalmyk, Nizhnevolzhsk, the joint Iran-Russian CCI, the Iran CCI, the Kazakhstan Republic CCI, and the CCI of the cities of Atyrau, Aktau, Aktyubinsk, and Uralsk. In 1999, they extended membership to the Azerbaijan and Turkmenistan CCI. ICBC also tries to include the Russian association called the "Great Volga" in the process of cooperation. The most recent ICBC meeting at this writing, in September 2000, was hosted by Astrakhan.

Migration and Labor Markets. In addition to food and goods exports, there is industrial cooperation in the case of Astrakhan enterprises acting as contractors or subcontractors in building and supplying gas and water in the Atyrau region, due to the shortage of highly skilled labor in Atyrau. Almost all commercial organizations working with Kazakhstan try to use the Russian-language migrants from Atyrau (except Kazakhs). They work as consultants, negotiators, and representatives of Astrakhan firms. Apparently, after large-scale oil development began in Atyrau, the outflow of the Russian-language population from Kazakhstan was reduced. All participants expressed the opinion that ethnic Kazakhs were poor workers. Even the organizations that have permanent representation in Atyrau try to engage Russian-language workers (Russians, Koreans, and Germans), hiring Kazakhs only in exceptional cases. One of the participants declared that the terms "labor force" and "Kazakhstan" were incompatible. Another person, a supermarket owner, declared that he would have to spend large sums of money to train Kazakhs before he could hire them as shop assistants.

The opportunity exists for cooperation on migration policies, since the Astrakhan region's policies were formed in a period characterized by a migrant influx from the conflict zones of the post-Soviet territories and based on factors that have since changed. The potential of the Astrakhan region to become the main point of growth for Caspian hydrocarbon production and transportation, for instance, is a key regional development that will stabilize economic growth and bring considerable investment flows to both the Astrakhan region and the contiguous territories of Kazakhstan. In fact, in 1997–2000, cross-border cooperation with the Atyrau region of Kazakhstan was more active owing to the investment inflow to the Tengiz oil field. The prospective trend within the next ten years will become the skilled-labor "export" from the Astrakhan region to set up the necessary infrastructure for the development of Kazakhstan oil. It will also be possible to draw in the Kazakh labor force of low and secondary qualification to the Astrakhan region. The growth in hydrocarbon production and transportation will create new jobs, where demand will exceed supply, especially for highly skilled labor, and it will also bring a rise in living standards. Under these conditions, the flow of poor immigrants from the Newly Independent States (NIS) will decrease and highly skilled workers from other Russian regions will prevail. However, the demand for unskilled labor cannot be met under the current "rules of the game."

To meet today's realities, migration policy should be reoriented toward attracting unskilled labor from the contiguous Kazakh and Russian territories to meet the needs of Astrakhan's changing labor market. A more successful migration policy would also stimulate the "export" of qualified, highly skilled manpower from Astrakhan to the contiguous Kazakh areas. The development of hydrocarbon resources in Kazakhstan brings the possibility of using an Astrakhan labor force because of the acute shortage of qualified manpower in Kazakhstan. In instituting these changes, the regional policy would again be in line with the international commitments of Russia, the Constitution of the Russian Federation, and federal legislation. Documents that regulate the attraction and use of the foreign labor force as well as the legislative position of foreign citizens and stateless persons (with some preferences given to Kazakh citizens) also should be passed. It would also be necessary to achieve an agreement with the bordering territories of Kazakhstan to open the markets to one another, including the labor market. In short, Astrakhan needs a regional migratory program, connected with programs of economic and social development, involving strict controls over the frontier with Kazakhstan and the legalization of the shadow economy.

Cultural Interactions. Cultural communications between the Astrakhan region and Atyrau were not broken after the disintegration of the Soviet Union: the traditional days of Kazakh culture are still celebrated in the region, and there is a memorial complex in the Volodarsky region (the mausoleum of an individual honored by Kazakhs). According to regional administration representatives, cultural communications have become more active since 1997, when the border area authorities received financing resources and the private organizations became active. Since then, real integration of the two regions has begun. The mutual measures on cultural exchange will help create an atmosphere of trust, for both Russians and Kazakhs alike.

Education and Research Institutions. The collaboration of universities and scientific research institutions takes place within the framework of the Caspian Universities Association. The main goals of the association are bringing together the leading scientists and specialists for complex learning in the region, searching for solutions to common problems, informing public opinion in the Caspian states, and consolidating efforts for the rational utilization and protection of the Caspian basin resources. The most important task of the association is to establish and develop a common educational and informational space in the Caspian region. The first constituent conference of the association (the General Assembly) was held in Astrakhan in September 1996, with the participation of the Astrakhan and Azerbaijan State Technical Universities; the Universities of Kalmykia, Daghestan, Turkmenistan, and Atyrau; and the Mazandran, Ghiljan, and Gorgan Universities of the Republic of Iran. The association also includes Baku State University (Azerbaijan), Aktau State University (Kazakhstan), and the scientific/industrial association Shilat (Iran).

It is important to note that in Astrakhan, as in the other Russian regions studied here, Kazakhstan citizens can and do receive education in its institutes, but the number is quite small. Moreover, because the population of the northern Kazakhstan regions as well as the Kazakhs who live in the Astrakhan region itself speak Russian well, there are no plans in Astrakhan now to teach in the Kazakh language.

Environmental Issues. Questions of ensuring ecological safety and controlling the sea shelf environment were raised in connection with the enlargement of oil production and oil exploration in the northern part of the Caspian Sea. But in the summer of 1999, the Astrakhan governor, the leaders of Atyrau and Manghistau regions of Kazakhstan, and the "Kazakhoil" president signed a communiqué in which they confirmed their intention to take all possible measures for preserving the ecological variety of the Caspian Sea and to forbid activity that would seriously harm the Caspian environment. This was the first initiative suggested at a regional level in the Caspian region. In another example—the Volga-Akhtuba flood lands, where the CPC pipeline is situated—about $365 million will be spent on increasing the safety of the pipeline. The pipe across the Volga River was not built on the riverbed, but below its level in order to contain the contamination in case of a break (Tjukaev 2000b, 3). As this is being written, some Astrakhan water towers also supply the Atyrau region with water, at no charge.

Further cooperation in this arena could occur, as Astrakhan citizens are anxious about the situation in Eastern Kashagan, situated 75 kilometers southwest of Atyrau and 200 kilometers southeast of Astrakhan. The mineral resources extracted include up to 24 percent hydrogen sulfide, a poisonous substance that could be blown by the wind into the Astrakhan region (Tjukaev 2000b, 1). There are also some doubts regarding the "OKIOK" project, which promises to follow "zero emission" technology—no marine pollution—but which plans to burn casing-head gases having a high content of hydrogen sulfide with its fuel sprays. Moreover, they are concerned about the environmental situation in Tengiz. The environmentally damaging operations in Tengiz, where gas production is three times higher than is allowable, can lead to soil erosion and earthquakes. An environmental movement against the project has formed in Kazakhstan, and Astrakhan ecologists support this activity of the Kazakh "greens."

Transborder Problems and Challenges

For those on the Russia-Kazakhstan border, the border is not only a barrier, but also a real factor of public concern and dissent. There is a whole range of issues for which the border and its transparency—or lack thereof—have important implications for both sides of the border. Some of these issues, such as education and health care, are of particular import for the Kazakhstan population, and maintaining the transparency of the border is critical from the Kazakh perspective. Many of those same issues, from the Russian perspective, are problematic and present additional financial burdens on the region. Still other issues affect both sides of the border, such as crime or drug trafficking, and the officials clearly believe the region would gain from strengthening control of the border.

Our research in the Omsk, Orenburg, and Astrakhan regions found that the border communities face a number of challenges to cross-border cooperation. Since many of these challenges turned out to be similar in each region, this section will summarize them, providing examples from the various regions. The primary issues were: criminal activity, ethnic and religious tensions, migration, delimitation of borders, and various technical issues such as border management and regulatory difficulties.

Criminal Activity

As on any border, criminal activity is a problem, ranging from trafficking in drugs, weapons, or people to road crime. For instance, respondents in the Omsk region noted the rapid growth of drug addiction in the region, claiming that nearly half of university students and at least one-third of high school children had had personal experience with drugs. Cattle theft is another local problem, with estimates ranging from 23,000 a year to twice that amount. Robbery of trucks and buses in the Omsk region (by gangs who know that cross-border prosecution is nearly impossible) was stopped only after special road-police troops were established and trucks and buses started moving in convoys, at a cost exceeding two million rubles a month. Residents in the Omsk region also fear that some parts of Kazakhstan are now a refuge for armed Chechen irredentists.

This fear was repeated by politicians in Orenburg, who were certain that the territory of their southern neighbor was turning into the base of activities of "the secret service agents of the foreign states" (Yelizarov 1997, 69–70).[15] It is reinforced by the uncontrolled migration of people from the Central Asian countries, Afghanistan, Pakistan, and China, across the territory of Kazakhstan, which contributes to the appearance within the Orenburg region of "the criminal national associations," with "the transit of narcotics and weapons" as one of its main activities (Savelzon 1999). These problems are seen as a potential threat to territorial integrity, particularly since the region is becoming the transshipping point of narcotics traffic.

Proximity to regions with well-organized drug trafficking (for example, 341 kilograms of drugs, including 220 kilograms of heroin, were seized in 1999) is also a problem in Astrakhan, which is facing an increasing crime rate (19,600 crimes recorded in 1999, a 21 percent increase from 1998) (Astrakhan Regional Administration 2000), two-thirds of which were classified as "grave." One serious problem is kidnapping, particularly of children. Other crimes involve firearms, murders, and robberies, all of which are increasing as well (over the last five years the number of premeditated murders has increased by 57 percent). A second reason for the higher crime rate relates to the corruption and criminal activity of those in charge of law enforcement. The distrust of the society regarding the militia is not baseless: in 1999, 62 actions were brought against 83 officers. Migration from the republics of the Northern Caucasus, Transcaucasus, and Central Asia was also blamed for the rising crime rate, with regional authorities calling it a destabilizing factor. Public opinion supports this thesis, with one newspaper report stating that every fifth crime is committed by those—citizens and non-citizens—without formal residence permits, 80–90 percent of whom are living in the region illegally. In addition, organized criminal groups are trying to gain some legitimacy through filling essential positions in the fuel and energy complex, in the financial sphere, and in the consumers' market. This has led the energy complex to establish and finance a special militia subdivision (complete with transportation, arms, and communications) to guard the important assets of the Astrakhan gas-processing plant.

Interethnic Conflicts

Some of the criminal threats described above are linked with the possible growth of religious extremism in the Central Asian states and the attempts at recruiting supporters of Islamic fundamentalism, both in the countries located to the south of the region and in the neighboring national territorial units of Russia (Bashkortostan and Tatarstan). For example, in the Orenburg region, the possibility of ethnic conflict is the most considerable challenge to the Southern Ural status quo: "The [region] is under the negative informational and criminal streams from the contiguous territories and is characterized by the focus of explosive factors of social and economical instability" (Raguzin and Pruss 1998, 81). The most probable zone of ethnic conflict is in those administrative units that directly adjoin the frontier and that have a higher share of native Kazakh population. Some 35.9 percent of native Russians and 31.9 percent of Kazakhs do not exclude the possibility of the interethnic conflicts, which are potentially stimulated by the situation of the Russians in Kazakhstan (Raguzin and Pruss 1998, 18–19). Commenting on the results of numerous sociological studies held in the region, representatives of the Orenburg administration note that "the situation of the Russians and Russian-speakers in Kazakhstan causes a boomerang effect in the border districts of the Orenburg region, [and] hostility is growing among the Russians toward the Russian Kazakhs" (Amelin and Vinogradova 1997, 117–118).

Increased migration into the Orenburg region also has brought growth in sympathy for the parties and movements on the extreme right of the Russian political spectrum. Those in Orenburg noted the potential danger to "the Russian passage" that arises in connection with some coordination of the course of three Turkish-Moslem state units —Tatarstan, Bashkortostan, and Kazakhstan. They fear re-creation of "the Idel-Ural state" and "the common Bashkir-Tatar state" at the expense of the Orenburg region. Also, Russian nationalists accuse the administration of "admitting 'Asians' [migrants and refugees]" and "turning the region into Babylon, of which the historical fate is known." Although fully one-fifth (20.4 percent) of those surveyed consider Russian nationalism to be "the spiritual revival of the Russian nation," and 14.8 percent believe it is "the country's way out of the crisis" (Raguzin and Pruss 1998, 47), general support for this nationalist position does not seem to be strong: 64.8 percent of the respondents regard Russian nationalism as "the destruction of the country, its international, historical basis" (Amelin 1999, 25–28).

Although generally relations between the different faiths in the Astrakhan region remain stable, Islamic fundamentalism is the one exception, with a perceived threat from the increasing influence of Islamic extremists, who are ready to implant the ideas of the Islam state illegally and by force if necessary. Interethnic tensions also are demonstrated by clashes of ethnic groups in the markets, fights among youth of different nationalities in the Limanovsky district in April 1998, and terrorist attempts on the railway in the Krasnoyarsky and Kharabalinsky districts in October 1999. A notable regional politician, Deputy Bozhenov, considers that the newly arrived, including Russians from Chechnya, differ from the point of culture and world outlook, and believes they must have time to adapt and to learn to understand and respect the local inhabitants. Nevertheless, in the opinion of the regional authorities, the situation in Astrakhan is currently under control, and the problem is exaggerated by the media, although authorities will continue to pay close attention (Barkov, Borovsky, and Volkov 2000, 3).

Migration

As described above, migration is blamed for many other problems, such as criminal activity and interethnic tensions. Immigration is indeed viewed by the regions as a challenge. In Omsk, for example, at least four-fifths of 6,000 total immigrants in 1999 came from Kazakhstan. Between 1993 and 1995, this migration influx had been mainly ethnic Russians, Ukrainians, and Belarusians (73 percent, 13 percent, and 14 percent, respectively), but since 1997 Armenians, Estonians, Latvians, and Germans have been immigrating in larger numbers (3.1 percent, 4.1 percent, 4.0 percent, and nearly 6.4 percent, respectively). This is interesting, since Russian migration authorities designated the Omsk region as "positive" for immigration in 1995 because its northern districts were suffering from depopulation trends. Emigration out of the German Azov district (the only national district in the region) reached a high of 14.4 percent in 1995. Both restrictions on the German side and emigration of ethnic Germans from Kazakhstan to Azov have now ameliorated the situation a bit.

The migration stream to and through the Orenburg territory from Kazakhstan and the Central Asian countries is a phenomenon of the post-Soviet era. The first groups to arrive were Russians and those who spoke Russian, followed by labor migrants from the Central Asian countries (Kazakhstan, Tajikistan, and Uzbekistan). Although most of these do not undergo registration, officials in Orenburg predicted that in 2000 no fewer than 10,000 labor migrants will arrive from Central Asia (Gorshenin 1999, 48). According to the data of the Orenburg Department of the Federal Migration Service, the number of registered migrants remained relatively constant at around 5,000 per year from 1994 to 1999, although the number of Kazakhs steadily increased. Also, according to official data, as high as 18 to 20 percent of all the migrants do not apply to the migration service and remain unregistered (Raguzin and Pruss 1998, 76–77). The region is not prepared to accept such numbers of migrants, as was demonstrated in discussions about whether or not to accept Chechen refugees (*Yuzhnyi Ural* 1999, October 29).

Public opinion in Orenburg about migration also is far from positive, with 64 percent of the study's respondents declaring that they do not accept migration and more than half feeling that migration has a negative influence on the Orenburg region (68 percent) and on Russia as a whole (52 percent), regardless of whether the migrants are Russian or from Central Asian countries. Experts see migrants as competitors to the native labor force and as placing additional strain on national and regional budgets. Sixty percent of the respondents considered it necessary to reinforce controls at the border crossings, and 30 percent of the advocates of this measure agreed with the idea of introducing a visa regime. Similarly, representatives of the Orenburg departments of the federal frontier guards, federal security services, and the heads of administrations of the border regions supported the idea of a visa regime, arguing that it can help combat the growth of the narcotic drug stream, smuggling, illegal immigration, and crime. Understandably, those who oppose the visa regime and tighter customs and frontier controls are the leaders of the regional Kazakh autonomy.

The majority of the survey respondents see the solution to the migration problem through the lens of "ensuring of the equal rights of the Russian-speaking population of Kazakhstan in the sphere of information, education, and culture." Only as a last resort do they speak about granting "privileges and credits for settling" to the migrants, a common point of view for people with difficult lives who regard the arrival of "aliens" as one of the sources of their troubles.

In the Astrakhan region, 40,600 migrants entered in the 1990s, half of whom came between 1995 and 1999. Many were forced migrants, because Astrakhan is near the conflict zones in Central Asia and the Caucasus, and many came from the former Soviet republics in the early 1990s. In addition to its physical proximity, they were attracted to its relatively low cost of living, relatively high living standards, and its tradition of peaceful coexistence with different nationalities and religions. The authorities of the border region focus on regulating the registration of temporarily residing persons, regulating residence in the bordering area, and easing the situation of involuntary migrants through provision of professional services and support.[16] These migrants also receive support from several federal programs, such as 16.9 million rubles under the "migration" and "children from the refugee and forced migrant families" programs, 30,000 rubles for lump-sum benefits, 1.6 million funded long-term building and real estate loans, and 14.2 million rubles as compensation for property lost in the Chechen Republic.

Nevertheless, anxiety regarding ethnic conflict, drug trafficking, and crime, along with public opinion and presumed menaces to social and political stability (for example, rising real estate prices, increasing property stratification according to nationality, an upset in the traditional ethnic balance of the population, and a growing unskilled labor force) has led regional authorities to tighten their migratory policy every year. In June 1993, the regional administration temporarily discontinued permanent registration in the region, and registration was allowed only for 45 days with possible extension.[17] In March 1994, the Administration Head Resolution tightened control over residing foreign citizens and persons without citizenship. Foreigners could receive permanent residence if they had close relatives in the region and with the permission of the committee, headed by the Governor.[18] A regulation to curtail the rights of the involuntary migrants to receive municipal housing passed under the Governor's pretext of safeguarding sanitary-epidemiological prosperity.[19] Subsequent efforts were aimed at returning the forced migrants to their permanent residences and putting pressure on Moscow either to direct the forced migrants to other regions or assign means for their support.[20] All the resolutions mentioned above are at variance with the international commitments of Russia, the Constitution of the Russian Federation, and federal legislation. But regional authorities believe that limiting migratory processes in the region is justified.

Public opinion in Astrakhan treats new arrivals negatively—regardless of citizenship, territory of departure, or migration types (permanent or temporary residence). Authorities and mass media often exacerbate the problem by speaking about thousands of illegal migrants (presumably from the Transcaucasus and Central Asia) without mentioning that the majority of them are Russian citizens from other regions who stay only for a short period. The citizens of the Transcaucasus and Northern Caucasus who do stay in the region specialize mainly in trading, although some are engaged in building and agriculture. The seasonal migrants from Kazakhstan (ethnic Kazakhs) do not influence the regional labor market. In most cases, they are engaged in casual agricultural work, unskilled construction, or low-paid piecework. Labor migration with the bordering Kazakh territories is practically absent because the bordering areas of both the Kazakhstan and Astrakhan regions are sparsely populated, with few settlements offering jobs and few Kazakhs, especially ethnic Kazakhs, meeting the labor-quality requirements. It is interesting to note that despite the negative perceptions regarding transit migration, the experts believed that the toughening of the passing regime must not concern the border area's inhabitants.

Delimitation

A fourth challenge to cooperation along this border is the still unresolved problem of delimitation of the border itself and the territorial claims on both sides. The Novowarsawka, Russkaia Poliana, and Cherlak districts were once part of Kazakhstan, and some Russian nationalists in the Omsk region talk about autonomy for northeastern Kazakhstan from Petropavlovsk to Ust-Kamenogorsk. A 1994 Friendship and Cooperation Treaty signed by the heads of all the bordering Kazakh and Russian regions tried to make some progress on this issue, but two polls—one in 1994 of 500 people and this study's survey in Schebarkul in 2000—found that around a third of non-Kazakhs in the Omsk region supported Russian sovereignty over northern Kazakhstan while around half the Kazakhs in the Omsk region supported Kazakhstan sovereignty in the same border districts. Orenburg officials had believed that the solution to the delimitation problem in its region would finally resolve the problem of Kazakhstan claims to some parts of its territory that were added after 1934 (Yakusheva

2000). However, since the process of delimitation is still in its initial stages, disputed territories remain unresolved.

Delimitation is a particularly key issue in the Astrakhan region because the oil and gas stakes are so high in determining natural resource use in the disputed territories. The delimitation process of the Kazakh-Russian frontier, including the 550-kilometer Astrakhan section, began in 1999 and at this writing is still only in its initial stages. The intergovernmental agreements in the eleven regions of Russia bordering upon Kazakhstan started in Astrakhan, since it has the most important commercial, economic, and strategic interests. The absence of agreements with Kazakhstan concerning the frontier and the use of disputed territories undoubtedly create conflict, particularly regarding territorial and natural-resource disputes.

In the Astrakhan region, the majority of the problems are connected with navigation, mineral-resource utilization, fishing rights, and environmental protection in the Caspian Sea. As an example, Kazakhstan fishes sturgeon but does not participate in replenishing the stocks. Similarly, Astrakhan water towers supply water to the Atyrau region, for which Kazakhstan does not pay. The heads of the local administrations, however, are reluctant to deal with this issue because they do not want to jeopardize their regular negotiations regarding use of Kazakhstan's space-vehicle launching site. Another example is the serious territorial disputes with Kalmyk in connection with the CPC oil pipeline construction. Kalmyk laid claim to Astrakhan lands in Shlansky district and only a separate agreement brokered by the CPC builders with Astrakhan collective farms on land utilization for the pipeline was able to put an end to the dispute (Tjukaev 2000b).

Border Management

The fifth challenge to cross-border cooperation involves technical issues related to border management. Resolving problems connected with the technical maintenance of the state border is not in the usual scope of regional administration competence, but rather falls within the sphere of activities of the federal power. Nevertheless, resolving problems related to the border has become the center of attention of the regional authorities, who influence implementing solutions in the most immediate way. The representatives of the federal agencies (the migratory service, customs and frontier guards) live in the regions and are often native to the area. Their destiny depends in many respects on the attitude of the administration (for example, their housing, salaries, and various other privileges). The administration forms its opinion about the results of their activities, influences the decisions made in Moscow, and ultimately determines the careers of the representatives of these structures.

In 1998 Omsk governor Leonid Polezhaev established a special borderline regime, a 5 kilometer-wide border zone on the Russian side with serious restrictions on freedom of migration and visiting. Even fiscal shortages have not forced the Omsk elite to reevaluate the necessity of this increased spending on customs and border guards. One local authority, who used to be a border guard at Khabarovsk Kraj in the Soviet period, stated his opinion that the need for serious border fortifications along the Kazakhstan border is even greater than on the Chinese border. At the same time, he doubted whether the current location of the border was fair. With the exception of the ethnic Kazakhs, none of the respondents objected to the idea of an official barrier border, disagreeing only on the role of the Cossacks as the border guard.

In Orenburg, the frontier is regarded as an area of heightened danger and higher responsibility; they believe it could stay "transparent" no longer (Savelzon 1999). At the same time, full-scale maintenance would be economically impossible due to the enormous budgetary resources required. The regional administration stressed that the availability of customs posts along the Orenburg section of the Russian-Kazakhstan borderline does not prevent border crossing "practically at any place" in the summer. This permeability promoted the increased "volume of the Russian raw materials and strategic materials exported to the Central Asian states," on the one hand, and the illegal import "of the bad-quality food products from the Republic of Kazakhstan to the oblast," on the other. Border maintenance presupposes that the actions taken in this connection would not destroy the already established direct relations ("at the grassroots level," as they used to say in Orenburg) with the executive authorities of the Kazakhstan regions. Although the technical part of the frontier status registration was to be determined by "the basic decisions of the heads of contiguous states," these decisions, nevertheless, should be taken "up to the suggestions from localities" (Savelzon 1999).

The final decision about seriously tightening the interstate frontier was made only in 1999 after an experiment showed that "there is a mass migration to the territory of the oblast from the states, which do not even border the countries of the former USSR" (*Orenburzhje* 1999a). Even with these increased posts and resources, maintaining the Russian-Kazakhstan frontier at its Orenburg section is not without significant problems, as verified by the author's own crossings. At present, only 150 border guards serve this section, and according to the head of the federal frontier guards in Orenburg, "the personnel have no modern means of communication or good motor-cars, and there is a keen need for financing." Orenburg journalists often write about the difficult situation of the frontier posts, such as the Orenburg-Kostanai customs post having only one old-fashioned jeep with which to patrol 100 kilometers (Urzhanov 2000).

Today, there are plans to increase the personnel of each of three detachments to 800 border guards. But even where the frontier posts are already functioning, they meet with the other difficulties, such as refusal of the border region's residents to cooperate closely with the border guards. The residents claim it is because they do not want to be "stool-pigeons," but the commander of the Orenburg frontier guards implied that their reluctance to coordinate relates to their active role in narcotics transportation (*Yuzhnyi Ural*, July 5, 2000). The border guards understand that the low living standards of the residents force them into abetting the traffickers, but that does not prevent both countries' frontier guards and customs officials from initiating acts of tyranny on ordinary citizens or businessmen and representatives of the industrial enterprises that cross the borderline. Extortion and bribes have become "the frontier scourge," said all the respondents of this research.

Related to the issue of border management in the Orenburg region is the extent to which the Cossacks participate in guarding the Russian-Kazakh frontier. The Cossacks are an integral part of the all-Russian state structure, so the Orenburg elite could not ignore them and, in fact, were eager to institutionalize the Cossack initiatives and to incorporate the local Cossack movement into the existing local power structures. They did so in August 1998, uniting the Cossacks of the

Orenburg, Cheliabinsk, and Kurgan regions, and unofficially those of Bashkortostan, thus restoring the borders of the territory of the Orenburg Cossack host.

On the basis of Presidential Decree No. 943 of 19 June 1996, the Orenburg administration rendered assistance to realization of "the experiment on the non-army guarding" of the frontier (Pilyugin 1997, 84), which caused sharp protests on the Kazakhstan side. The Cossack activists were included in the process of completing the local detachments of the frontier guards (*Orenburzhje* 1999a). At the same time, however, the Orenburg administration opposed the Cossacks' guarding the frontier independently, because it could bring "imbalance to the whole border region" if they were to act independently. The situation in this sphere, however, has begun to change. The Cossacks can be used only by the regional administration, which in turn is able to influence the federal powers to exert pressure on Kazakhstan for achieving solutions to problems of the disputed sections of the territory to their profit.

Business Difficulties

The sixth obstacle to cross-border cooperation raised by focus group respondents involves another set of technical issues—challenges in doing business in Kazakhstan, which included an overwhelming amount of paperwork, having to give bribes to authorities, banking complications, and transportation problems. Focus group participants were very negative regarding the paperwork, citing the fact that no fewer than 15 different documents must be repeated on both sides of the border (certificates, licenses, veterinary certificates, transport documentation, and so on). All this paperwork results in transportation delays (and leads to food spoilage) and stresses on drivers. Most documentation issues are resolved privately, via the second problem, bribes.

It seems obligatory to cooperate with authorities to conduct business in Kazakhstan, through bribes or private communications. According to the unanimous opinion of businesspersons and customs officers, bribes also are common in the customs arena. The Russian customs officers take bribes in cases of incorrect documentation, whereas Kazakh customs officers take bribes with or without a reason. The Russian customs officers have more or less "fixed" tariffs, but the Kazakhs take a bit more from the same firm each time. Border crossings have improved recently due to some simplifications on the Russian side. In general, the system of interactions with Kazakh authorities is similar to the Russian one, except that, according to one of the respondents, "If you render a service to any official in Russia, you can hope for gratitude. There is no such system in Kazakhstan." But despite these difficulties, none of the experts surveyed sensed any direct counteraction to introducing Astrakhan capital in Atyrau. This "reluctant openness" to Astrakhan capital is most likely due to the fact that Kazakhs themselves realize that they do not have the capacity to organize the infrastructure needed for modern hydrocarbon production in their region.

The third difficulty relates to carrying out banking payments, caused first by the non-convertibility of Russian and Kazakh currency (the accounts are conducted by means of dollars); and second by some peculiarities of Kazakh legislation. If you convert tenghe into dollars at the bank one day and the money transfer is fixed for the next day, it is by no means certain that you will receive the sum of dollars you have bought. If in the course of the transaction the tenghe falls, the sum transferred will be less. The problem is made worse in Kazakhstan because there the period of transfer is longer.

Fourth are the significant transportation problems. The route from Astrakhan to Atyrau shocked all the participants in the boundary cooperation survey. The drivers of heavy haulers refuse to go to Atyrau, stating that it is easier to go to Moscow backwards than to go to Atyrau. According to all the experts surveyed, the absence of an adequate arterial highway between Astrakhan and Atyrau is the main obstacle to increased cooperation.

The respondents attribute these technical difficulties to two factors. First, the border area lacks a policy that recognizes the unique border region circumstances. It has no system of preferences to stimulate economic and other interactions with the contiguous territories of other states, nor are there legal mechanisms at the regional level. The legislation does not reflect the fact that Astrakhan and Atyrau are contiguous territories; there is no difference in required documents and customs duties whether the goods are imported from Astrakhan or another region of Russia. Second, Kazakh legislation, even more so than the Russian, lacks procedures for implementing its measures.

This in turn creates bureaucratic obstacles because officials can interpret the laws rather freely. This begins to explain the psychological incompatibility between Kazakh and Russian partners: the agreements and the rules of business activity in Kazakhstan are constantly changing and the Russian partners are hard-pressed to keep up.

All participants in the discussion noted that they needed the authorities' assistance for efficient collaboration with Kazakhstan. None of them lives in Kazakhstan. In crossing the frontier individually, they have no difficulties, and so they are opposed to tightening the control of the frontier crossing and to abolishing the non-visa regime for the inhabitants of the Astrakhan and Atyrau regions. The experts surveyed believe that transit migration via Kazakhstan negatively influences the situation in the region and that it must be limited, but not at the expense of border-area residents.

Conclusions

What conclusions, then, can be drawn from the study of these three Russian regions about the current situation and possible developments in the arena of transborder interactions and cooperation along the Russia-Kazakhstan border? Even before the breakup of the Soviet Union, interaction among the Russian regions and their Kazakhstan neighbors was sparse. This was in large part due to the Soviet Union's highly centralized transportation infrastructure throughout the whole country, and in these regions in particular. The border of each region exceeds 500 kilometers, but no more than three to five paved roads and only one or two railroads cross the border in each region. This is even true for the Astrakhan region, which is considered the transport junction that links Russia with Central Asia, India, the Crimea, and Transcaucasus. For these reasons, it is clear that no serious trade or economic contacts existed among Kazakhstan and two of the three regions (Omsk and Astrakhan) in the Soviet era, a trend which continues in the post-Soviet era as well, as less than 15 percent of exports or imports connect the Omsk or Astrakhan regions to Kazakhstan, and not one joint Russian-Kazakhstan venture for economic cooperation has been established in either the Omsk or Astrakhan region.

From the Kazakhstan perspective, there is little economic interest in the bordering Russian regions, because ethnic Kazakhs are minorities in the border districts of the Astrakhan and Orenburg regions. In the Omsk case, however, the situation is slightly different because of Russian ethnic—but by no means political—domination in Kazakhstan's border regions. And because the Kazakhstan political establishment tends to function as some kind of ethnic semi-democracy, ethnic Russian business in Kazakhstan is not favored, nor is establishing new links with its "northern neighbor."

There are, however, two important areas in which transborder cooperation does exist. The first is in the Orenburg region, where there is a considerable amount of economic cooperation: up to 85 percent of foreign trade in the region is Kazakhstan-oriented imports of raw materials from the Emba oil region and chromium from Khromtau. Because the adjacent Kazakhstan regions are industrially underdeveloped and no serious investment in refining industries is made there, Orenburg's industrial cities of Novotroitsk and Orsk remain crucial for Kazakhstan's well-being. The industrial giants, in turn, depend on the neighboring regions of northwestern Kazakhstan for agricultural products and raw materials. The majority of this trade, however, is either on a barter basis or is conducted by third-country economic agents. Even so, in the Orenburg region there are some joint Russia-Kazakhstan ventures (but their relative number is declining, from 15 percent in 1995 to less than 7 percent in 1999).

A second area in which transborder cooperation is taking place is the Astrakhan role in hydrocarbon production, both in the transport of oil and gas from existing operations (for instance, in Tengiz) and the potential hydrocarbon resources of the Caspian shelf adjacent to the Astrakhan region, Kazakhstan, and Turkmenistan. Astrakhan transport capabilities and its technical know-how and skilled labor force will be key in helping Kazakhstan develop its hydrocarbon industries.

But with the exception of these two examples, new economic links across the border in all three regions are virtually nonexistent. Commercial ventures across the border meet with considerable obstacles including payment problems, excessive bribes, and documentation difficulties. Joint ventures are rare, and bureaucratic red tape on both sides of the border continues to discourage cooperation. For some time, "shuttle" exchanges were in operation, but since 1998 these smallest of business links have also nearly stopped. In the Orenburg region, a small amount of trade occurs among residents on each side of the border, but of late even that has begun to decline.

So economic cooperation of the neighboring regions of Russia and Kazakhstan was not the main source of the transborder links in most cases and has become even less so. Where cooperation did exist, it was mostly of a donor-recipient relationship rather than mutual cooperation. As the impact of the Soviet legacy declines, this type of "cooperation" will decline as well. Because of the scarcity of road infrastructure, few habitual contacts ever existed on the basis of private life either, at least for the Russian-speaking majority of the population; the case is slightly different for the ethnic Kazakhs, who have strong family and clan ties to spur transborder visits and contacts.

The much faster decline of educational services in Kazakhstan than in neighboring Russian regions has made higher education of Kazakh students in the cities of Omsk, Orenburg, and Astrakhan a common practice. But in most cases the graduates do not return to their home countries, making the education interaction more a migration technique and less a form of transborder cooperation. A similar decline in Kazakhstan's medical facilities continues to draw the Kazakh population over the border to seek medical services in the Russian regions. Providing these services constitutes an additional burden on resources in the Russian regions.

Due to large illegal immigration influxes, both the public and the local and regional authorities see the border as a peril. Migration is considered the most daunting problem of the frontier because it is linked to crime, ethnic and religious conflicts, espionage, and drug trafficking. These problems, in the opinion of the authors of this report, have led to the joint efforts by Russian federal authorities and the regional border authorities to delimit and fortify the frontier. The experiences of these three Russian regions also make clear the importance of proper delimitation of the border. Territorial disputes in all three regions are causing tension and conflict, especially in the case of Astrakhan, where the use of vast hydrocarbon resources—and therefore vast sums of revenue—is at stake.

In less than ten years, the situation at the border has changed dramatically. The total transparency of the border in 1991 to 1994 was first decreased by establishment of a paramilitary border guard and further decreased by the regular military border forces now in operation. But because much of the borderline is located either in the steppe or in the deserts and semi-deserts, maintaining the border is so costly that neither Russia nor Kazakhstan, singly or in concert, can establish total border control. Thus, leaks remain large enough for nearly unhindered drug transportation and illegal migration into Russian regions, causing still more tensions in transborder relations.

The collapse of the Soviet Union was accompanied by the process of delimitation of the states that have risen in its ruins, a process which continues. All these states, including Russia, need to establish their identities and choose a strategy for moving forward politically, culturally, and economically. In doing so, their shared Soviet past, a key component of which is the absence of a developed civil society, continues to dominate their thinking and their choices. In continuing to define themselves, they will at the same time need to define their relations with their neighbors and the kind of cooperation they are willing to foster. Let us not forget that the status of the border as an official state border was established less than ten years ago in the three regions studied. It is still very early in the process of moving out of the Soviet past. Only time and changing circumstances will make clear the need to cooperate in solving common threats and problems. Only in acknowledging common interests will these regions be able to overcome the fears that interfere with their fruitful interaction. Only then will the line that divides them become one that unites them.

Notes

1. In cooperation with the Orenburg sociologist Professor E.M. Vinogradova.
2. This unexpected refusal could, perhaps, be related to the uncertainty resulting from the administrative reforms initiated by President Vladimir Putin.
3. A 1995/1996 treaty signed with the federal government on mutual delimitation of commission created the necessary legal prerequisites for Orenburg to implement the regulations which, as a national-territorial formation, allow the region to create agreements on cooperation with

bordering regions. This occurred in January 1995, during the formulation of the treaty between the Governments of the Russian Federation and the Republic of Kazakhstan.

4. The Orenburg region itself, however, was the Soviet raw materials "periphery," with its extracted and refined oil sent to the Volga region and central Russia, and the natural gas sent to European Russia, Ukraine, and Eastern Europe.

5. Districts sharing a land frontier with Kazakhstan (from north to south) include: Akhtubinsky, Kharabalinsky, Krasnoyarsky, and Volodarsky. The districts that have an outlet to the Caspian Sea (from east to west) include Volodarsky, Kamyzyansky, Ikryaninsky, and Limansky.

6. The region is indeed rich in natural resources—hydrocarbon resources, gas and gas condensate, sulfur, oil, and salt. There are also large fields of gypsum, mineral colors, argils, glass-making sands, potassium salts, bromine, and iodine. Mineral and freshwater production are also important.

7. One example was the Russian government's May 2000 decision on the sale of the state package of shares of the Orenburg oil company, ONAKO. It is supposed that its future owner will be one of the largest Russian oil monopolists, LUKoil company, since its representative became president of ONAKO the following month. Orenburg feared that the situation would result in the withdrawal of its activity beyond the region, refusal to cooperate with Kazakhstan, and a general reduction in a number of its enterprises (*Yuzhnyi Ural*, June 24, 2000b).

8. At times it seemed the only way to motivate post-1991 widespread transborder contacts in the Orenburg section of the Russia-Kazakhstan borderline was to support the production capacities of the industrial enclaves—Orenburg, Orsk, and Novotroitsk, where considerable numbers of workes were employed. In some cases the industrial giants are the factor that forms the towns, and in the absence of significant financial assistance from the federal government, the basis for the regional, municipal, and district budgets; they are thus the source of social stability.

9. During the post-Soviet period, $132.5 million was invested in the oblast economies (Yelagin 1999). Further, for seven months in 1999 the average wage-rate in Orenburg oblast was 386.6 rubles, while living costs were equal to 873.7 rubles (*Orenburzhje* 1999b.)

10. For 1996 data, see Mirkitanov (1997, 7). V.I. Mirkitanov was then deputy-chief of the Orenburg oblast administration and the head of the Department of International and Foreign Economic Relations. For 1999 data, see Gorshenin (1999, 47).

11. For the text of the Treaty see OGAU 1997: 203–205.

12. V.V. Amelin is the head of the department of interethnic relations of the Orenburg oblast administration.

13. For a list of Deputies of the Legislative Assembly of the Orenburg oblast of the second convocation, see Raguzin and Pruss (1998, 234–238).

14. Future cooperation in this area is likely, since Astrakhan firms built the floating platform for Caspian drilling at the request of the international marine works consortium (OKIOK) in Kazakhstan, which was created by nine of the largest oil and gas companies of the world. The negotiated contracts guarantee that, in the event of successful drilling results on the northern Caspian shelf, the subsequent orders for construction and modernization of the technical means for marine oil production and an accessory fleet would be placed with the Astrakhan shipbuilding facilities. The regional administration carries on the negotiations with Kazakh partners for placing other orders, making loans against mutual securities for purchasing and building ships for the Kazakh fleet.

15. G.N. Yelizarov was the head of the Federal Security Service Department in the Orenburg oblast.

16. For the Resolution of the Regional Administration Head, no. 190, item 3.4 of May 19, 1999, see the "Consultant Plus" data base, www.consultant.ru.

17. The Resolution of Astrakhan Region Administration Head, June 28, 1993, no. 100. "On stabilizing the criminal situation in the region," item 35; the temporary regulations on the registration order of citizens from other regions of Russian Federation and abroad. (The Appendix to the Resolution, no. 100, item 4.) (See the "Consultant Plus" data base, www.consultant.ru.)

18. Temporary regulations on stays of foreign citizens and persons without citizenship in the region. (The Appendix to the Resolution of the Regional Representative Assembly March 16, 1995, no. 36, item 16.) (See the "Consultant Plus" data base, www.consultant.ru.)

19. The Resolution of Astrakhan Regional Administration Head "On the measures, ensuring the sanitary-epidemiological prosperity in Astrakhan region." April 27, 1995, no. 110, items 4.1; 5, 6, 7.2. (See the "Consultant Plus" data base, www.consultant.ru.)

20. The complex of the primary measures to strengthen control over the registration regime for nonresidents in Astrakhan region. (Approved by the Resolution of the Administration Head, April 29, 1998, no. 171, items 4, 6.) (See the "Consultant Plus" data base, www.consultant.ru.)

Works Cited

Amelin, V.V. 1999. "Etnopoliticheskaja situatsija I mezhetnicheskije ot-noshenija v Orenburzhje." Orenburg: Izdatelskiy tsentr OGAU.

Amelin, V.V., and E.M. Vinogradova. 1997. "Sostojanije mezhnatsionalnykh onnoshenij v prigranichnykh s respublikoi Kazakhstan raionakh Oren-burzhja (sotsiologicheskij aspekt)." In *Orenburzhje i respublika Kazah-stan: prigranichnyje aspekty sotrudnichestva.* Orenburg: Izdtelskiy tsentr OGAU.

Astrakhan Regional Administration. 2000. "Obespechenie pravoporitadka" ("The criminal situation"). <www.adm.astranet.ru>.

Barkov, L., D. Borovsky, and O. Volkov. 2000. "Vahhabits on the Volga." MN *Time*, February 22, no. 26.

Borisyuk, N.K., and V.A. Sivelkin. 1997. "K voprosu ob ekonomicheskoi inte-gratsii s prigranichnymi raionami Kazakhstana." In *Orenburzhje i re-spublika Kazahstan: prigranichnyje aspekty sotrudnichestva.* Orenburg: Izdtelskiy tsentr OGAU.

Futurianskii, L.I. (ed.). 1996. *Istorija Orenburzhja. Uchebnoje posobije.* Oren-burg: Orenburgskoie knijnoie izdatelstvo.

Gorshenin, S.G. 1999. "Novoje prigranichje: k voprosu geograficheskoi na-pravlennosti gosudarstvennoi vneshneekonomicheskoi politiki." *Etno-panorama*, Orenburg, no. 1: 46–50.

Kolosov, V., et al. 2000. *Geopolitical Situation of Russia; Representations and Realities.* Moscow: Art-Courier Publishers.

Laskov, A.P. 1997. "Nekotoruje itogi vneshnei torgovli Rossii s respublikoi Kazahstan." In *Orenburzhje i respublika Kazahstan: prigranichnyje as-pekty sotrudnichestva.* Orenburg: Izdtelskiy tsentr OGAU.

Mirkitanov, V.I. 1997. "Ukreplenije prigranichnogo sotrudnichestva—trebo-vanije vremeni." In *Orenburzhje i respublika Kazahstan: prigranichnyje aspekty sotrudnichestva.* Orenburg: Izdtelskiy tsentr OGAU.

OGAU. 1997. *Orenburzhje i respublika Kazahstan: prigranichnyje aspekty sotrudnichestva.* Orenburg: Izdtelskiy tsentr OGAU.

Orenburzhje. 1999a. Dryndin V. "Granitsa Rossii i Kazahstana ne stanet gran-itsei razdor." October 5.

———. 1999b. "Oblast v tsifrah i faktah." October 2.

———. 1998. July 4.

Pilyugin, A.P. 1997. "Orenburzhje vnov stanovitsya zonoi pogranichnogo kontrolya. In *Orenburzhje i respublika Kazahstan: prigranichnyje aspekty sotrudnichestva.* Orenburg: Izdtelskiy tsentr OGAU.

Raguzin, V.N., and A.P. Pruss. 1998. *Formirovanije grazhdanmskogo obshestva v Orenburzheje.* Orenburg: Pechatnyi Dom "Dimur."

Savelzon, V. 1999. "Granitsa (tchyast vtoraja)." *Orenburzhje,* July 8.

Tjukaev, V. 2000a. "200-kilometrov trubi prinesut nam sviche 1 mlrd. dollarov" ("200-kilometer pipeline will bring over $1 billion"). *Volga*, February 2, no. 23.

———. 2000b. "Sroyiteli neftyinoy trubi pomogayut astrakhanzam" ("The builders of the oil-pipeline help Astrakhan population." *Volga*, April 26, no. 61.

Tsykler, V.A. 1997. "O problemakh prigranichnogo ekonomicheskogo sotrudnichestva." In *Orenburzhje i respublika Kazahstan: prigranichnyje aspekty sotrudnichestva.* Orenburg: Izdtelskiy tsentr OGAU.

Urzhanov, B. 2000. "Po obe storony Tobola." *Yuzhnyi Ural*, July 14.

Volga. 1999a. A. Jelkin. "Nadeyus, chto vostorjestvuet razum," no. 202, October 20.

———. 1999b. "Budget 2000: there are reserves for income increasing." no. 246, December 23.

Yakusheva, V. 2000. "Chuzhoi zemli my ne hotim ni pyadi." *Yuzhnyi Ural*, July 12.

Yelagin, V.V. 1999a. "Prigranichoye sotrudnichestvo na uroven sovremennyh trebovanii: Orenburzhje i respublika Kazahstan." In *Orenburzhje i respublika Kazahstan: prigranichnyje aspekty sotrudnichestva.* Orenburg: Izdtelskiy tsentr OGAU.

———. 1999b. "Sotrudnichestvo kak natsionalnaia ideia." *Orenburzhje.* May 29.

Yelizarov, G.N. 1997. "Na zashite bezopasnosti dvuh gosudarstv." In *Orenburzhje i respublika Kazahstan: prigranichnyje aspekty sotrudnichestva.* Orenburg: Izdtelskiy tsentr OGAU.

Yuzhnyi, Ural. 2000a. "Zastavy vsegda natseku." July 5.

———. 2000b. "Chto zhdyot 'ONAKO'?" June 24.

———. 1999. October 29.

APPENDIX

APPENDIX

The Development of Free Movement in the European Union

Sandra Schmidt and John Salt

THE CONCEPT of free movement is a cornerstone of the European Union and a basic right of the citizens of EU member states. This right is accompanied by a series of wide-ranging economic and social entitlements and enables those employed in other member states than their own to benefit from protections equal to those afforded to nationals. Table A.1 briefly outlines the development of free movement in the European Union, with reference to the relationship with EU regional policy and cross-border regional cooperation.

We first outline the evolution of economic integration and its accompanying steps toward political union. While the vision behind European integration was political, the rationale behind the concept of free movement in light of such integration is primarily economic. We then review the role of regional policy in promoting social and economic cohesion, good neighborly relations, creation of a European labor market, and related policy issues such as the role of regional authorities and programs in the European Union.[1] Free movement and regional policies seem to have evolved independently, however, with the former taking a top-down approach for national-level macroeconomic and political reasons and the latter using a bottom-up approach in response to recognition of regional and local-level problems.

TABLE A.I
Major Steps Toward Free Movement in the European Union and the Role of Cross-Border Regional Cooperation

EU Level	Main Provisions Regarding Free Movement	Developments on the Regional Level
GENESIS: THE 1950S–1970S		
1951 Treaty of Paris		Council of European Municipalities and Regions
1952 European Coal and Steel Community	Free movement for workers in the relevant industries	
1957 Treaty of Rome		
1958 European Economic Community		
THE 1960S–1980S		
1965		First Commission Communication on Regional Policy
1968 Regulation 1612/68, EEC	Completion of Common Market labor policy; free-movement rights for EC workers and their families	
1969		Second Commission Communication on Regional Policy
1971 Regulation 1408/71, EEC	Application of social security schemes to employed persons, self-employed persons, and to members of their families moving within the EC	
	Free-movement rights for self-employed EC workers	
1973		
1975 European Regional Development Fund		
1985 Schengen Agreement		
1986 Single European Act (SEA)		
CONSOLIDATION AND NEW CHALLENGES: THE 1990S		
1990	Extension of free-movement rights to non-workers	INTERREG Community Initiative Adopted
1993 The Maastricht Treaty	Citizenship of the European Union (Art. 7)	Creation of the Committee of the Regions (COR)
1994	Eures network set up by Commission	Creation of transparency for a European labor market
1998 The Amsterdam Treaty		Expansion of the COR's remit

Evolution of Free Movement

Although the 1957 Treaty of Rome and the entity it created, the European Economic Community (EEC), generally are associated with the commencement of European economic integration and free intra-EEC movement rights, there are several earlier examples of countries that had agreed to the free movement of labor before the establishment of the EEC. One is the European Coal and Steel Community (ECSC), established in 1952, which coordinated economic and social policies and resources in the coal and steel industries of the same countries that later constituted the EEC.

Precursors

In 1954, Denmark, Norway, Sweden, and Finland established a common labor market within which workers could move to accept or seek employment (Olsson 1953). Of the three historical precursors to the EEC, this agreement was the most advanced. Employment offices in the four countries systematically informed one another of vacancies and exchanged details of job applicants. Thus, the job placement of another member state's national was typically pre-arranged. Freedom of movement in the Nordic common labor market applied to all citizens irrespective of whether they were employed. Complementary policies were introduced as well, such as the Nordic social treaties, which removed barriers in the field of social protections.

In 1957, the European Coal and Steel Community (ECSC), comprising Belgium, France, the Federal Republic of Germany, Italy, Luxembourg, and the Netherlands, committed itself to the removal of barriers restricting movement of labor within the coal and steel industries of the six member countries. However, the practical result of this freedom of movement was small, due to the restrictive Community labor-card system. Only skilled workers in specific occupations could receive a Community labor card, and then only after two or three years of employment in an ECSC member state other than their own. Unskilled workers, however, could move between ECSC countries without labor cards in the same way as workers in any other industry;

many skilled workers may have done so as well (Hunter and Reid 1970). Work permits for employees in private industry were abolished for nationals of the Benelux countries (Belgium, the Netherlands, and Luxembourg) in 1960. This meant that the freedom of movement conditions of the common labor market within the Benelux countries came into effect eight years before they were fully implemented in the rest of the EEC.

Labor Market Integration

From the beginning of the European integration process, free movement of workers has been a guiding principle. Article 48 of the 1957 Treaty of Rome, which extended the coal and steel common market to all economic sectors of the member countries, stipulates that "freedom of movement for workers" entails the "abolition of any discrimination based on nationality between workers of the Member States as regards employment, remuneration and other conditions of work." In the Treaty of Rome free movement was understood as the right to seek employment and the right to establishment for EC nationals. The 1986 Single European Act, which came into effect in 1987, prepared the way for the creation of an EU market, without internal frontiers, while the 1993 amendments, known as the Maastricht Treaty, established a more general right for EU nationals to move and reside within the Union.

The initial rationale behind free movement was primarily economic (Böhning and Stephen 1971; Dahlberg 1968; Rochcau 1968), although its political underpinnings should not be discounted (Feldstein 1967).[2] In the Preamble to the Treaty of Rome, the six founding Member States declared their intention to "ensure the economic and social progress of their countries by common action in eliminating the barriers which divide Europe." From a political point of view, the founding fathers of the EEC considered the Treaty of Rome as only the beginning of a process leading to ever-closer integration. Freedom to move between member states can be interpreted as part of that process, fostering greater political unity by allowing the nationals of one country to work and settle in another and creating a sense of social belonging within the Community.[3]

The establishment of a common market was not, however, just a mechanism to produce labor market equilibrium and reduce disparities between member states by guaranteeing equal access to jobs to all Community citizens; it also was a way to achieve economic growth by creating an exclusive pan-European labor market. Article 48 stipulates that "the free movement of workers shall be ensured within the Community not later than at the date of the expiry of the transnational period [in 1970]." Thus, all discrimination by nationality among European Community nationals was to be abolished by that time. "Community migrant workers should have preferential treatment.... If the Community is to retain any control over its labor market, this must imply a discrimination against third country immigrants" (Shanks 1977, 33).[4]

Transitional Policies

Once the decision to allow and promote free movement had been made, progress was rapid. The first set of rules on free movement was announced in August 1961 and free movement of labor came into full operation about a year and a half ahead of schedule, in July 1968 (Böhning 1972, 10).[5] The speed of the operation spoke of a commitment at national levels. The main provisions of this policy were as follows:

- Any EEC worker had free access to employment offered in another EEC country if after three weeks no national worker had been found.

- Terms and conditions of employment were similar to those offered to nationals.

- Work permits were automatically extended after one year.

- There was no restriction on job changes after two years.

- Family and dependents were freely admitted once housing had been obtained.

- Social security rights were similar to those enjoyed by nationals in the country of residence.

The removal of obstacles to free movement was part of a wider set of measures against discrimination between member nationals. One of the fundamental aims of the EEC, as expressed in Treaty Article 3(c), was to realize "an internal market characterized by the abolition, as between Member States of . . . obstacles to the free movement of . . . persons. . . ." This is reflected in detailed provisions in European law providing for comprehensive equal treatment between nationals and migrants, with respect to employment and work conditions, trade union rights, and housing, as well as vocational training and education.[6]

Over the years, equal treatment was also extended to social security rights, another obstacle to mobility. European law also gradually extended equal treatment to other areas such as residence, culture, and political participation (Goodwin-Gill 1978). Such treatment, however, did not extend to the nationals of non-EEC member states. In fact, by 1967, there were several ways in which the member countries of the EEC gave priority to employees of other member states over those from outside the Community in recruitment, entry, and dismissal of such third-country workers.

The Treaty of Rome thus outlined the terms and conditions of movement and settlement of Community workers, including their employment, social security, and civic rights. The permanent removal of the institutional barriers to discrimination between national and Community workers derives from a commitment to wider economic integration, not from the particular circumstances of national labor markets (Hunter and Reid 1970). The 1968 regulation on free movement of labor by which the common labor market policy was fully established specified the following:

- Community workers were entitled to go to another country to take up work or look for it for a specified period of time.

- Work permits for EEC member nationals were abolished.

- Workers had full rights of residence.

- Community workers were given priority over third-country workers.

- National workers could no longer be given priority.

The right of EEC workers and their families to stay in a Member State for the purpose of employment is recognized in Article 48(3)(c) EC. The scope and formal aspects of this right were defined in a Council Directive in 1968[7] on the abolition of restrictions on movement and residence within the Community. The right to permanent residence of self-employed workers (and non-EEC nationals who are their family members) and to establish themselves in a member state other than their own was granted by an equivalent Council Directive in May 1973.[8]

Additional Progress

The free-movement cause received an enormous qualitative boost in the mid-1980s when France and Germany decided in 1984 in Saarbrücken to virtually eliminate border controls on each other's nationals. The next year, they were joined by the Benelux countries, in the 1985 Schengen Agreement. When the Schengen Agreement came into force in March 1995, it had expanded to include most other member states. Today, all but Denmark, the United Kingdom, and Ireland have ratified the agreement and all EU members share cross-border police data through the Schengen Information System. Although the Schengen Agreement is regarded by many as the "motor of European integration," disputes between member states continue, most notably intermittent arguments between the Netherlands and France about the liberal Dutch drug policy, France's concerns about terrorist threats, and a disagreement between Belgium and Spain about Belgium's refusal to extradite Basque terrorists.

The signing of the Single European Act (SEA) in 1985 was another critical qualitative step in Europe's quest for integration. The SEA introduced the concept of an internal market (a Community-wide market which operates under the same conditions as a national market) as an extension of the Common Market. The internal market required "elimination of all obstacles to intra-Community trade in order to merge the national markets into a single market" and set its sights on achieving an internally borderless Europe by the end of 1992.

In 1990, three directives adopted by the Council[9] paved the way for extending free movement rights to all EC nationals regardless of whether they are pursuing an economic activity in member states, as long as they are covered by health insurance and have sufficient resources. The next year, in a communication on the lifting of internal border controls in the Community, the Commission stressed that the continued existence of formalities and checks at internal borders "would undermine the political dimension of the objective laid down" in Article 8A of the SEA. These principles found their voice in Article 8A(I) of the Maastricht Treaty on European Union, which states that "[e]very citizen of the Union shall have the right to move and reside freely within the territory of the Member States, subject to the limitations and conditions laid down in the Treaty and by the measures adopted to give it effect."

The EU free-movement system thus operates within the context of an integrated group of states with similar economic, social, and political goals and conditions. It was neither designed nor implemented to ease movement across particular parts of borders nor to create transborder regional economic areas. The intent of the principles underlying it was to reduce the relevance of nationality within the Union by adopting a concept of "European citizenship." Since the right to stay indefinitely in a member state is recognized under EU legislation, EU migrant workers and their families, after an initial period, had to be entitled to social security benefits as a result of their mobility.[10] Hence the EU's determined foray into social policy.

Free Movement Today

The Treaty of Rome, as fine-tuned at the Community's and, since 1992, the Union's periodic "constitutional conventions," prohibits discrimination on grounds of nationality regarding employment, pay, and other working conditions between a country's own citizens and the nationals of the other member states. This general principle is implemented by a number of Treaty provisions, including free movement of workers (Article 48),[11] the right of establishment (Articles 52–58), free movement of services (Articles 59–66),[12] and legislation adopted under the Treaty that guarantees equality not only in employment and for tax purposes but also in social policies. Numerous European Court of Justice decisions have made plain the fact that member states may virtually never favor nationals over Community/Union nationals for employment.

At the heart of the provisions on both establishment and provision of services is the principle of non-discrimination regarding nationals of member states or companies established in member states, with increasingly narrow exceptions on the grounds of public policy, public security, and public health. Notably, free movement does not allow workers to enter another member state in order to take advantage of its welfare system. An unemployed worker, though, who is receiving benefits in his/her own country, is entitled to seek work in another member state while continuing to receive benefits in the home state, for a period of up to three months, a process one author has called "search unemployment" (Lundborg 1997). In fact, despite the elimination of internal border controls implicit in the free movement of EU member nationals—a policy that increases the opportunities for nationals to move so as to avail themselves of another EU member state's more comprehensive social and economic policies—it has not led to a substantial increase in intra-Union movements. A key reason for the lack of large-scale migration may be the massive regional redistribution programs such as structural and cohesion funds, which focus on the development of the entire EU space and address the region's economic inequalities.

Development of Regional Policy

Cross-border cooperation in such areas as managing ethnic conflicts, promoting mutual understanding, stimulating social and economic development, and enhancing integration, is a well-established feature of postwar Western Europe. Various regional programs have been established to overcome obstacles to interregional cooperation such as language barriers, cultural differences, stereotypes, and the legacy of the Second World War. The aim of such cross-border regional cooperation has been to improve neighborly relations and to bring new activities to public life, though there is little evidence that regional campaigns for more open borders have actually stimulated such cooperation. However, some states worry that too much regional or interregional autonomy could erode their own central authority or induce alliances between regions and the European Commission that would eventually bypass them.

Euroregions

The emergence of Euroregions coincided with the formation of the European Economic Community, beginning with the establishment of a region around Enschede in the Netherlands and Gronau in Germany in 1958. A Euroregion is a region in the sense of a voluntarily constructed geographical entity that shares such characteristics as cultural, economic, or social ties among constituent parts in different countries (Wolters 1994). Euroregions must fit into the public and private legal systems of at least two countries. The aim of public bodies in these regions is to promote the common interests of the participating municipalities, districts, or cities in such fields as economics, culture, environment, and transport. In this capacity, Euroregions are "governed" by a common board and administration composed of subnational public authorities on both sides of one or more common national borders. External funding organizations, such as INTERREG, as a condition for providing grants insist on organizational forms that can act as a legal entity for cross-border activities (Hrbek et al. 1994, 46–50).

Committee of the Regions

The Committee of the Regions (COR), set up in 1993 by the Maastricht Treaty, is intended to give local and regional authorities a stronger role in cross-border cooperation. It is an advisory assembly of the European Union composed of 222 representatives of local and regional authorities. The COR must be consulted by the Commission and the European Parliament on a number of issues such as education, vocational training, health, culture, transnational European networks, and economic and social cohesion. The Committee was established to ensure that the public authorities closest to the citizen—for example, mayors, city and county councilors, and regional presidents—are consulted on European Union (EU) proposals of direct interest to them, especially when they are responsible for implementing these policies after their adoption. The members of the COR are responsible both for providing the other European institutions with the local and regional point of view on Union proposals and for informing their citizens about Community policies that are decided and administered by the

European Union. The COR has no role in the implementation of border controls.

Regional Development and Structural Funds

As discussed earlier, the ultimate objective of EU structural (and regional) development programs is to work toward achieving economic and social cohesion within the European Union. EU structural policy focuses on large structural infrastructure projects, while regional development programs focus directly on engaging subnational governments and private actors with the Commission. Resources are targeted at actions that help bridge the gaps between the more- and the less-developed regions within the EU and promote equal employment opportunities between different social groups, according to certain priority objectives. In particular, the European Regional Development Fund (ERDF), established in 1975, targets disadvantaged regions. Its resources are used mainly to finance improvements in infrastructure, as productive investment to create and maintain permanent jobs, and in local development, human resources, and the environment. Border issues per se have played little part in the ERDF.

The establishment of the Regional Development Fund linked regional policy closely with social and industrial policy, such as vocational training and the identification of potential industrial locations (Shanks 1977). The ERDF also co-financed the Community Initiatives, a set of economic and social development programs launched in 1989 and focused on transnational, cross-border, and interregional cooperation in a "bottom-up" method of implementation.[13]

In 1990, the INTERREG Community Initiative was adopted to prepare border areas for a Community without internal frontiers. It enables the Commission to foster cross-border cooperation and to endow the resultant Euroregions with legal and economic means. In 1994, for example, INTERREG spent 800 million ECU[14] on Euroregions, of which 150 million ECU were available for cross-border cooperation between EU countries and Eastern European countries. According to EU "additionality requirements," the funds must be matched by national and subnational authorities. Initiatives include the development of cross-border contacts and commercial networks between small and medium-sized firms; establishment of trade organizations, professional organizations, and cross-border planning groups; cooperation in the fields of education, research, and culture; and support for training and employment measures, particularly for those affected by changes arising from the establishment of the single market. Often it is the possibility or expectation of these types of funds that leads to regional cross-border activity.

Recent Debate on Free Movement

In January 1996, the Commission decided to establish a "High-Level Panel on the Free Movement of Persons" whose role was to investigate the legal, practical, and administrative problems that restrict the right to free movement for EU citizens and to propose possible solutions. The Commission was aware that the rules on free movement were not applied effectively and that by now the internal market should have been a reality. Chaired by Mrs. Simone Veil, the panel submitted its report (the so-called Veil Report) in 1997. Its main conclusion was that, with a few exceptions, the legislative framework for the free movement of persons in the EU was established, and that the majority of problems could be solved without legislative changes. It recommended that member states improve cooperation, "particularly in relation to frontier regions, information for the public, training for the competent authorities in the Member States, and an improvement in the protection of individual rights" (European Commission 1998, 89–90).

Notes

1. See, for example, Swann 1992, 8–9.
2. Strong national interests also were at work, as France, Belgium, and Luxembourg were short of labor, and Germany was moving that way, while Italy and the Netherlands had high unemployment, especially in certain regions.
3. For example, Feldstein (1967, 46) concluded that intra-EC migration fostered political integration because "time may indeed be the melting pot's

flame and . . . the influx of ex-Community workers may distinguish the 'Community we' from the 'foreign they' all the more sharply." A similar view was proposed by Deutsch et al. (1954) in a thesis on nation building and European integration in which it was argued that increased contacts and exchanges transmit greater mutual responsiveness, a notion of "we-feeling" and a sense of identity and community, irrespective of whether they are guided by institutions (which might in fact hinder the process). The neo-institutionalists disagreed, arguing that institutional mechanisms or legally binding arrangements were needed to sustain interregional cooperation or to make it effective (March et al. 1989; Keohane 1989).

4. In reality, though, the problem of a European-wide labor exchange system still has not been solved today, as work permits to third-country nationals are supposed to be issued only when no EU national can be found to fill a vacancy, but it is nearly impossible for employers to advertise job vacancies across the whole of a union of fifteen countries and in twelve languages, even for highly specialized staff.

5. Why was free movement achieved ahead of schedule? Before 1961 intra-EC labor migration took place under bilateral labor and social agreements. Similarly to non-EC workers during the 1960s and 1970s, access to employment was offered in a particular enterprise, subject to employment and residence permits; permits were renewed on an annual basis; change of occupation could take place after five years; and some social security schemes were more restrictive than for nationals.

6. The principle of non-discrimination as it applies to free movement of labor is elaborated in EC secondary legislation, particularly in Council Regulation 1612/68/EEC.

7. Article 4(1) of Council Directive 68/360/EEC of 15 October 1968 on the abolition of restrictions on movement and residence within the Community, *Official Journal*, special edition 1968–69, p. 485.

8. Article 4(1) of Council Directive 73/148/EEC of 21 May 1973 on the abolition of restrictions on movement and residence within the Community for nationals of other member states with regard to establishment and services, *Official Journal*, 1973, L 192/14.

9. Directive 90/364/EEC of 28 June 1990 on the right of residence, *Official Journal*, 1990, L 180/26; Directive 90/365/EEC of 28 June 1990 on the right of residence for employees and self-employed persons who have ceased their occupational activity, *Official Journal*, 1990, L 180/28; and Directive 90/366/EEC of 28 June 1990 on the right of residence for students, *Official Journal*, 1990, L 180/30, re-issued as Directive 93/96/EC of 29 October 1993, *Official Journal*, 1993, L 317/59.

10. EU law (Article 51 EC) coordinates national social security arrangements in order to ensure that EU nationals moving between member states are

afforded adequate social security protection, but it does not create a uniform supranational social security system.

11. This includes "the right to take up, maintain, or pursue activities as self-employed persons and to set up and manage undertakings, in particular, companies and firms," under the conditions laid down for its own nationals by the law of the respective country.

12. The right to provide services is covered by the Articles 59 to 66, with Article 59 providing that restrictions on freedom to provide services within the Community shall be abolished in respect of nationals of member states who are established, other than that of the person for whom services are intended. The intention is to allow EU nationals (and European Economic Area nationals, such as Swiss and Norwegians) offering a service within one member state temporarily to provide services in another member state, without going so far as to establish themselves in that second member state under Article 52. As long as there is a cross-border element, the service provider may move to the second member state or remain in the original member state in order to provide the service. As in the case of right of establishment, companies established as service providers in the member states have the same rights as individual EU-EEA nationals.

13. Community Initiatives address specific problems that are Europe-wide, such as improving labor-market integration of vulnerable groups, especially migrants and refugees, development of human resources, management of industrial change, social inclusion, and the transnational character of the actions to be implemented.

14. The ECU was the currency unit in the European monetary union that preceded the Euro.

Works Cited

Böhning, W. R. 1972. *The Migration of Workers in the United Kingdom and the European Community.* London: Oxford University Press for the Institute of Race Relations.

Böhning, W. R. and D. Stephen. 1971. *The EEC and the Migration of Workers: The EEC's System of Free Movement of Labour and the Implications of UK Entry.* London: Runnymede Trust.

Dahlberg, K.A. 1968. "EC Commission and the Politics of the Free Movement of Labor." *Journal of Common Market Studies* vol. 6, no. 4.

Deutsch, K., et al. 1954. *Political Community at the International Level: Problems of Definitions and Measurement.* Garden City, New York: Doubleday.

European Commission. 1998. Report on the Report of the High-Level Panel on the Free Movement of Persons Chaired by Mrs. Simone Veil. European Commission, Committee on Civil Liberties and Internal Affairs, c4-0181/97.

Feldstein, H.S. 1967. "A Study of Transaction and Political Integration: Transnational Labor Flow within the European Economic Community." *Journal of Common Market Studies* vol. 6, no. 1.

Goodwin-Gill, G. S. 1978. *International Law and the Movement of Persons between States.* Oxford: Clarendon Press.

Hrbek, Rudolf, et al. 1994. *Betrifft: Das Europa der Regionen: Fakten, Probleme, Perspektiven.* Munich: Beck.

Hunter, L.C., and G.L. Reid. 1970. *European Economic Integration and the Movement of Labor.* Industrial Relations Center Research Series No. 9. Kingston, Ontario: Queens University.

Keohane, R. 1989. *International Institutions and State Power.* Boulder, Colo.: Westview Press.

Lundborg, P. 1997. "The Free Movement of Labor between Sweden and the New EU Members," in *Bigger and Better Europe? Economic Effects of EU Enlargement.* Ministry of Finance, Stockholm, 37–75, Government Official Reports 1997/156: Final Report from the Committee on the Economic Effects of European Enlargement.

March, J., et al. 1989. *Rediscovering Institutions: The Organizational Basis of Politics.* New York: The Free Press.

Olsson, B. 1953. "The Common Employment Market for the Northern Countries." *International Labor Review* vol. 68.

Rochcau, G. 1968. "Free Movement of European Workers and Its Limits." *Migration News* vol. 17, no. 2.

Shanks, M. 1977. *European Social Policy Today and Tomorrow.* Oxford: Pergamon Press.

Swann, D., ed. 1992. *The Single European Market and Beyond.* London: Routledge.

Wolters, M. 1994. "Euroregions along the German Border." In *Die Politik der Dritten Ebene: Regionen im Europa der Union,* ed. Bullman. Baden-Baden: Nomos Verlag.

Contributors

Gustavo del Castillo V. is a researcher at El Colegio de la Frontera Norte in Tijuana, B.C., Mexico, specializing in issues pertaining to economic integration in North America, on which he has written three books. His current research involves how workers can work more effectively within globalized institutions, such as the World Trade Organization, and be participants in the decision-making process. Dr. del Castillo earned his Ph.D. from the University of Texas at Austin and has taught at the University of California at San Diego and San Diego State University. He has been a Senior Fellow at the Center for U.S.-Mexican Studies (UCSD), the Overseas Development Council (Washington), the Center for Trade Policy and Law (Carleton University, Ottawa), and the International Development Research Centre (IDRC) in Ottawa.

Jacqueline Hagan is co-director of the Center for Immigration Research and an associate professor in sociology at the University of Houston. Her research focuses on community impacts of U.S. immigration policy, social networks and immigrant incorporation, and migrant deaths at the U.S.-Mexico border. She is currently investigating the effects of immigrant deportations on immigrant households, mental health conditions of immigrants separated from their families, and the impact of religious networks on Central American migrant circuits. Dr. Hagan earned her Ph.D. at the University of Texas at Austin.

Malgorzata Irek is an associate researcher at the Department of Comparative Cultural and Social Anthropology, Europa-Universität Viadrina, Germany. She earned her Ph.D. in Sociology in 1992 from Free University of Berlin, West Germany, where she studied ethnology and sociology and earned a Thyssen Stiftung scholarship. Her previous research includes studying the informal economy (of ethnic minorities, illegal Poles, and cross-border traders), perceptions of race, and American Ethnic Literature, in which she obtained an M.A. in Poland. Dr. Irek's post-doctoral research focused on foreigners' perception of the transforming Poland. Her publications include two books and several articles.

Grigorii G. Kosach is a professor in the Political Sciences Department, Institute of Asian and African Studies, Moscow State University. He has published studies of the problems of the formation of political parties and movements in the Arab world and Central Asia and international relations in the Middle East. He also studies the Muslim movement in Russia and the problems of Russian regionalism, as well as interethnic relations in Russian regions.

Alexei S. Kuzmin is a professor at the Russian State University for Humanities and the research director of the Institute for Humanities and Political Studies. He also is a member of the board of the Russian Political Sciences Association and the vice-president of the Russian branch of the International Association of Constitutional Law. Dr. Kuzmin is an authority on post-Soviet politics and theoretical investigation of social and cultural transformations and also investigates the problems of Russian regionalism and domestic and foreign politics and policies. He has authored numerous books and papers on mathematics, cultural and social theory, theoretical archaeology, constitutional law, and political science.

Viktor Larin is director of the Institute of History, Archaeology and Ethnology of the Peoples of the Far East, Russian Academy of Sciences, Far Eastern Branch. Having earned his Ph.D. in history, he is a specialist on East Asian countries (Chinese history) and Russian Far East-China cooperation. Dr. Larin has published more than 70 articles in magazines and newspapers as well as four books.

Deborah Waller Meyers is a policy analyst at the Migration Policy Institute. Until July 2001, she was an associate in the International Migration Policy Program at the Carnegie Endowment for International Peace. Her work has focused on U.S. immigration and refugee policy and process, international borders, and the U.S. relationship with Mexico and Canada, and she has written a number of articles on these and other immigration-related issues. Ms. Meyers previously worked for the U.S. Commission on Immigration Reform, the U.S.-Mexico Binational Study on Migration, the Inter-American Dialogue, and RAND. She earned her M.A. from George Washington University and her B.A. from Brandeis University.

Vladimir I. Mukomel is the director of the Center for Ethnopolitical and Regional Studies, a member of the Russian Sociological Association, and a member of the CIS Research Center on Forced Migration and Russian Economic Society. With an M.S. in Economy, M.S. in Computer-Aided Design, and an M.S. in Demography, Mr. Mukomel has served in various advisory capacities in the Russian Federation. His main interests are migration and refugee issues, ethno-demography, national minorities, socioeconomic consequences of conflicts, and the computer simulation of social processes. He has published about 80 articles and eight books and monographs on the above problems.

Demetrios G. Papademetriou is co-director of the Migration Policy Institute. Until July 2001, he was a senior associate and the co-director of the International Migration Policy Program at the Carnegie Endowment for International Peace. His research is focused on evaluating the adequacy of U.S. policies and administrative structures and practices in meeting U.S. objectives in the immigration and refugee areas, the migration politics and policies of European and other advanced industrial societies, and the role of multilateral institutions in developing and coordinating collective responses to international population movements. He is also the co-founder and co-chair of *Metropolis: An International Forum for Research and Policy on Migration and Cities.* He has been the chairman of the Migration Committee of the Organization for Economic Cooperation and Development (OECD), the director for immigration policy and research at the U.S. Department of Labor, and the executive editor of *International Migration Review.*

Dr. Papademetriou received his Ph.D. in Political Science from the University of Maryland and has been a faculty member at the University of Maryland, Duke University, the Graduate Faculty of the New School for Social Research, and the American University. He has published widely, with over 150 books, monographs, journal articles, and opinion pieces on the immigration and refugee policies of the United States and other advanced industrial societies, the impact of legal and illegal immigration on the U.S. labor market, and the relationship between international migration and development.

Nestor Rodriguez is co-director of the Center for Immigration Research and an associate professor in sociology at the University of Houston. His research focuses on U.S. immigration, intergroup relations, urban development, and global sociology. He is currently working on the effects of the 1996 U.S. welfare and immigration laws on immigrant households; stress and depression among immigrants separated from their families; and evolving relations between African-Americans and Hispanics in the United States. Dr. Rodriguez earned his Ph.D. at the University of Texas at Austin.

Anna Rubtsova is a project associate with the migration and citizenship program at the Carnegie Moscow Center. She graduated from the Moscow People's Friendship University, where she was a post-graduate fellow. While working at the Carnegie Moscow Center, she also participated as coordinator of the non-Carnegie project on ethno-political monitoring organized by the UN High Commissioner for Refugees. Ms. Rubtsova has worked on the problem of cross-border cooperation at the Russia-China border, and she has contributed a number of articles to magazines and books.

John Salt is a professor of geography at University College, London, where he is also director of the Migration Research Unit. He has published widely on European international migration and has worked with the European Commission, the Council of Europe, the OECD, and various United Kingdom government departments. Dr. Salt earned his Ph.D. from the University of Liverpool.

Sandra Schmidt completed her Ph.D. in political science at Southampton University on the development of a common immigration policy in the European Union, based on a comparative analysis of immigration policy making in Germany, France, and the United Kingdom. She presently holds a Jean Monnet Fellowship at the Robert Schuman Centre (European University Institute), developing a comparative research project on labor immigration in the European Union.

Andrea Witt is a doctoral candidate in political science at Humboldt University, Berlin, focusing on cross-border cooperation (in Germany and the United States) and on the impact of local and regional actors on regional, economic, political, and social development. Ms. Witt is an American Political Science Association Congressional Fellow, and has held fellowships at Millersville University (Pennsylvania) and at the German American Center for Visiting Scholars (Washington, D.C.). Formerly a free-lance journalist and editor in Germany, she was a reporter and newspaper editor at the German-Polish border. Ms. Witt earned her Diplom (M.A.) in Political Science from Free University, Berlin and her undergraduate degree at Philipps University, Marburg, Germany.

Index

Single European Act, 310–15

Sister Cities Pact (Pacto de Ciudades Hermanas), 92, 98

Slubice, Poland/Frankfurt-Oder, Germany: demographics and economics, 215; education cooperation between, 183, 216–17; irregular economic activity, 216; levels of cooperation between, 216–17

Solis, Luis, 5, 9

Southeastern Michigan Council of Governments (SEMCOG), 70

Southwest Border Regional Commission (SBRC), U.S.-Mexican, 143

Suifenhe: crime in, 251; free trade zone, 237; personal relations with, 243; Russia-oriented economy of, 234, 247–48. See also Heihe

Supranational institutions: of European Union, 176. See also European Union (EU); NAFTA

Tengiz oil field, Kazakhstan, 278–80, 282, 284. See also Caspian Pipeline Consortium (CPC)

Tijuana: Department for Migrant Issues, 137; economic growth and socioeconomic development, 126–27; El Colegio de la Frontera Norte (COLEF), 140–41; manufacturing firms in, 124–25; maquiladora industry in, 124–25, 136; migration and migrant-related issues in, 137; Municipal Institute for Migration, 139; NGOs operating in, 128; service sector in, 124–27. See also San Diego/Tijuana region

Tomás Rivera Policy Institute survey, 17

Trade: Canadian-American Border Trade Alliance, 69; NAFTA influence on U.S.-Canadian, 45; narcotics trade on U.S. Mexican border, 142, 151;

Nogales, Arizona as foreign trade zone, 147–48; Red River Trade corridor, 71; of Russian border towns with Chinese towns, 247, 259; through Laredo, 90–92; United States-Canadian bilateral, 45, 48–50; volume in Detroit/Windsor region, 51; with Kazakhstan, 276. See also Shuttle traders

Transborder communities. See Cross-border communities

Transportation Equity Act for the 21st Century, United States, 70

Treaty of Ghent, 56

Treaty of Rome: free movement provisions in, 309–13; prohibition of discrimination under, 314–15

Treaty of Zgorzelec, 202

U.S. Border Patrol: inspections at Nogales, 150; Operation Blockade, 94; treatment of undocumented workers, 142

U.S.-Canada Auto Pact, 45, 57

U.S.-Canada Free Trade Agreement, 71

U.S.-Canada Open Skies Agreement, 45

U.S.-Canada Pre-Clearance Agreement, 45

U.S.-Canadian border: Binational Regional Initiative Developing Greater Education, 72–73; border crossings, 62–68; Border Trade Alliance, 69; Cascadia Project, 69–70; Cross-Border Crime Forum, 75; environmental issues, 73; Golden Horseshoe Educational Alliance, 73; policy recommendations for, 18–19; proposals concerning border inspections, 78–80; proposals concerning infrastructure, 78; proposals concerning personnel, 76–78; proposed conceptual solutions, 80-82; trade

Carnegie Endowment for International Peace

THE CARNEGIE ENDOWMENT is a private, nonprofit organization dedicated to advancing cooperation between nations and promoting active international engagement by the United States. Founded in 1910, its work is nonpartisan and dedicated to achieving practical results.

Through research, publishing, convening and, on occasion, creating new institutions and international networks, Endowment associates shape fresh policy approaches. Their interests span geographic regions and the relations between governments, business, international organizations, and civil society, focusing on the economic, political, and technological forces driving global change. Through its Carnegie Moscow Center, the Endowment helps to develop a tradition of public policy analysis in the states of the former Soviet Union and to improve relations between Russia and the United States. The Endowment publishes *Foreign Policy*, one of the world's leading magazines of international politics and economics, which reaches readers in more than 120 countries and in several languages.

The Migration Policy Institute

THE MIGRATION POLICY INSTITUTE (MPI) is an independent, nonpartisan, nonprofit think tank dedicated to the study of the movement of people worldwide. The Institute provides knowledge-based analysis, development, and evaluation of migration and refugee policy issues at the local, national, and international levels. It aims to meet the rising demand for pragmatic responses to the challenges and opportunities that large-scale migration, whether voluntary or forced, presents to communities and institutions in an ever more integrated world. MPI grew out of the International Migration Policy Program, which was founded in 1989 at the Carnegie Endowment for International Peace to provide analytical and intellectual guidance to a number of the most important migration policy debates of the 1990s.

MPI's work is organized around four thematic pillars. Under the first, *Migration Management*, MPI focuses on how different states manage the flows of people across their borders and how their social institutions adapt to these flows. In the second pillar, *Refugee Protection and International Human Rights*, MPI uses a combination of legal and social science research to track new developments in thinking, law, and practice in the realm of refugee protection and proposes ways to reconcile the protection needs of refugees and the policy priorities of sovereign states. The *North American Borders and Migration Agenda*, the third pillar, enables MPI to use the results of its extensive research to provide an intellectual framework for discussing concrete steps toward cooperative management of common borders and movements of people in North America. Finally, through the *Immigrant Settlement and Integration* pillar, MPI works with researchers, advocates, and officials of national, state, and local governments to understand better how newcomers and receiving communities interact and to develop an analytical framework and a plan of action for improving this interaction for the benefit of all.

Migration Policy Institute
1400 16th Street, N.W., Suite 300
Washington, D.C. 20036-2257
202-266-1940
www.migrationpolicy.org